AF600459

SUMMONING THE DEAD

SUMMONING THE DEAD

Essays on Ron Rash

Edited by
RANDALL WILHELM *and*
ZACKARY VERNON

Foreword by
ROBERT MORGAN

The University of South Carolina Press

Published by the University of South Carolina Press
Columbia, South Carolina 29208

www.sc.edu/uscpress

Manufactured in the United States of America

27 26 25 24 23 22 21 20 19 18
10 9 8 7 6 5 4 3 2 1

Library of Congress Cataloging-in-Publication Data
can be found at http://catalog.loc.gov/

ISBN 978-1-61117-838-8 (cloth)
ISBN 978-1-61117-839-5 (ebook)

Bonding Fire

For Bob Cumming

A spark takes hold in a glen
in Scotland's midlands and burns
winter and summer, and when
hands tending that spark grow cold

passed on to daughter and son
fire passed hearth to hearth to fire
a bride's wedding night passion,
light an old man's corpse candle,

part heirloom, part talisman,
cradled and nursed like a child
in the ship's hold when the clan
sailed west to Charleston, then west

to east Tennessee, the first
carried by wagon, by hand,
huddled by when a panther
cried out at night and when night

turned slantland white when they came
into the Blue Ridge where they
raised their hearths over a flame
two centuries old, two more

passing until water came
to douse that valley, to douse
the hearth of one who remained
to tend that fire, who refused

to leave the valley until
that fire left with him, the truck's
windows left up lest wind still
the pail of sparks his lap held.

Ron Rash

CONTENTS

FOREWORD

Robert Morgan

In the past three decades, there has been a surge of writing about southern Appalachia, its history, folklore, music, crafts, religion, and storytelling. Most outstanding has been the fiction and poetry written in and about the region. Beginning with Jim Wayne Miller's poetry and essays in the 1970s, Jeff Daniel Marion's magazine the *Small Farm,* and Lee Smith's novels, especially *Oral History* and *Fair and Tender Ladies,* this renaissance has included such outstanding works as Charles Frazier's *Cold Mountain* and Jayne Anne Phillips's *Machine Dreams,* and more recently the novels of Wiley Cash and the poetry of Rose McLarney and Jesse Graves. But no writer of the southern highlands has achieved greater recognition than Ron Rash, in his short stories, novels, and poetry. Rash's rise to prominence may seem sudden and meteoric to some, but in fact it has had a long foreground.

It seems that when a culture is fading, or is recently dead, it becomes available in a special way for treatment in fiction. Hawthorne's great novels and short stories are an excellent example, written, and read, just as the Industrial Revolution transformed the culture created by John Winthrop, the Mathers, Samuel Sewell, and others. There is certainly an element of nostalgia in this phenomenon, but also a drive, a need, almost an obsession, to understand the past, to bring alive a sense of who we were, and how we became who we are. The novels of Faulkner and other southern writers answered this desire in the twentieth century, portraying with intimacy and intensity a South going or gone, in all its contradictions and complexities. Nobody has addressed the contradictions and complexities of the rapidly evolving culture of the southern highlands more memorably than Ron Rash. His work encompasses both past and present, life in cotton-mill towns at the foot of the mountains, and in remote coves during the Civil War. The stories of his first book, *The Night the New Jesus Fell to Earth,* are among the finest comic writing we have, taking their place alongside Fred Chappell's *I Am One of You Forever.* The poems of Rash's volume *Waking* evoke the lives of mountain people in firm, lyrical lines in a wide range of styles and forms. His later stories bring to life a culture wrenched painfully apart, almost beyond recognition, by deracination, meth, and other contemporary addictions. His best-known novel, *Serena,* tells the story of the robber barons' destruction of the timber on the highest peaks a hundred years ago.

I first met Ron Rash about two decades ago, just before he began publishing his work. At that time he was teaching at Tri-County Technical Community College near Clemson, South Carolina. His workload was five or six courses each semester, many of them classes in English composition with large enrollments. It seemed impossible that anyone with such a teaching load could get his own writing done. But with persistence, discipline, patience, and extraordinary talent, Ron kept writing and sending out his work. His first novel won the Novello Prize in 2002, and he was invited to serve as visiting writer at Lenoir Rhyne University. Then he was appointed Parris Professor at Western Carolina University. His career is an example to any aspiring writer. I have often been asked if I have any advice for ambitious young writers, and my answer is one word, "persistence." It has been thrilling to watch Ron grow as a writer and achieve such prominence. All along I have admired both the quality and the diversity of his work. Besides writing in many genres, he has written in many different voices and from many points of view, of textile towns and cove farms. My own hunch is that his best work is still to come.

Ron's first novel was called *One Foot in Eden,* a title borrowed from the Scottish poet Edwin Muir. The title suggests the way his work bridges and connects different worlds. Ron is the son of a college professor of art, but his summer vacations were spent with his grandparents on their farm in the mountains near Boone, North Carolina. There he acquired both a love and close knowledge of the woods and rural life. Both his parents worked in textile mills before they became teachers, and Ron's *Eureka Mill* is a classic portrait of life in a mill town, a culture now gone, as the industry has moved jobs abroad in the past few decades. Ron's work also bridges the gap between literary culture and popular culture, traditional music and country music, ballads and modernist poetry.

Since World War II life in the southern mountains has been transformed significantly. The peaks and valleys of the Cherokees' wide hunting grounds, once settled by small subsistence farmers, are now accessible by superhighways. The Cherokees themselves manage prosperous casinos and other tourist industries. The waterfalls, mountain haze, and thrashing whitewater streams are still there, but the people have changed. Mountainsides are covered by expensive houses owned by retirees and summer inhabitants. Golf courses, resorts, nursing homes, condominiums, and malls fill the valleys. Asheville is so crowded it is almost impossible to find a parking place. Much farm and construction labor is done by Hispanic immigrants, and signs in stores are now often in Spanish. Community colleges dot the landscape. The majority of voters in elections are nonnative. It is this rapidly evolving world that Ron Rash also portrays definitively in much of his fiction. It is a special pleasure to celebrate Ron's achievement and to know that he belongs to us, and to this region, as well as to southern and American literature at large. This collection of essays indicates the impact his work has already made, and it is clear that his writing belongs to the future as well as the present.

ACKNOWLEDGMENTS

We would like to thank the helpful and encouraging staff of the University of South Carolina Press, particularly Bill Adams, Jim Denton, Bob Ellis, Linda Fogle, and Jonathan Haupt, for their assistance and guidance in developing this collection. Special thanks to Ron Rash for his support of this project and his willingness to work with us, Robert Morgan for his kindness in writing the foreword for this book, and for our contributors for creating the insightful analyses found within these pages. We also thank Bob Cumming of Iris Press, Betsy Teter of Hub City Press, and Mark Watson of Press 53 for their kindness and generosity. Thanks also to Louisiana State University Press for permission to reprint an excerpt from Robert Morgan's poem "Honey." Thanks as well to Penguin for allowing us to reprint a passage from "October Crossing." From *Terroir* by Robert Morgan, copyright © 2011 by Robert Morgan. Used by permission of Penguin Books, an imprint of Penguin Publishing Group, a division of Penguin Random House LLC. We also gratefully acknowledge the *Southern Quarterly* for allowing us to reprint a section of Jesse Graves's essay included in this volume. In developing this collection of diverse critical approaches, our desire is to deepen and invigorate the significant cultural, aesthetic, environmental, and political issues that Rash's poetry, short fiction, and novels explore. We hope these chapters will provide a productive foundation and catalyze new research in the burgeoning field of Ron Rash studies.

INTRODUCTION

The Hum of Resurrection—Raising Rash to Critical Light

A battered lighter flares in darkness. On a table spread with mill cloth, a mason jar assumes sudden shape, its lid uncapped and brimming with moonshine, and "in the almost silence / of house-creak and time's / persistent tracking of eternity," a ritual summoning begins (*Eureka Mill* xv). The poet touches flame to liquid, and soon a "blue trembling rises," transforms to smoke, and merges with "all elements" in the shadowless night, its dark energy "whispering out the window" curling into the North Carolina mountains and "into the black bony dirt" of his grandfather's grave. Readers of Ron Rash may recognize the ritualistic incantation and haunting sublimity of "Invocation," the opening poem in *Eureka Mill* (1998), Rash's penetrating look into the faded histories of the cotton-mill system in Chester, South Carolina. The book's pages are filled with ghosted bodies and lost voices from the poet's personal, familial, and cultural past. The incantatory prologue "Invocation" grooms the reader for a journey that slides into the folds and gaps of time, where the dead speak and spin their tales through spirals of forgotten history. Forgotten, that is, except for the poet's ritual longing and humble patience, awaiting:

> a tobacco-breathed haint, shadowless shadow,
> bloodless blood-kin I have *summoned*
> to hear my measured human prayer:
> Grandfather guide my hand
> to weave with words a thread
> of truth as I write down
> your life and other lives,
> close kin but strangers too,
> those lives all lived as gears
> in Springs' cotton mill
> and let me not forget
> your lives were more than that.
> (*Eureka Mill* xv–xvi, emphasis added)

"Summoning the dead" to "weave with words a thread of truth" has been and remains one of the clearest declarations of Ron Rash's project as a poet, short-story writer, and novelist.

Rash's fierce dedication to preserving the lives and customs of southern Appalachia shapes the backbone of his narrative vision and transports readers into stark and violent worlds teeming with ghostly and human presences. Treading the borderlands between past and present, Rash's characters battle a host of human, ecological, psychological, and temporal perils. Victims of war, poverty, disease, corruption, and the vicissitudes of the human heart, the men and women of Rash's Appalachia brave the hardships of life with a stubborn will to survive, despite the darkness pulsing through landscapes rife with suffering, cruelty, and sorrow. But Rash's artistic vision is never nihilist or drowning in despair. Even in the blackest of nights in Rash's cosmos hope flares doggedly, and the healing warmth of bonding fires[1] shine through the darkness, annealing wounds and heartache, soothing the bloodied breast, raising the dead to the greater light of day.

Although Rash has often written through the lens of history, it is a fundamental feature of his aesthetics that time is never past—that there *is no was*—no tense where human presence and action is inert, invisible, or irrevocably lost. Calling forth through the vortex of time, Rash's work summons the past in startling shapes to speak to us firmly in the present. Rash's dark and clear vision reveals an obsession with penetrating surfaces—physical, moral, historical, and psychological—and marks the writer's *ars poetica* as a passion for discovering the mysteries that lurk unseen, disembodied, just out of reach. *Summoning the Dead* runs both ways in Rash's work, performing as conduit for his compulsive dipping into history and for raising archetypal power and universal themes that charge his precisely rendered stories of a regional world on the brink of becoming history itself. Ghosts, dreams, and visions haunt Rash's texts with a stubborn materiality that collapse temporal and spatial boundaries to foreground the inexorable pressure of the past on the present. Rash's oft-quoted line—"I am haunted still"[2]—regarding the Civil War atrocity at Shelton Laurel in 1863 makes clear that his dedication to and obsession with the vagaries of human existence and the silent gaps of history are fundamental in generating his artistic vision.

As ephemeral as "Invocation" is, with its mystic and supernatural calling forth of the dead, in most of Rash's work one has to dig into the natural and psychological worlds in which his characters strive to find voice and meaning. For example "Good Friday: Shelton Laurel, 2006," a poem in *Waking* (2011), published five years after *The World Made Straight* (2006), which deals extensively with the Civil War massacre, attests to Rash's consistent probing into a violent past written into the region itself. A hundred and forty three years after the killings, a farmer still works the land in "morning's sun-sprawl," but the poet stands vigil over hallowed ground and reveals where light fails—the marble marker of a mass grave that "darken[s] Shelton ground" (*Waking* 60). In the space beyond the farmer's vision, Rash calls forth the shade of twelve-year-old David Shelton as silent witness to the human brutality, cruelty, and paranoia that burns in the human heart. While the twenty-first-century farmer "sows his field the old way," the landscape "unrolls like a palimpsest" behind him (*Waking* 60), suggesting an attempt to live with and to deny the bloody past and the human capacity for evil etched into the land and its people in layers of violent history throbbing just beneath the surface.

Summoning the Dead also taps into Rash's concerns for human malevolence and environmental destruction that bury, drown, or silence both victims and victimizers. In a great many of Rash's poems and stories, characters desperately search for something, to break physical, historical, psychological surfaces to explore what waits below, beyond, or within, whether it is for speckled trout, a giant sturgeon, drowned bodies, an underwater valley, or an old jacket and a memory of a night long forgotten. "Time is but the stream I go a-fishing in," Thoreau famously remarked,[3] and the same is true for Rash, but what Rash's characters dredge up from Appalachian history is far more "rich and strange" than anything in Walden Pond.

Rash's characters strive obsessively for meaning that often eludes their grasp. The unknown lurks in various forms in his work: in burials and drownings, in floods and fires, in impenetrable gorges and underwater valleys. Mystery emerges in ghostings and dreams, in ecstatic rituals and repressed memories, in secrets and suspicions, in neuroses and uncanny objects. Through Rash's configuration of space, action, and imagery, characters (and readers too) are allowed entry into these boundary zones of the seen and unseen, of knowledge in the act of recovery, and of the past's firm footprint on the present. Wading into memory Rash's characters seek to rend the veil and access submerged signs of the personal and regional unconscious that turn and twist and reform in their minds. These disturbing tales stir up the bottom waters churning beneath the surfaces of Rash's tension-loaded texts and, like finding the key to the proverbial Jungian door,[4] often raise the undiscovered to light.

It is in this spirit that we have chosen *Summoning the Dead* for the title of the first collection of critical essays on the work of Ron Rash. Central to Rash's concerns and work as a writer, *Summoning the Dead* begins in many ways "where the map ends" in current Rash studies. With contributions from seventeen scholars working in diverse fields, each reading Rash's poetry and fiction through a variety of theoretical and critical lens, our goal is to raise the discussion of Rash's work and to promote new and innovative ways of understanding his literary art.

To give structure to the variety of critical approaches to Rash's work in this collection, we have divided the essays into three parts: (1) "The Natural World," (2) "Intertextual Streams," and (3) "War, Memory, Violence." The essays in the first part examine Rash's work in relation to the natural world, and each writer has employed theoretical strategies from the burgeoning fields of agricultural, environmental, animal, and food studies. In the second part, the contributors have analyzed the web of intertexuality pervading Rash's work, pointing out that Rash's work alludes to a dizzying array of texts from Shakespeare to Welty, from *The Mabinogion* to *The Sound and the Fury*, and from Beowulf to Heaney. In the third part, contributors have analyzed Rash's obsession with war, violence, and memory and have provided significant readings of the recurring traumas Rash's characters endure because of their connections to the Civil War, World War I, and the contemporary drug wars in southern Appalachia.

Zackary Vernon's essay, the first of the opening part, "The Natural World," explores Rash's relationship to James Dickey's infamous novel *Deliverance* (1970). The essay argues that both *Deliverance* and Rash's *One Foot in Eden* (2002) can be read as responses to the Southern Agrarians' manifesto *I'll Take My Stand: The South and the Agrarian Tradition* (1930). Dickey's novel provides a Cold War fantasy about postapocalyptic Agrarian culture in Appalachia, while Rash's work provides a historically accurate account of agriculture in the region and in doing so provides a sharp critique both of the Agrarian's romanticization of southern agriculture and Dickey's unflattering depiction of Appalachia.

Frédérique Spill has also written about Rash's *One Foot in Eden,* but her essay focuses on the ways in which water plays a prominent role in this novel as well as in Rash's other fictional and poetic works. Using a range of philosophical and ecocritical texts, Spill's essay examines how humans have struggled in Rash's texts, with varying degrees of success, to harness the forces of the natural world. Dams and man-made lakes, in particular, have haunted the literary imagination of Rash, and Spill's essay repeatedly demonstrates the central role these hydrological efforts have played in Rash's work. Furthermore the essay contends that water becomes a powerful and pervasive symbol that Rash has used to explore a range of issues, including regional identity, literary narratology, memory, trauma, and human finitude.

Building on Edgar Allan Poe's "single effect" theory, Brian Railsback's essay argues that Rash has created a unique environmental discourse that shatters the overly reductive binary between ecophobia (antagonism toward nature) and biophilia (love of the natural world). Instead Rash's characters display both polar opposite tendencies as well as many positions in between; therefore Rash's work conveys how people so often inhabit complicated, if not contradictory, environmental positions. Railsback's essay also asserts that Rash's style relies on "narrative rooted in the land in an Emersonian ideal (language that hews closely to the natural artifact)." While Rash's depiction of the natural world can appear to be dark and even deterministic, his fiction is also punctuated by moments of spirituality and the possibility of both personal and environmental renewal.

Jimmy Dean Smith's essay continues to explore the intersections between environmentalism and spirituality by investigating Rash's relationship to Flannery O'Connor. On multiple occasions Rash has acknowledged his indebtedness to O'Connor's style and thematic content. Smith has augmented existing critical conversations about this indebtedness by analyzing the appearance of endangered or extinct plants and animals (such as ginseng, panthers, Carolina parakeets, American chestnuts, or speckled trout) in each writer's work. The theological underpinnings of Rash's fiction, like O'Connor's, is often informed by and indeed inspired by interactions with animals that inhabit his "spirit country."

Erica Abrams Locklear's essay elucidates several of Rash's works by showing the central role of Appalachian food and foodways in his literary and cultural projects. From fried chicken and apple stack cakes to ramps and collards, food plays a central role in many of Rash's works. His depictions of food celebrate the traditions of the region, but they also highlight the times of abject poverty and food scarcity that have transpired periodically throughout the region's history. In addition Abrams's essay points out that regionally specific foods and foodways tell complicated histories of people dwelling in particular locations as well as how such locations are penetrated, both historically and in the present, by national and international networks of cultural and economic exchange.

The second part of the collection, "Intertextual Streams," begins with an essay by Randall Wilhelm that examines the crucial role that narrative images play in Rash's work. Wilhelm's essay argues for the importance of vision, citing Rash's statement that "vision is central to everything I do." Employing visual and affect theory with object-relation studies, Wilhelm has examined how Rash's work uses visual tropes, particularly "pictures of the dead" and the framing of grief and mourning to shape an alternate discourse that speaks to characters' vision and their ability to see—or not see—the physical world or undead energies. Through a selection of visual episodes, Wilhelm's essay shows Rash's complex weave of visual tropes that create narrative mystery, affective vibrancy, and thematic wonder.

Jesse Graves has framed his essay in the context of the Appalachian poetry renaissance and the ambitious and prolific careers of Robert Morgan, Fred Chappell, Jeff Daniel Marion, Maggie Anderson, Katherine Stripling Byer, and Michael McFee. Focusing on the mountain South, such writers have given voices to the Appalachian region that remain distinct from American and even southern literature. Although surprisingly diverse in content and style, these poets have tended to use poetic formalism. Graves's essay focuses on the poems of Morgan and Rash in order to examine why syllabics and other tendencies toward form have become important elements in the poetry of Appalachia, and also as models by which to examine the impact of this movement. In addition to the common investment in poetic formalism within the Appalachian literary tradition, Morgan's and Rash's lives share many cultural similarities; both writers grew up in the mountains of the Carolinas, and both have familial roots in agriculture and industry in southern Appalachia. Morgan's and Rash's poems draw heavily from their personal and familial histories in order to examine their native region as well as how it has evolved in recent years.

Mae Miller Claxton's essay provides a reading of several of Rash's fictional works—*The World Made Straight* (2006), "Their Ancient, Glittering Eyes" from the collection *Chemistry and Other Stories* (2007), and *Serena* (2008), alongside Eudora Welty's well-known story "A Worn Path." In interviews Rash has said that he has been deeply influenced by Welty's fiction, noting "A Worn Path" in particular as being the model for a key scene in *Serena.* Rash, like Welty, has written about the human condition in such a complex way that everyday experiences often gain mythic qualities. Claxton's essay also argues not only that Welty's work helps us comprehend the complexity of Rash's work, but also that Rash's work can facilitate a fuller understanding of Welty's work as both writers have helped us to see each other's vision more clearly.

Martha Greene Eads's essay contends that Rash's work follows that of a long line of southern writers, most notably Flannery O'Connor, in that his landscape is "Christ-haunted." Focusing on Rash's recent collection of short stories *Nothing Gold Can Stay,* Eads has demonstrated how Rash's work uses violence to spur his characters toward awareness in a way that is similar to much of O'Connor's fiction, particularly the epiphanic moments that so often conclude her stories. However, unlike O'Connor's work, Rash's work is often devoid of overt Christian ideology, and his characters seek substitutionary atonement from the people around them rather than from spiritual sources.

In the first of two essays about Shakespeare's *Macbeth* and Rash's *Serena,* Barbara Bennett has catalogued an impressive array of connections between these texts, focusing considerable attention on representations of gender. In Shakespeare's play Lady Macbeth calls on the spirits to "unsex me here," indicating her desire to replace her feminine attributes with masculine ones. Lady Macbeth ultimately undermines stereotypical gender roles, and in doing so she seems to alter the basic order of the universe, causing unexpected and even supernatural consequences in the environment. Serena similarly subverts gender roles, and she is seen by the people around her as being "beyond gender" and "the equal of any man." Serena's adoption of certain hypermasculine attributes ends up disrupting both the social and natural worlds of which she is a part. Building on feminist scholars such as Judith Butler and Carole S. Vance, Bennett's essay critiques the cultural, rather than biological, limitations placed on women living in masculinist societies.

Extending the analysis of *Macbeth* and *Serena,* Tripthi Pillai and Daniel Cross Turner have given a provocative reading of this relationship by suggesting that Shakespeare's play catalyzes undead reverberations that haunt Rash's novel. Many macabre elements are contained in both works (corpses, bloody daggers, uncanny prophesies, spectral life forms, unnatural if not supernatural figures, stillborn babies). Moreover Pillai and Turner's essay suggests that the many allusions to *Macbeth* in *Serena* act as undead influences, bringing forth the voices of the dead. As a remediation of Shakespeare's early modern British play, Rash's contemporary Appalachian novel responds to a swarm of calls. Shakespeare's famed "Scots tragedy" finds resurrection or a kind of resurrection (the eerie afterlife of the undead) in Rash's Scots Irish tragedy. Cultivating a complex intertextual narrative with such deep connections to past authors and characters has enabled Rash to create a meaningful dialogue between the living and the (un)dead.

The third part of the collection, "War, Memory, Violence," begins with an essay by Adam J. Pratt in which he has provided a detailed account of the Shelton Laurel Massacre. This massacre occurred in January 1863, when Confederate troops in Madison County, North Carolina, executed thirteen nonmilitary Union sympathizers, most of them old men and young boys. Pratt's essay analyzes the existing historiography about the massacre and, more broadly, how the memory of the Civil War has transfixed the imagination of Appalachians from the 1860s to the present. While the legacy of the Civil War has been studied from a wide variety of vantage points, its reception among past and present Appalachians requires further investigation, as Appalachians were and are sometimes still split in their attitudes toward the war and how best to deal with its lingering questions and traumas. Surveying the historiographical literature about this topic provides much needed new insights into Rash's complex interrogation of the Shelton Laurel Massacre and the Civil War as well as the ways in which these events have led to social fracturing in various communities in southern Appalachia. Ultimately Pratt's essay argues that a more nuanced and honest reckoning of the region's troubled relationship with the Civil War will contextualize and further explicate Travis Shelton's story.

Extending the discussion of the Shelton Laurel Massacre, John Lang's essay examines how the massacre has impacted Rash's literary imagination. Rash has written about the Shelton Laurel Massacre most directly in *The World Made Straight,* but he has also alluded to it in a range of other texts, both fiction ("Dead Confederates," *Saints at the River,* and *The Cove*) and poetry (*Among the Believers, Raising the Dead,* and *Waking*). Lang has provided a comprehensive survey of the numerous allusions to the massacre that occur in Rash's work as well as how these allusions change over time. Lang's essay argues that this atrocity has played such an abiding role in Rash's artistic vision owing to the fact that, in Rash's own words, he is "haunted still."

Edward J. Whitelock's essay explores how Rash's fiction responds to traditional southern cultures of honor, which he has traced back to the Scots Irish and Welsh immigrants who came to the region in the eighteenth and nineteenth centuries. Building on Bertram Wyatt-Brown's seminal text *Southern Honor: Ethics and Behavior in the Old South* (1982) as well as more recent works by Edward L. Ayers, Grady McWhiney, and Richard E. Nisbett and Dov Cohen, Whitelock's essay illustrates how southern honor was used, in the stratified culture of the Old South, as a means of maintaining or even improving one's status in the eyes of society. Rash's fiction adds to ongoing conversations about the function of southern honor both in the past and present, and Whitelock has convincingly demonstrated that southern honor is a central but heretofore unacknowledged theme that is pervasive throughout all of Rash's novels.

Thomas Ærvold Bjerre's contribution to the collection examines Rash's *The Cove* (2012), a novel that remains understudied by scholars and critics. Although *The Cove* deals less directly with war than some of Rash's other works, it provides an intimate examination of what occurs back home both to those soldiers who return as well as those family members who are left in their absence, some for only a time and some permanently. Moreover, the novel offers a fuller understanding of World War I and its profound ramifications in small communities in the rural South, and it resonates compellingly with contemporary political concerns regarding prejudice and xenophobia.

While the other contributors to this part of the collection have explained Rash's relationship to violence associated with war, this part concludes with a study by James Eric Ensley of a very different type of violence: cultural colonialism. Attentive to the need to assert the voices of native Appalachians into national and international conversations in order to more accurately depict the region, Ensley's essay warns that the task for Appalachian studies scholars is similar to postcolonial studies scholars in that they must avoid ventriloquizing their subjects in the quest for cultural authenticity. Postcolonial criticism is particularly relevant to the study of Appalachia if we understand the region to exist, as Rodger Cunningham famously wrote, in a state of double alterity—this is, it functions as an Other both for the South and the nation. Summoning theorists ranging from Homi K. Bhabha to Gayatri Spivak to Edward Said, Ensley has offered a productive reading of Appalachia as a postcolonial literary space, and his essay contends that Rash's work gives voice to a subaltern culture by depicting Appalachian identity as one that is peripheral to the United States and is thus more closely related to other peripheral postcolonial territories across the globe.

Our hope is that this collection will help to remedy the fact that Rash's fiction and poetry remain understudied and undertheorized. Rash's work, with its popular and scholarly appeal as well as its invaluable social critiques and celebrations, is increasingly relevant and important on both local and global levels, and thus it warrants ongoing academic attention. Rash's work encourages readers and critics alike to understand Appalachia in all its complexity, and Rash has consistently provided portrayals of the region that reveal the beauty of its cultures and landscapes as well as the social and environmental pathologies that it has and continues to face. The landscapes, peoples, and cultures that emerge in Rash's work (and that are examined in the essays in this collection) represent and respond not only to Appalachia or the South, but also to national and global cultures as well. Firmly rooted in the mountain South, Rash's artistic vision weaves the truths of the human condition and the perils of the human heart in a poetic language that speaks deeply to us all.

Notes

1. Mythology and regional practices of bonding fires, or "bonfires," vary throughout Great Britain. In Rash's work the ritual most often resonates with the Scots Irish, and Welsh traditions. Whether these fires were set for protection from evil, for homage to water spirits, or for warding off demonic presences, in Rash's poem "Bonding Fire" the light in darkness assumes familial and ancestral power passing "hearth to hearth" as generations leave the highlands and immigrate to the Blue Ridge Mountains, the "flame / two centuries old" that burn with the ties that bind (*Waking* 17).

2. Rash has used this phrase in many interviews and in his nonfiction essays about the Shelton Laurel Massacre in Madison County, North Carolina. See Bjerre and Lang for lengthier discussions and analyses of this important trope in developing Rash's historical consciousness.

3. See Thoreau 400.

4. See Jung 103–7.

Works Cited

Bjerre, Thomas Ærvold. "'The Natural World Is the Most Universal of Languages': An Interview with Ron Rash." *Appalachian Journal* 34 (2007): 216–27.

Jung, Carl S. *Man and His Symbols.* New York: Dell, 1964.

Lang, John. *Understanding Ron Rash.* Columbia: University of South Carolina Press, 2014.

Rash, Ron. *Waking.* Spartanburg, S.C.: Hub City, 2011.

———. *Eureka Mill.* Spartanburg, S.C.: Hub City Press, 1998.

Thoreau, Henry David. *A Week on the Concord and Merrimack Rivers, Walden; or, Life in the Woods, The Maine Woods, Cape Cod.* New York: Library of America, 1985.

Part I

THE NATURAL WORLD

STRANGE AGRARIANISMS

Transmutations of *I'll Take My Stand* in James Dickey's *Deliverance* and Ron Rash's *One Foot in Eden*

Zackary Vernon

In writing his debut novel *One Foot in Eden* (2002), Ron Rash entered headlong into Dickey country, and this was no small feat for a first-time novelist. James Dickey looms large in the American, southern, and Appalachian literary imaginations. His fiction and poetry still garner critical and scholarly attention, and his novel *Deliverance* (1970) remains a significant cultural phenomenon despite the fact that it was published nearly half a century ago. Emily Satterwhite claimed that *Deliverance* "continue[s] to shape national perceptions of the Appalachian region" in the twenty-first century (131), and that the film adaptation (1972) "continues to be the single most prominent pop cultural reference to Appalachia" (23). Even within the region, *Deliverance* shapes perceptions of Appalachian popular culture. This is readily apparent if one travels through the lower mountain South, particularly in the tourist destinations of northern Georgia, northwestern South Carolina, and western North Carolina; there you will inevitably see allusions to *Deliverance,* such as the nearly ubiquitous bumper stickers and T-shirts that read "PADDLE FASTER, I HEAR BANJO MUSIC!"

Rash entered or, one could say, *invaded* this Dickey-centric landscape in that *One Foot in Eden* bears striking resemblance to the plot and predominant themes of *Deliverance.* Dickey's novel follows a group of four Atlanta suburbanites who endeavor to paddle down a "wild" river before it is dammed to create a hydroelectric reservoir; Dickey's river is based on two rivers in northern Georgia, the Coosawattee and the Chattooga, both of which were threatened during the 1960s with damming projects and hydroelectric plants. The Chattooga, where the film adaptation of *Deliverance* was shot, begins around Cashiers, North Carolina, then forms the border of South Carolina and Georgia, and finally travels through parts of northern Georgia. *One Foot in Eden* is also about the damming of a river to create a hydroelectric reservoir, and Rash's river is based on the Keowee, which runs through the northwestern corner of South Carolina, not far from the Chattooga. In addition Rash's novel, like Dickey's, explores how humans' cultural connections to the landscapes around them change as these environments are irrevocably altered.

However, Rash's novel is far from a mere attempt at mimicry. Instead Rash's project in *One Foot in Eden* is to critique much of *Deliverance,* especially its unflattering depiction of southern Appalachia, by providing a more nuanced and realistic portrayal of the region. In doing so Rash focuses his narrative on the lives of the region's natives, rather than interlopers from elsewhere, in order to show how the creation of a large-scale dam and reservoir affects indigenous cultures and economies by dismantling agricultural communities. This thematic preoccupation places Rash within a long tradition of southern and Appalachian authors who have written about the South's relationship to agriculture. While this tradition extends back to the nation's founders—most important, Thomas Jefferson—it increased in popular appeal in the early to mid-twentieth century as a direct result of the Southern Agrarians' manifesto *I'll Take My Stand: The South and the Agrarian Tradition* (1930). Dickey himself was intimately familiar with Southern Agrarianism, and he transmutes it in strange and unexpected ways in *Deliverance.* Rash, too, transmuted this tradition in *One Foot in Eden* but did so in order to counter the very different but equally romanticized agrarian narratives presented in *I'll Take My Stand* and *Deliverance.* In contrast Rash's work provides an agrarian narrative that is remarkably *un-strange* in that it is far more accurate and evenhanded than anything the Southern Agrarians or Dickey ever penned.[1]

The Uses and Limits of Southern Agrarianism

If scholars and public intellectuals in the fields of environmental, agricultural, and food studies employ the term "agrarianism," they must do so only after acknowledging its troubling legacy within the context of the American South. If we are fully cognizant of the racism, classism, and misogyny that are pervasive in texts like *I'll Take My Stand,* we may then, and only then, reappropriate the term and employ it in the contemporary context. We may even be able to return to the works of the Southern Agrarians and reevaluate them, confronting their problematic elements, while also exploring the potentially positive ramifications of their platform. My purpose in this chapter is to highlight the baggage associated with the Southern Agrarians; however, I do not want to simply bring up the Agrarians in order to denounce them yet again. Rather I aim to acknowledge their potential contributions to American environmental philosophy and agricultural activism in order to investigate the various transmutations of Southern

Agrarianism, both positive and negative, that have developed in the twentieth- and twenty-first-century American literary canon.

The core group that would later make up the Southern Agrarians began to coalesce when several talented writers, calling themselves "the Fugitives," banded together at Vanderbilt University just after World War I. By the mid-1920s, the Fugitives became increasingly uncomfortable with what they saw as the tenants of modernity, namely commercialism, materialism, industrialization, intellectual condescension, and an absence of an ethical foundation. As a result the group took on a new title, the Agrarians, and in 1930 published *I'll Take My Stand.* The authors of this manifesto include John Crowe Ransom, Donald Davidson, Frank Lawrence Owsley, John Gould Fletcher, Lyle H. Lanier, Allen Tate, Herman Clarence Nixon, Andrew Nelson Lytle, Robert Penn Warren, John Donald Wade, Henry Blue Klime, and Stark Young. Ransom believed ardently that the book cultivated a central unified argument, and to stress this unity he drafted "A Statement of Principles" to serve as the introduction to the book. Although Ransom first wrote this introduction, all twelve of the authors assisted in editing it, and ultimately all subscribed to its content. The introduction encapsulates the overarching aim of *I'll Take My Stand* in that it suggests that humankind is fundamentally unfulfilled, both psychologically and spiritually, in an industrial society. Conversely the Agrarians suggested that fulfillment is more easily attained in an agrarian society, and they problematically chose the Old South as their primary model. The fact that antebellum agriculture was built on the backs of slaves was rarely recognized by the Agrarians. While Frank Lawrence Owsley conceded that slavery was part of the agrarian system and indeed one facet of the ideological schism that led to the Civil War, he, like the other Agrarians, whitewashed southern history by arguing that slavery was "only one element and not an essential one" (73).

Despite the fact that some of the Agrarians, especially Stark Young, were willing to advocate or at least wax romantic about a return to a large, plantation-esque system of agriculture, most of the Agrarians tended to support a return to small-scale subsistence farming. In his essay "The Hind Tit," Lytle contended that "it is in fact impossible for any culture to be sound and healthy without a proper respect and proper regard for the soil" (203). Lytle spent the vast majority of the second half of "The Hind Tit" describing, in great detail, the life of a "provincial" subsistence farming family that possesses a deep and satisfying sense of community. To combat the pitfalls of industrial societies, Lytle suggested that farmers become independent of the cash economic system and self-sufficient for all their daily needs. By producing and preparing their own food, making their own clothes, and tending the upkeep of their own houses and properties, farmers could feasibly "live in an industrial world without a great deal of cash"

(244). Additionally Lytle argued that if southerners and indeed all American citizens in agricultural communities were to disregard "the articles the industrialists offer for sale," then they could reaffirm local folkways: "return to our looms, our handcrafts, our reproducing stock. Throw out the radio and take down the fiddle from the wall. Forsake the movies for the play-parties and the square dances" (244). Such traditions, Lytle implied, could continue to thrive in agricultural communities but not in industrialized ones.[2]

While *I'll Take My Stand* generally fails to address specifically the social and agricultural problems the South faced in 1930, most of the Agrarians—with the exception of Davidson—noted that they were presenting an ideology and not a practical blueprint for how to change an industrial society back into an agrarian one. Their principal objective was only to point out that "if a community, or a section, or a race, or an age, is groaning under industrialism, and well aware that it is an evil dispensation, it must find the way to throw it off" (xlviii). With that in mind, *I'll Take My Stand* should be studied for its revolutionary impulse rather than its practical importance. Southern Agrarianism has engendered a range of ideological responses in southern and American culture, and various writers have conceived it as an anecdote for the cultural pathologies of particular times and places. I will now turn my attention to one such example, *Deliverance,* in order to see how Dickey transmuted the Agrarian platform for the atomic age.

James Dickey's Apocalyptic Agrarianism

After World War II, James Dickey studied both literature and anthropology at Vanderbilt University. While there he became increasingly interested in the debate between agrarianism and industrialization. Donald Davidson was the only Agrarian still at Vanderbilt when Dickey was there, although he later served as Andrew Lytle's assistant at the University of Florida (Dickey, *Self-Interviews* 33, 35) and became a close friend of Robert Penn Warren (Hart xviii). Dickey has said that when he arrived at Vanderbilt the debate over agrarianism and industrialization "was no longer a burning question, but it was still in the air" (*Self-Interviews* 34). Consequently Dickey steeped himself in the writings of the Fugitives and the Agrarians. In particular he was fascinated by *I'll Take My Stand* (1930), which in his 1970 *Self-Interviews,* he claimed "is still very powerful" (34). However, according to Dickey, the best book of the Fugitive-Agrarian body of work was Davidson's *Regionalism and Nationalism in the United States: The Attack on Leviathan* (1938). Dickey described its significance to him: "Davidson points out that you belong to a specific time and place where you can see the same things and a certain number of the same human beings every day. . . . This is the way human beings were meant to live. This is the way they can root down into a place and develop their own way of life in harmony with the environment. . . . I'm really convinced of the truth and necessity of what Davidson points out: that differences give richness and variety to life and offset the terrible monotony that we're drifting toward in Americanizing the whole world, where eventually there won't be anything but a supermarket culture" (35).

Owing to his desire to achieve this "way of life in harmony with the environment," Dickey remained preoccupied throughout his career with the work of the Southern Agrarians, and that work undoubtedly influenced his thinking. The question I will take up in this section of the chapter is whether Dickey drew on this influence in writing *Deliverance* and whether a distinctly Southern Agrarian worldview is present, problematically or not, in the novel. To address this question, I will focus on two characters, Ed and Lewis, to determine whether their conceptions of humanity's relationship with the environment resonate with *I'll Take My Stand.*

Early in *Deliverance,* as the men are driving toward the river in north Georgia, Ed and Lewis spend much of the trip discussing the possibility of nuclear annihilation. Although little critical attention has been paid to *Deliverance* in the context of nuclear proliferation, the novel is marked by an undercurrent of atomic anxiety. Dickey himself was particularly fixated on this issue, because during his service in World War II, he witnessed the bombing and subsequent destruction of Nagasaki (*The One Voice* 96). On one hand Ed and Lewis's conversations exemplify Cold War America's anxiety about a nuclear warfare–induced apocalypse. On the other hand, though, these conversations are uniquely southern, because Lewis's fascination with postapocalyptic life seems to be informed by Dickey's own fascination with Southern Agrarianism. While Dickey's characters represent the alienated work force of an industrialized society, they cannot conceive of achieving an agrarian dream via a rededication to an agriculturally based society; instead Lewis believes an agrarian society would be possible only in the aftermath of some kind of apocalyptic nightmare, such as the dropping of an "H-bomb" (44), which would return humanity to a more elemental and perhaps even sustainable existence in southern Appalachia.

Emily Satterwhite argued, "*Deliverance* manufactured a rural, premodern Appalachia set apart from consumer society and its purportedly banal suburban lifestyle that, despite the predatory nature of the mountain villains, somehow managed to activate readers' romance with authenticity" (156). In the novel Lewis is enamored by the same kind of "romance with authenticity" that Satterwhite identified in readers, and his return to an "authentic" society is predicated on the dismantling of contemporary American culture. He says, "I think the machines are going to fail, the political systems are going to fail, and a few men are going to take to the hills and start over" (Dickey, *Deliverance* 42). He then asks Ed: "Where would you go when the radios died?" (44). This question alludes directly to Andrew Lytle's contribution to *I'll Take My Stand.* In perhaps the most evocative moment of his essay, which I mentioned briefly in the previous section of this chapter, Lytle entreated southerners to abandon mass-produced commodities in order "to avoid the dire consequences and to maintain a farming life in an industrial imperialism" (244). Lytle believed that such a return to the farm would have far-ranging cultural and artistic ramifications, and he famously entreated his readers to reinvigorate region-specific folkways, saying, "Throw out the radio and take down the fiddle from the wall" (244). In Lewis's imagination southerners, so long inundated by popular culture, are no longer capable of destroying the proverbial radio; therefore Lewis envisions an apocalyptic scenario through which the choice is negated, the radio dies, and the surviving people of the South head back to the hills and begin anew in a more elemental existence. Lewis's vision culminates in a distinctly agrarian philosophy as he tells Ed how he would live after the fall of society and the necessitated return to the land: "If everything wasn't dead, you could make a kind of life that wasn't out of touch with everything, with the other forms of life. Where the seasons would mean something, would mean everything. Where you could hunt as you needed to, and maybe do a little light farming, and get along. You'd die early, and you'd suffer, and your children would suffer, but you'd be in touch" (Dickey, *Deliverance* 44). If the narrative ended here, then we could certainly argue that, through Lewis, Dickey was promoting a distinctly Agrarian perspective at the heart of which is the small-scale subsistence farmer. But, of course, the narrative does not end here. Lewis, the mouthpiece of the Agrarian platform, albeit a strange and mutated Cold War inflection of that platform, is bested by nature early on in the novel. His leg is broken in a whitewater rafting accident, and his apocalyptic agrarian philosophizing is swiftly curtailed.

Unlike Lewis, Ed hates the rural South and repeatedly demeans Lewis's romanticization of this apocalyptic form of Southern Agrarianism. Ed labors under an antipastoral impulse, which he employs to deflate the myths and idealizations that Lewis propagates. Ed says, "You'd think that farming was a healthy life, with fresh air and fresh food and plenty of exercise, but I never saw a farmer who didn't have something wrong with him, and most of the time obviously wrong; I never saw one who was physically powerful, either. Certainly there were none like Lewis" (Dickey, *Deliverance* 56). Assessing Lewis's perspective in relation to Ed's, Barnett Guttenberg argued, "In his will to dominate, Lewis is part of the devitalized society which dams the river; he, too, stops the stream of primal energy. His overriding will must be broken before he can join Ed in a right relation to nature" (84). Yet Ed's "right relation" to the environment—be it natural or not—is highly debatable. When the men first set out on the river,

Ed never feels "civilized" (Dickey, *Deliverance* 76) in the natural world. The first time that Ed says "We were civilized again" occurs after the men pass an industrial chicken-processing plant that is polluting the river with trash and animal by-products. This is at least the second time on the river that the men have seen signs of human cultivation. Prior to encountering the processing plant, the men had floated past a farm; however, Ed associates civilization not with the farm but rather with the processing plant and the pollution in the river. If the farm represents the agrarian garden, then the factory suggests the Leo Marxian machine in the garden, and ironically it is the latter that Ed finds comforting. Ed does not begin to feel fully at ease in the rural South until the men set up their camp; after pitching their tents and, in effect, creating a small city on the edge of the river, he says, "I felt a good deal better; we had colonized the place" (83). Although Ed does implicitly lament the environmental degradation of southern Appalachia later in the novel, he never mourns the cultures—including agricultural communities—that are displaced by the construction of the dam. To Ed the flattening of regional diversity is fundamentally a boon for society, and he seems to welcome the eradication of the "natives" and the homogenization of the region.

For Ed, in the perennial battle between the desire to preserve and the desire to colonize the natural world, the latter impulse inevitably wins. For Lewis the "supermarket culture" of upper-middle-class Atlanta suburbanites is already ubiquitous, and, as a result, he must imagine a more extreme catalyst—in this case a nuclear apocalypse—for cultural change to occur. However, in *Deliverance,* such a change does not appear to be imminently forthcoming, and, by the end of novel, Dickey's characters, Lewis included, no longer seem interested in such an extreme transformation. Having experienced the "wilderness" and in turn assuaged their sense of malaise, the men return to the suburbs of Atlanta, and their subsequent retreats from the suburbs are far less, to use Lewis's term, "wild." In the last pages of the novel, Ed and Lewis buy houses on a man-made lake. This is, of course, highly ironic given their extreme reactions against the damming of a wild river in the opening of the novel. It appears that contentment for these characters stems not from the urban center or the undisturbed wilderness but rather, as in the final scene, from a man-made, hydroelectric lake, which represents a balanced, albeit fabricated, space that is simultaneously wild and domesticated. Thus Lewis seems to be disabused of his apocalyptic Agrarian dreams, and Ed's antiagrarian worldview is largely vindicated. Yet, in his own strange way, Dickey has brought us back to agrarianism, because the man-made lake is similar to agriculture in that it conflates the built and the natural and, as a result, affords the characters some semblance of wildness without actually having to enter the wilderness. Since small-scale agriculture in the United States has largely become a thing of the past, the liminal space of the man-made lake seems to be the best option these suburbanites can muster in their postagrarian world.

Rash's Rebuke of I'll Take My Stand *and* Deliverance

Ron Rash's relationship with *I'll Take My Stand* has been far less documented than Dickey's, and he has not had the personal connection to the Southern Agrarians that Dickey surely had. However, in an interview in 2006, I asked Rash about the Southern Agrarians, and he confirmed that he had read *I'll Take My Stand.* However, Rash was quick to critique the Agrarians, saying, "I read *I'll Take My Stand.* . . . But there is a kind of romanticizing of that [agricultural] lifestyle. You get a sense that some of those Agrarians, a few of them, envision themselves as plantation owners essentially. Somebody else is going to be doing the hard work." Rash's skepticism about *I'll Take My Stand* and the Agrarian platform more broadly is evident throughout *One Foot in Eden,* which confronts romanticized agrarian stereotypes and ultimately undermines them by providing a more realistic depiction of the region's agricultural communities.

Like Dickey, Rash was already a well-known and respected poet, but it was the publication of his first novel that made him a national best seller and garnered several major awards, including the Appalachian Book of the Year. *One Foot in Eden* revisits material that Rash previously used in his three poetry collections, *Eureka Mill* (1998), *Among the Believers* (2000), and *Raising the Dead* (2002). As in many of the poems featured in these collections, the narrative of *One Foot in Eden* is set in the Jocassee Valley, an area of upstate South Carolina that was flooded in the 1960s to create a massive hydroelectric reservoir. Randall Wilhelm explained Rash's continued fascination with this historical circumstance by asserting that his "characters fear the encroaching flood that will drown their land, their ancestors, and their agrarian way of life. The novel expresses Rash's genuine fear of cultural erasure—that an entire way of life and its people can vanish so easily" ("Introduction" 13). In the aforementioned interview, Rash stated, "When I wrote *One Foot in Eden,* part of what I wanted to do was resurrect that valley." Rash went on to explain that he had been "obsessed" with the Jocassee Valley since he lived near the area in Oconee County during the 1970s. While teaching at a rural high school there, Rash spent a great deal of time talking to locals and learning about "what had been lost" when the hydroelectric reservoir was created and how it displaced so many people who had lived and, in most cases, farmed in the area. Rash dramatized the flooding of the Jocassee Valley in *One Foot in Eden,* and in doing so, he has given life to a people and a culture that had once existed in "Jocassee"—a Cherokee word that appropriately means "valley of the lost."

While *Deliverance* is told from the perspective of Ed Gentry, an Atlanta suburbanite who ventures into the mountains of southern Appalachia for a weekend lark, *One Foot in Eden* is narrated by five different characters, all of whom are locals living in and around the Jocassee Valley as the flood project is initiated. The central story, both narratologically and thematically, is about Billy and Amy Holcombe, a young couple who own and operate a small farm in the valley that is about to be flooded. The story's drama begins because Billy is infertile—an apt metaphor for a novel about the deterioration of agriculture in southern Appalachia. Unable to conceive a child with Billy, Amy makes love with and is ultimately impregnated by a neighbor named Holland Winchester. When Holland finds out about the pregnancy and begins making demands of Amy, Billy murders him. Much of the rest of the novel is concerned with Billy hiding the body, as the local authorities—particularly Sheriff Alexander, one of the novel's narrators—search for the body in order to drum up enough evidence to convict Billy. As in *Deliverance,* solving the story's central murder depends on finding the victim's body. Wondering where Billy might have hidden the body, Sheriff Alexander thinks, "*Your best chance was the river, your only real chance, because water can keep things covered up*" (43). Although Billy does not hide the body in the river, he knows that "the law needs a body to claim a murder" (130). The characters in *Deliverance* share a similar conviction, and in both novels the dead bodies are hidden and then submerged by floodwaters, which cover up the characters' secrets forever. Burying bodies in both novels also evokes the notion that agriculture in the region is on the decline as people sow death, rather than life, in their local landscapes.

Billy and Amy Holcombe not only drive the overarching drama of *One Foot in Eden;* they are also central to Rash's project of depicting southern Appalachian agriculture as fairly and as accurately as possible. While the Holcombes are not subsistence farmers because they grow cash crops and are thus imbricated in a wider network of capitalist commerce, they are precisely the kind of small-scale farmers that the nostalgically minded Southern Agrarians would have commemorated. So in tune are Billy and Amy with the agricultural settings around them that they constantly use farming-based metaphors to understand and explain their lives. For example, in describing her difficulty getting pregnant, Amy says that she is "fallow as a December corn field" (66). In another scene she states, "Each time my blood flowed it seemed it was our hearts' blood that was flowing, like our hearts that had once swelled so full of love for one another was shriveling like tomatoes in a drought" (75). Similarly, when Billy thinks about Amy having sex with Holland, he imagines "him between her legs like a plow in a furrow" (118). For both Amy and Billy, these agricultural metaphors help to structure and interpret the events, both good and bad, of their lives. Thus, the Southern Agrarians might argue that they are autochthonous people who understand themselves and derive their livelihoods through the agrarian culture to which they are inextricably bound. This interpretation, however, is increasingly difficult to maintain as Billy and Amy's story continues.

In *One Foot in Eden,* Billy is a kind of self-made, independent farmer; he says, "By the time I'd met Amy I'd paid enough of the bank loan to finally call the twenty acres I'd bought from Joshua Winchester my own. That had been a big doing for me. The only land Daddy and my Uncle Joel could claim was what dirt they carried under their fingernails" (121). However, as proud as he is of his land ownership, Billy also acknowledges the negative facets of the farming life he has established. For instance he says that he and his mule worked as hard as they could "to make a living from this scratch-ankle mountain land but no matter how hard [they] worked there'd be things [they] couldn't do nothing about. All [they] could do was keep the reins tight and hope for the best" (138–39). Billy is also fully aware of how difficult small-scale farming can be on people, both physically and psychologically (141); and yet they continue to derive pleasure from their farm until they are forced to abandon it. "It's a pretty place," Amy says, seeing the farm for the last time. "I don't notion I knew how pretty till these last few days" (186). When the floodwaters displace the Holcombe family, they, like so many in the Jocassee Valley, move to a nearby town, and Billy begins to work in a mill. Although their lives have undoubtedly been difficult on the farm, Billy and Amy struggle constantly to acclimate to life in town as well as at the mill. Consequently they mourn the loss of their farm (187) and long to get "a place out in the country" (188).

If the Holcombes remain throughout most of the novel agrarian insiders, then Sheriff Alexander is both an insider and outsider. In this sense it is Alexander who has, as the title of the novel suggests, one foot in either world—the rural and the urban, the agricultural and the industrialized; however, Rash refuses to permit his readers from thinking that either of these worlds is an "Eden." Instead Alexander provides a candid assessment of each world, finding much to celebrate and critique in both. While Alexander's family's livelihood is still tied to working the land, he no longer has to worry about agricultural concerns like the weather. Alexander is distanced from agriculture and his family because he went to Clemson College, joined the police force, and now lives in town. So alienated is he from his family that, in one scene, when he enters a field on the family farm that his brother is working, he says that his brother "stared at [him], the same way he'd stare at a stump in his field or anything else bothersome" (18). His brother then says, "You ain't needed anything up here for a long time" (18). As a result of his sense of exile from his family and their agricultural pursuits, Alexander says that he "was the ghost, haunting a valley where [he] no longer belonged" (55).

Yet, within the cast of characters in *One Foot in Eden,* Alexander is the best person to assess the split between agrarianism and industrialization, because he has both farmed and worked a "dead-end job in a cotton mill" (49). Having labored throughout his youth on his family's farm, Alexander remembers "how it felt to hoe tobacco—how the sweat stung your eyes and your back stayed bent so long you felt by day's end you'd need a crowbar to straighten yourself" (14–15). The worst part of farming, he contends, is "knowing no matter how hard you worked, it might come to nothing" (15). While Alexander reminds himself, "Don't pretend you miss such a life as this" (15), he cannot help but feel a pull toward agriculture, and he dreams of leaving the police force and farming with his family once again. In one flight of fancy, he says, "I'd farm this land until Carolina Power ran us all out and drowned these fields and creeks and the river itself. However long that was, it would give me some time to be a son and a brother again, maybe even learn how to be an uncle" (40). But what Alexander seems to lack is precisely what his father has always possessed—"the love of a place that connected you to generations of your family" (49).

Shortly after making these statements, Alexander witnesses Billy's struggle to adjust to life at the mill, and at this point he provides his most balanced assessment of the pros and cons of working on a farm and at a mill:

> He'd work in a mill where he'd get a paycheck at the end of every week and not have to worry anymore about drought and hail and tobacco worms.
>
> Other changes he wouldn't like as much, things that would make him miss being behind a horse and plow. He'd have to ask permission to get a drink of water or take a piss. The work would be the same thing day after day, week after week, the mill hot and humid as dog days all year round. He'd breathe an unending drizzle of lint he'd spend half his nights coughing back up.
>
> His work would give him no satisfaction, but he'd have a wife and child to go home to when the mill whistle freed him at day's end. There were men who would envy that about him if nothing else. (56)

Alexander's conflicted responses to his agricultural heritage in southern Appalachia closely resemble those of Rash's own family members. Rash said, "I can remember my grandmother telling me about some of my relatives who worked in mills and how there was a kind stability there. Though you could get hurt and lose your job and not get any kind of compensation, you knew at least that you were going to get a paycheck. You knew you weren't going to plant a crop and work on it three months and then have a hailstorm or a drought or a tobacco barn burnout or any those kinds of things. They didn't romanticize the agricultural world they came from; nevertheless, one thing all my relatives have done is they all want to be buried back in the mountains. So that landscape and that place continue to have a pull on them" (Vernon "Interview"). Similarly, in

One Foot in Eden, Sheriff Alexander wants to be buried in his ancestral home; he says, "When I had become a deputy I had made out my will and stipulated that I was to be buried here in Jocassee with the other Alexanders. I hoped I would be in that grave before they built the reservoir so when the water rose it would rise over me" as well as all those who had come before him in that place (57).

Throughout *One Foot in Eden,* Rash clearly drew on the experiences and perspectives of his family members. In doing so he was able to provide a portrait of the region in a time of accelerated transition. With regard to the continually transmuted legacy of agrarianism in the American South, Rash's portrait of both agriculture and industry in the region is relatively unproblematic in that it takes into account both the positive and negative facets of each culture. While the Southern Agrarians romanticized the life of large- and small-scale antebellum farmers and while Dickey contemplated an agrarianism catalyzed by a nuclear apocalypse, Rash's depictions of the region's agriculture and industrialization are comparatively un-strange in that he opted for accuracy in cataloguing this particular chapter in the history an ever-evolving region.

If Rash entered Dickey country with the publication of his first novel, then now, after the publication of his four volumes of poetry, six novels, and six short-story collections, we could say that Rash has firmly planted his own flag in this literary and geographical landscape. Furthermore Rash's landscape has been cultivated with care and honest conviction, and it ultimately provides a far more accurate depiction of southern Appalachia than Dickey ever achieved. Although *Deliverance* may continue to haunt the minds of Appalachians and shape national and international perceptions of the region, it seems increasingly possible that in the years to come readers may approach *Deliverance* as an early novel that happens to be set in Rash country.

Notes

1. Owing to space constraints, my focus in this chapter will be on the debut novels of Dickey and Rash. I have discussed Rash's poetry in this context in a previous essay. See Vernon, "The Role of Witness." However, there is much work to be done on the relationship between the poetry of Dickey and Rash as well as on how that relationship is configured in response to Southern Agrarianism. For a more extended analysis of "the large-scale shift . . . from agrarian to industrial values" and how this historical shift is explored in Rash's poetry, see Wilhelm, "Ghostly" (25).

2. Alexander Karanikas argued that the Agrarians' use of the Old South to buttress the Jeffersonian ideal of the small-scale yeoman farmer rendered their argument fundamentally flawed. While subsistence farming may have been a desired goal in frontier conditions, it most often resulted "from misfortune or incompetence, not from any conscious desire" (Karanikas 65). The subsistence farmer "had no greater wish than to make a lot of money, build himself a big white house, purchase slaves, and emulate the leisurely 'good life' of the rich, cultivated gentleman." Scholars in Appalachian studies have also

noted that the ideal of the subsistence farmer was largely a myth. For example Wilma Dunaway stated, "Contrary to long-standing stereotypes, there were few subsistent producers in Southern Appalachia" (20). Ronald L. Lewis also pointed out that "the idea that Appalachia was the land of subsistence farmers until recent times is under serious reevaluation" (25).

Works Cited

Dickey, James. *Deliverance.* 1970. New York: Delta Trade Paperbacks, 1994.

———. *The One Voice of James Dickey: His Letters and Life, 1942–1969.* Ed. Gordon Van-Ness. Columbia: University of Missouri Press, 2003.

———. *Self-Interviews.* Recorded and edited by Barbara and James Reiss. Baton Rouge: Louisiana State UP, 1970, 1970.

Dunaway, Wilma A. *The First American Frontier: Transition to Capitalism in Southern Appalachia, 1700–1860.* Chapel Hill: University of North Carolina Press, 1996.

Guttenberg, Barnett. "The Pattern of Redemption in Dickey's *Deliverance.*" *Critique* 18.3 (1977): 83–91.

Hart, Henry. *James Dickey: The World as a Lie.* New York: Picador USA, 2000.

Karanikas, Alexander. *Tillers of a Myth: Southern Agrarians as Social and Literary Critics.* Madison: University of Wisconsin Press, 1966.

Lewis, Ronald L. "Beyond Isolation and Homogeneity: Diversity and the History of Appalachia." *Back Talk from Appalachia: Confronting Stereotypes.* Ed. Dwight B. Billings, Gurney Norman, and Katherine Ledford. Lexington: University Press of Kentucky, 1999.

Lytle, Andrew. "The Hind Tit." *I'll Take My Stand: The South and the Agrarian Tradition.* 1930. Ed. Louis D. Rubin, Jr. Baton Rouge: Louisiana State U P, 1979. 201–45.

Owsley, Frank Lawrence. "The Irrepressible Conflict." *I'll Take My Stand: The South and the Agrarian Tradition.* 1930. Ed. Louis D. Rubin, Jr. Baton Rouge: Louisiana State UP, 1979. 61–91.

Ransom, John Crowe, Donald Davidson, Frank Lawrence Owsley, John Gould Fletcher, Lyle H. Lanier, Allen Tate, Herman Clarence Nixon, Andrew Nelson Lytle, Robert Penn Warren, John Donald Wade, Henry Blue Klime, and Stark Young. *I'll Take My Stand: The South and the Agrarian Tradition.* 1930. Baton Rouge: Louisiana State University Press, 1979.

Rash, Ron. *One Foot in Eden.* New York: Henry Holt, 2002.

Satterwhite, Emily. *Dear Appalachia: Readers, Identity, and Popular Fiction since 1878.* Lexington: University Press of Kentucky, 2011.

Vernon, Zackary. Interview with Ron Rash. October 12, 2006. Clemson, S.C.

———. "The Role of Witness: Ron Rash's Peculiarly Historical Consciousness." *South Carolina Review* 42.2 (Spring 2010): 19–24.

Wilhelm, Randall. "Ghostly Bodies and Worker Voices: Power and Resistance in Ron Rash's *Eureka Mill.*" *South Carolina Review* 42.2 (Spring 2010): 25–36.

———. "Introduction: Blood Memory." In *The Ron Rash Reader.* Ed. Randall Wilhelm. Columbia: University of South Carolina Press, 2014. 1–32.

"LIKE A DAM BROKE OPEN"

Water and Narrative in Ron Rash's *One Foot in Eden*

Frédérique Spill

"The pain of water is infinite."
Gaston Bachelard, *Water and Dreams*

Water—which Gaston Bachelard called "the universal liquid" (60) and which Edgar Allan Poe described in "The Sleeper" as "the pure element"—plays a major role in Rash's fiction and poetry. The characters in Rash's writing are often shown struggling with water, and their hubristic efforts to master the natural world are forcefully illustrated by the obsessive recurrence of images of the dam and man-made lake that irreversibly transformed the Jocassee Valley. Though this dam was completed in 1974,[1] water-related issues began long before, altering—and very profoundly so—the habits, traditions, and beliefs of the people living in the valley. With compelling variation, Rash's works reimagine the key motif of man's (and sometimes woman's) exploitative struggle with nature—their efforts to contend with, let alone master, nature's inherent, unpredictable forces. The antithetical power of water—at the same time life giving and destructive—is at the core of Rash's poetics. This leitmotiv took shape in two books published in 2002, the first of which—a collection of poems with a programmatic title *Raising the Dead*—engendered the second, Rash's debut novel *One Foot in Eden,* thus confirming the flowing quality of his imaginative and creative processes.

Both books are responses to the same event: the drowning of an ancient Appalachian valley by Duke Power Company to match the needs and expectations of modern life—amenities, services, and leisure. The flooding that literally erased an entire landscape awakened Rash's urge for remembrance, as well as his sense of obligation toward the mishandled dead, to whom he pays a belated homage. Haunting images of the buried valley, the "place of the lost" (*Raising the Dead* 75; *One Foot in Eden* 214), surface in memory of the dead that literally had to be *raised,* as they were disinterred and displaced in order to allow humans to flood the valley and claim power over the natural world there. Rash asserted, "At Jocassee, there is only the water; not even the place names remain. It's simply terrifying to me, at Jocassee—the erasure—of lives, of graves, of farmland, of flowers, of names. All erased" (qtd. in Higgins 49). The main concern at the core of *Raising the Dead* and *One Foot in Eden* is that the lost should not be forgotten, and water provides a powerful medium for addressing this concern. While in interviews Rash has repeated that he considers water to be "a conduit between the living and the dead" (Bjerre, "The Natural World" 225), the power of water and its attendant images also contribute to reasserting the indefectible bonds that tie the living with the dead. For Rash water is a privileged metaphor of memory, of its flux, reflux, and unpredictable emergence at the surface of everyday life. Rash's prose and poetry formally echo this essential fluidity between themes, times, and places, as the past often merges with the present, as the regional specificity broadens into the universal, and as stories and histories are inextricably commingled.

This chapter will first explore the metaphorical power of water, as major upheavals in Rash's characters' lives are systematically associated with either water or its absence. I will also examine how the tensions generated by the dam project, the flooding, and eventually the lake conjure up images of the finitude of human life. I will then highlight the crucial role water plays in the narratological construction of Rash's *One Foot in Eden.* Ultimately I argue that water and water-related imagery help define the categories of place, time, plot, and character, while operating as the privileged symbol of the fluid forms adopted by memory and writing. Gaston Bachelard's poetico-philosophical reflections on water and imagination, *Water and Dreams,* will be the main secondary reference used throughout this chapter; building on Bachelard I hope to convey the centrality of water in Rash's literary imagination.

Slipping into Finitude: "Too much too soon disappears"

In *One Foot in Eden,* sense of place is chiefly conveyed to characters by the nearby presence of the river, which is an essential element of the novel's topography and functions as a main landmark. Much of the novel takes place on Billy Holcombe's land, one boundary of which is delimited by the river. The river operates as a liminal space between the familiar world Billy shares with his wife, Amy—a world of hard daily farm work—and the wild beyond, where lurking snakes await their prey and where the local "witch," Widow Glendower, gathers plants out of which she makes strange concoctions. Beyond the river awaits a landscape where seemingly anything can happen. Consequently, crossing the river amounts to accepting the unruliness of the wild. The novel's most grisly scenes—the handling of a corpse that needs to be hidden from the law, the disposing of the remains months later—take place "across the river" in this "wild" space.

While the river is at times a menacing force, it is also a presence that can be trusted. As Amy pays a visit to Widow Glendower, on her way to the latter's secluded cabin, the creek, a tributary of the river, is the only landmark she can trust as darkness and snow have obscured the familiar trails. A reassuring element in the landscape, the river naturally orients Amy's—and many other characters'—sense of direction. "Walk[ing] the river a ways" (*One Foot in Eden* 13), as Sheriff Alexander says, certainly has a redeeming value: his purposeful connection with the river at a critical moment in his life reveals his intention to do things "right," while probably also indicating his desire to escape the sordid present with which he has to contend. Nearly twenty years later Amy's child, Isaac Holcombe, in a state of shock as the long delayed revelation of his true identity has finally been revealed to him, also spontaneously goes to the river: "I followed the river down stream, not really knowing where I was going. It was like my mind moved so fast it was taking my body right along with it" (179). In the ontological disorientation he then experiences, Isaac walks to the familiar river of his childhood—a river whose banks are, ironically, about to vanish underwater. Bachelard, the master of poetic spaces, discussed the power of water on human consciousness: "The human mind has claimed for water one of its highest values—the value of purity. How could we conceive of purity without the image of clear and limpid water, without this beautiful pleonasm that speaks to us of *pure water?*" (14). At the very moment Isaac's innocence is corrupted, it is symbolic that he should revert to the cradle of purity that also was the central locus of his childhood.

Although the dam is created and the valley is flooded throughout the two-decade span of the novel, which dramatically alters the characters' sense of place, water will remain the only constant element in the landscape. The level of the river, whether low or critically high, often operates as a key element in the setting and contributes both to the characters' livelihoods and psychological well-being. For example the river's sudden disappearance in summer signals how the stability of ordinary life can quickly shift to the extraordinary. The effects of extended periods of heat impact both the landscape and characters; the drought causes a lengthy period of agricultural inactivity and, as a result, sharpens people's obsessive hope for rain on which their yearly crops and living conditions ultimately depend. While the city dwellers and white-collar workers can afford to be indifferent to rain, this is obviously not the case with the farmers. Sheriff Alexander, who has one foot in both worlds, understands these different relations to weather and rain: "Before I got in my car I glanced at the sky.

Like it mattered to me, a man with a certain paycheck come rain or drought" (*One Foot in Eden* 10). The dependence of the mountain farmers on contingent elements like the weather further highlights the isolation of the community, which seems far beyond the margins of the modern world. The contrast between the demanding efforts it takes to work the land, all the more so when drought desiccates the natural world, and the prospect of that same land's absurdly quick disappearance also underscores the gap separating two worlds operating in two radically different timeframes. While Billy has spent most of his life laboring to grow crops on land he is proud to claim as his own, Isaac is told "not to plant anything" (167), which he interprets as an insult to his "father" Billy's vocation: "But Daddy had told the Carolina Power man it was our land for a few more months yet, and he'd damn well do what he pleased" (167). This cultural gap is further reinforced by the superstitions associated with rain. *One Foot in Eden* repeatedly evokes the local beliefs regarding rain: "The old folks claimed you could kill a blacksnake and lay it on the fence and it would bring rain" (124). It seems that the dry, snakeskin-like bottom of the river asks for the sacrifice of a blacksnake to recover its wet smoothness.

The characterization of Billy also reveals how rain and its lack shape characters' lives. Indeed, as drought and emotional turmoil weigh on him, Billy mostly appears as a desiccated, incapacitated figure—a modernized version of the Fisher King of the Grail legends. While Billy is deeply affected by the withering of the world around him—"most everything that surrounded me had seemed to lay down to die" (*One Foot in Eden* 117)—he himself is portrayed as being contaminated by the environment around him and thus a shriveled version of himself. Indeed his disabilities (his limping, his sterility) and limitations (his questioning his own courage) are persistently hinted at. The long-expected rain toward the end of Billy's section of the novel takes the form of a deliverance; it significantly entails an unlikely sense of peace and ease: "It wasn't long before drops of rain tapped the roof and that's the best sound ever I've known to make a body drowsy" (154). At the same time, the possibility of renewal is evoked as "the splats of rain [turn] dust back to dirt" (155); while the quick succession of monosyllables is suggestive of raindrops, the way *dust* and *dirt* alliteratively echo the metamorphosing effects of water on nature and humans. The general impression is that the return of rain contributes to Billy's own slow straightening, both physical and psychological, while his crops are fortunately saved and new life develops in Amy: "I felt the young one stir again and told myself my luck had changed, was changing with every drop of rain that fell on my thirsty fields" (155). The evocation of drought through the image of thirst is particularly striking as it associates humans and nature in the grasp of a similar fate; at the same time, the ultimate reversal—drowning by water—is also suggested. Bachelard said, "It is important to note in passing this new *inversion* that attributes a human action to a material element. Water is no longer a substance that is drunk; it is a substance which drinks" (54).

Such binary oppositions as drought and rain or sterility and regeneration are likely to be made more complex as contradictory metaphors surreptitiously come to the surface. Amy's "curse" (*One Foot in Eden* 75), her unfulfilled pregnancy, is represented by the inexorable return of her monthly flow. Meanwhile her making love with Holland, and truly enjoying the guilty experience, is compared with "a flood" (74), which thus becomes a metaphor for being overcome—flooded—by pleasure. Yet Amy tries hard to resist the flood, endeavoring not to be carried away. While in the act, she focuses her attention on mundane remembrances of "quilt-washing day[s]" (84). Symbolically this memory is associated with water, whiteness, and the removal of stains, thus obliquely figuring Amy's awareness of her shame. But the "hot and bubbling" (84) cleansing water also refers to her exhilaration, designating a very likeable sensation: "It was a good, pure feeling to be out in the river on a warm spring day. . . . It was knowing something could be made clean no matter how soiled and dirty it got" (85). Pain and pleasure, disgrace and grace, corruption and purification are indissolubly intermingled; therefore water imagery thematizes the intricacy of human experience and its often conflicting urges.

Later Amy registers the very moment Holland makes her pregnant through the joyful images of a well and a spring: "Then I felt something else, something deep inside me, a kind of brightness *welling up* and spreading all through my body like *spring water* when it *bubbles out* of the ground. At that moment I knew certain as anything ever in my life that Holland's *seed* had *took root* inside me" (*One Foot in Eden* 88, emphasis added). While this primal scene takes place in a natural cradle, the spring water is intimately associated with the symbolism of springtime, the season of burgeonings, births, and rebirths. While Amy's most intimate desire—that is, procreating—is being fulfilled, she is also somehow born again as a woman. Indeed, while suggesting the intrinsic life of nature, the *bubbling out* Amy sensuously evokes designates the simultaneous experiences of new life "[taking] root inside her," her overwhelming pleasure, and a flowing sense of unity between woman and nature. Last, in their very magnitude, Amy's birth pangs catalyze in her an oceanic feeling, which points to her flourishing sense—however illusory—of her own limitlessness (101). The radical ambivalence of water imagery reaches a peak in Amy's depiction of her newborn baby as "drowned-looking" (102). As Amy fears for the life of her newborn, her feelings sink toward "the ocean bottom" immediately after she has enjoyed the elation associated with mountain peaks. She experiences a state of nadir before reaching her zenith: an all-pervading sense of finitude thus replaces the previous impression of infinity.

One Foot in Eden is scattered with images evoking the fragility of life, relentlessly pointing to the essential transience of all things. The flood that finally erases the valley is certainly the most striking image of impermanence in the novel, as well as in *Raising the Dead,* but there are echoes of the wider picture to be found at every level of the text. For instance, as he observes the pool of blood—what is left of Holland after Billy disposes of his body—Billy realizes that most of the trace has already partly vanished: "The ground stained dark where Holland had laid but the *dust* had already drank up his blood. Another few minutes and you wouldn't be able to tell a man's life had *spilled* out there" (131, emphasis added). As Holland's blood has been "swallowed," such vampire-like representations of nature, which are prone to erase man and the memory of him "in a few minutes," foreshadow the future disappearance of the whole community.

While life's end is often represented as a *spilling,* which conjointly suggests an *emptying* that evokes violent deaths, the turning point—the "tumble" (107)—between life and death takes the form of a *slipping.* The story that lies at the core of *One Foot in Eden,* as the rising water uproots the dead and carries the living away, is encapsulated in the poetical shift from *spill* to *slip.* While Rash's writing often features "slick rocks" ("Compass Creek," *Raising the Dead* 17), many of his characters, "not trusting even the ground beneath them" (*One Food in Eden* 35), "[risk] a slip in the river" (33, 34). The recurrence of the verb *slip*—"slipping on a slick rock" (43), "slipping free" (46), "slipping off in the dark" (47)—always contains an impending threat: that of losing one's balance and becoming prey to the irresistible power of waters. This is how Billy's crossing of the river with his horse, Sam, and Holland's corpse is portrayed: "The water ran slow, the stones under our *feet* green and slick. I took my time, tucking my *feet* in white pockets of sand amongst the rocks. . . . Halfway across Sam's legs splayed out in front of him. He near went *tumbling* and kicking into the whitewater downstream, taking me and Holland with him, but he found his balance. We got the rest of the way without *slipping* and sloshed out of the river into Carolina Power land" (*One Foot in Eden* 132, emphasis added). As they cross the river, the balance of man and animal is lost, and they both make great efforts to recover their endangered stability. Meanwhile the clear and peaceful beauty of the river makes the probability of drowning and the precariousness of the characters' lives even more dramatic.

Similarly, as she walks in the snow toward Widow Glendower's cabin for advice and a remedy for Billy's sickness, Amy's tumble downhill portentously foreshadows her later fatal slipping in the river: "The land was *s*id*l*ing and snow *sl*icked the ground. I tried to hold my balance but soon enough I *sl*ipped and *sl*ided down and down" (*One Foot in Eden* 106, emphasis added). The prolonged alliteration in /s and l/ materializes Amy's plunge down the snowy hill.[2] As in the case of Billy's crossing of the river, Amy's tripping feet (and there are countless references to feet) echo the novel's title. Indeed the phrase "one foot in Eden," which Rash borrowed from Orcadian poet Edwin Muir's own *One Foot in Eden*—the title of a poem and that of a collection—plunges the novel into a mythico-biblical dimension that suggests from the outset that the plot about to unfold will take the reader both into Appalachia and beyond. Furthermore this title, which establishes the indefectible link between poetry and prose and the essential porosity of the genres, also contains a sense of promise, which is inseparable from the risk of a terrible loss. Indeed, as dramatically illustrated in the 2004 short story "Something Rich and Strange," placing one's feet in two different places is a precarious and dangerous posture. The young girl in the story "wants to wade into the middle [of the river] and place one foot in Georgia and one in South Carolina so she can tell her friends in Nebraska she has been in two states at the same time" (*Something Rich and Strange* 221). Quickly the reckless young girl becomes the victim of the sly, deceptive waters of the river. Although they appear "shallow and slow," there is a strong "current surging under the smooth surface" (221)—a current that is about to absorb her as "she takes another step and the bottom is no longer there" (222). Consequently to have "one foot in Eden" is by no means a comfortable position. The expression designates an unfinished movement, as if temporarily frozen, that may or may not lead to the achievement of a desirable condition.[3]

In *One Foot in Eden,* the symbolical dimension of such losses of balance is last highlighted by Isaac's "grip[ping] the railing" (172–73), as he is about to enter Mrs. Winchester's house and learn she is his grandmother and that Holland is his true father. This gesture can be interpreted as Isaac's ultimate endeavor to cling to the world he is familiar with and that, he senses, is about to vanish. As the truth slowly imposes itself on him in the dense cloud of "kerosene fumes" from Mrs. Winchester's self-immolation (174), Isaac's eyes start watering as a response to the fire and the revelation, the effect of which reaches a peak in his sense of drowning; he states, "I felt like I was drowning" (174). Similarly, when Holland's corpse is "raised into the sky" (136) as Billy has hoisted it up to hide it in a tree, the images Billy conjures are again those of a drowning: "I took Sam's rein and walked with him out into the stand of yellow poplar, Holland's body circling slow as it raised into the sky *like a body caught in a suckhole below a waterfall.* I looked at Holland dangling from that white oak and tried not to see it as a sign of my own future" (136, emphasis added). Like most evocations of mortality in the novel, the corpse's rise to heaven (or hell) paradoxically invokes water rather than air. Billy cannot prevent himself from contemplating drowning; this is foreboding in that his own end will be the result of drowning in the floodwaters that will carry him away, together with his love and his land, in a single vengeful current.

Water and Narrative

Throughout *One Foot in Eden,* there is an unbroken, almost aqueous, quality to the narrative itself. Indeed, though divided up into five clearly separated sections, the novel manages to take the form of a single flow. While distinguishing between the five different perspectives that contribute to the development of the story, adding up streams and tributaries to the main current, the metaphoric dams that fragment the narrative also make it clear that the fluid continuity of the story is by no means disrupted by such delimitations. The five headings—which refer to the five character-narrators as archetypes, replacing proper names with characterizing social functions[4] that further open up the singularity of individualities into a universal dimension—are also reminiscent of the headstones that are evoked throughout the novel. But even headstones are doomed to be carried away by water, which demands that graves be displaced. Similarly the current of the narrative actually seeps through the small-scale metaphoric dams that separate each section and announce the emergence of a new stream that will follow a current of its own with a voice of its own, while gradually augmenting a single river. *One Foot in Eden* thus achieves its unity and unique beauty through plurality and diversity. The essential porosity of the five narratives is due to the resurfacing of the same key elements and themes.

The narrative structure of *One Foot in Eden* echoes the fluidity of memory. Indeed, far from following a straight line, each of the five narratives takes the form of meandering curves, as frequent returns to the past are likely to interrupt the advance of the present. This meandering pattern is all the more complex as the evocation of the same events, especially in the first three narratives, rests on a constantly reshuffled version of chronological time. The story is consequently told in the form of continuous shifts through time, as the past of each character-narrator colors his or her own perceptions of the present. In most cases the past takes the form of harrowing existential questions that densify the present. Such intrusions of the past into the present create momentary disruptions in the narrative, but they also constantly remind the reader of how the past informs the present. Images of the future—the dam/"damn" project,[5] the planned flooding of the region—foreshadow the dramatic blurring of both time and place, making the need to remember what is about to be "erased" all the more necessary and difficult. Memories of his thwarted career as a football player, of his war wound, and of the consequences on his life choices keep resurfacing and interfering throughout the sheriff's murder investigation, and his monologue significantly concludes with a memory of his own baptism in the river. While the omnipresence of water thematizes the permeability of time, this final image reconciles the sheriff's conflicting perception of himself and the world around him with the acceptance that the near future, fated to take the form of an all-erasing immersion, will be but a prelude to the ultimate disappearance of all things.

A constant element of the narrative—in the past, present, and future—water consistently contributes to the novel's sense of time, and it provides much of the pacing and tension in the narrative. Indeed the rising level of water, which threatens to take everything along with it, generates an increasing sense of urgency that peaks in the novel's fourth section, which is narrated by Isaac: "'That water's not waiting for anyone.' I looked toward the river and knew the truth of what he said. The tobacco was already underwater, and the land I stood on would soon be. I was in a race with the water to see who would get to the cabbage first" (*One Foot in Eden* 168). As the water inexorably rises, the flood, which, up to Isaac's section, had been only a distant threat, increasingly becomes a reality and, as a result, quickens the pace of the narrative. While water contributes to the novel's pacing, it does not simply operate as a narrative function; it also plays a major poetical role in the narrative. Water conveys one of Rash's favorite metaphors of time, which often takes the form of a pool of water: "I drove out of the valley, the sun *sinking* into the trees. By the time I got on the blacktop, twilight had *turned* the strange color it always does in August, a pink *tinged* with green and silver. That color had always made it seem like time had somehow *leaked* out of the world, past and present *blending* together. My mind *skimmed* across time like a water spider *crossing* a pool" (19, emphasis added). This passage is scattered with verb forms pointing out two apparently conflicting movements: the horizontality (*skimmed, crossing*) and verticality (*sinking*) of water and of time are indeed educed conjointly, conjuring at the same time images of surfaces and images of depths. Through these water-related images, the evocation of time as a chronological sequence of events—hence a flat, linear surface—becomes indissociable from its depiction as a profundity, the cradle of memories having become impervious to clear temporal distinctions. Hence the multiple images of elements merging and becoming indistinct: *turned, tinged, leaked, blending.* The gerund forms show this blurring process at work. In the last pages of the sheriff's monologue, the merging of time and water recurs as memories surface with renewed intensity: "I dreamed of water deep as time" (51). In *Raising the Dead,* the poem "Deep Water" similarly interlaces categories (time and place) within a memory of water: "Soon that squared pool of water / flickers as if a mirror, / surfaces memory of when / this deep water was a sky" (14). While the lake operates as the mirror reflection of a past remembrance, the future (*soon*) merges with the past (*when, was*), and water and sky appear to be reversible.

Water thus generates the overall sensation that categories are blurred, as in a dream. Time in Rash's writing is inextricable from place. Water allows the poetical synthesis of place and time. As the sheriff depicts "the sun sinking into the trees" (*One Foot in Eden* 19), the temporal evocation of the end of the day cannot be dissociated from the simultaneous sense of place; the central form *sinking* indicates the leaking of one category into another, while the overall blending is further emphasized by the intertwined alliteration in /s/ and assonance in /i/. The "liquid quality" of language, which Bachelard defines as "a flow in its overall effect, water in its consonants" (14), is thus realized.

The combined motifs of sleeping and forgetting repeat, with some variation, the same liquid sense of blurring that allows a momentary escape from the real world. By contrast the moment of waking, which is also described through water imagery, marks the return of blunt, bare reality. "Then it all came rushing on me like a dam broke open," says Billy (*One Foot in Eden* 142) after indulging in a few hours of willed forgetfulness. It is quite striking, of course, that the undeniable truth that imposes itself on him (in this case his own responsibility as a murderer) should be evoked through the image of a broken dam that carries all things away. The portentous significance of his truth makes all other things weightless. The same kind of violent image is likely to be associated with the sudden surfacing of memories: "Then another memory tore into me" (197). In Isaac's case the return of the repressed—deeply buried allusions to his likeness to his birth father Holland—similarly takes the form of a breach, triggering a general sense of flooding. While sleep, whether literal or figurative, allows a transitory blurring between what is and what is not, waking brings back the return of reality, as a kind of vengeance. Water, in the various forms it is likely to take (the peaceful splattering of rain or the violent breaking of a dam) thus contributes to representing multiple and conflicting states of being.

Conflicted emotions are likewise prone to be evoked in terms of water. As the sheriff remembers his own father as a young man, the distance between father and son is ominously evoked through the image of a lake: "Though we sat five feet apart, it seemed a lake had spread out between us, but it was something wider and harder to get across" (*One Foot in Eden* 38). A few pages later, as the uninterrupted flow of his reflections and remembrances runs on, the sheriff defines solitude as man's essential condition: "But we lived in the here and now. You tried to find something to fill that absence. Maybe a marriage could cure that yearning, though mine hadn't. Drink did it for many a man besides Williams" (49). While Hank Williams and rain compose the two-voice soundtrack of existential melancholy, solitude is evoked as a void that demands to be filled, however precariously and by whatever substance, for man to have a chance to cope with living.

Following this scene Alexander contemplates the naturalist William Bartram's ominous idea of the mountains as an ocean: "*The mountainous wilderness appearing undulated as the great ocean after a tempest*" (*One Foot in Eden* 51). While eliciting a reversed image of Creation, the "*dry* land" returning to its initial condition as "waters" (Genesis 1:9), Bartram's words evoke the deliquescence of all elements. Moreover the way these words dissolve into the sheriff's thoughts is suggestive of how various histories and narratives eventually comingle and how the same images proliferate in a constant recycling of ideas in Rash's writing. For instance the poem entitled "Bartram Leaves Jocassee" also revolves around Bartram's prophetic imagining of "the lake's coming" (*Among the Believers* 61) and, with subtle variations, quotes the same words in italics. In "Calenture" the image of "Appalachian / hills unfolding in waves" (*Waking* 28) can be interpreted as a leitmotiv of Rash's imagination. While the fluid and flowing quality of memory is thus pointed out, what is also suggested is the way water literally irrigates remembrance: "water gives beauty to all shadows, it gives new life to all memories" (Bachelard, 66).

In *One Foot in Eden* the images of memory sustained by water are multiple: water incorporates individual memories as well as the traumatic memory of a whole community. It also artfully keeps the collective memory of earlier texts and writers alive. The unheralded emergence of other writers' words or privileged figures in Rash's writing, together with the fluid recurrence of the same or similar images within his own work,[6] seems to partake of a general vision of literature as made of a single, uninterrupted outflow, whose energy and perpetuity are fostered by individual streams.

At its own small scale, the structure of the novel can be considered to be echoing the broader way literature develops, in the form of separate threads that eventually weave into a single text.[7] As some critics or interviewers have noted, *One Foot in Eden* belongs to the southern subgenre of flood literature that includes novels such as William Faulkner's *The Wild Palms,* Robert Penn Warren's *Flood,* Madison Jones's *A Buried Land,* and, more recently, William Gay's *Provinces of Night.*[8] Undercurrents of intertextuality can be found throughout *One Foot in Eden,* further highlighting the essential fluidity of literary themes and images. Faulknerian echoes are numerous. For example the buzzards attracted by the decaying body of Billy's plow horse Sam are evocative of the buzzards that circle in the sky above Addie Bundren's coffin in *As I Lay Dying.* The tension of Amy's forbidden yet growing desire, the fulfillment of which soon becomes inexorable, is reminiscent of Dewey Dell's elliptical narration of "the first time me and Lafe picked on down the row" (Faulkner, *As I Lay Dying* 26). Also, in *Raising the Dead,* Rash's poem "The Request," in which sons "gave their word / to honor [a mother's] dying words" (50), can be interpreted as a much-condensed version of *As I Lay Dying.* Finally, the minute description of the uninterrupted heat and drought in *One Foot in Eden,* together with the tension and need for action they generate, may be regarded as a tribute to Faulkner's "Dry September." In this way images and homages keep circulating in Rash's writing. While Rash has gracefully acknowledged his peers and predecessors, he has also rejuvenated familiar figures by engulfing them in the fluid current of his own creation.

It is from water that some of the most evocative poetic figures of *One Foot in Eden* and *Raising the Dead* emerge. Rash's use of water imagery and symbolism provide the textual ground in which his most beautiful and intricate flowers take root. The boundless diversity of its uses place water at the heart of Rash's poetics. From rivers, currents, and lakes, rain and snow, drought, floods, and deluge come the undercurrents of a writing that is often characterized by its rich complexity, as similar images are prone to elicit both dread and desire. Forever reminding the reader that life is flux and that one cannot step twice in the same river,[9] the symbolism of water in Rash's writing is multifaceted and often contradictory, both "rich and strange." While the "universal liquid" is an essential element of the landscape Rash has called his own, water offers multiple occasions for the here and now to merge with the far beyond. In both *Raising the Dead* and *One Foot in Eden,* Rash raised his voice both as poet and novelist, and water can be considered his first matter, the primary color in his stylistic toolbox. As Bachelard reminded us, "the region we call home is less expanse than matter; it is granite or soil, wind or dryness, water or light. It is in it that we materialize our reveries, through it that our dream seizes upon its true substance. From it we solicit our fundamental color" (8). For Rash water is the very stuff of which dreams are made.[10]

Notes

1. In the "Notes" concluding *Raising the Dead,* Rash provided the reader with precious elements of clarification: "In the early 1970s, despite fervent opposition by the valley's inhabitants, Duke Power Company built a dam to create Jocassee Reservoir. Both the living and the dead were evicted, for hundreds of graves were dug up and their contents reburied in cemeteries outside the valley. The reservoir reached full water capacity in 1974. In Cherokee *Jocassee* means 'place of the lost'" (*Raising the Dead* 75).

2. While she slips on her way up, Amy finds proper balance as she walks down, once things are settled: "The snow had hardened up and made a crunching sound every time I laid my foot down, but it wasn't slippery and I made my way down the river without much bother. The rest of the way home was trifling easy for the sun was out bright by then" (*One Foot in Eden* 111). Once again, symbolically, the recovery of balance marks the disappearance of a temporary menace, and the character's return to a precarious form of equilibrium.

3. Thomas Ærvold Bjerre interpreted the title of the novel as follows: "This is perhaps what the title connotes: one foot in a mythic agrarian Eden and one foot in harsh reality" Bjerre, "Ron Rash 235).

4. The characters-narrators are, indeed, respectively identified as follows: "The High Sheriff," "The Wife," "The Husband," "The Son," and "The Deputy." The actual names of the characters appear only incidentally in the flow of the narrative.

5. Rash played cunningly with homophony through one of his secondary characters, Roy, who thus voices the community's collective response to their common fate: "They'll do what they *damn* well please. Just ask them farmers that lived down there where Santee-Cooper Reservoir is" (*One Foot in Eden* 135, emphasis mine).

6. For more information on Rash's recycling of his own material, see Wilhelm.

7. It may be useful to remember that the word "text" comes from the Latin *textus,* which means "style or texture of a work." It literally designates a "thing woven," from past participle stem of *texere,* i.e. "to weave, to join, fit together, braid, interweave, construct, fabricate, build" (Online Etymology Dictionary, http://www.etymonline.com/index.php?l=t&p=13).

8. Some of these works probably inspired Rash. For more on genre and literary influences in the novel, see Bjerre and Vernon.

9. The actual quote from Heraclitus reads as follows: "In the same river we both step and do not step, we are and are not" (Kaufmann 20).

10. See Shakespeare's *The Tempest:* "We are such stuff / As dreams are made of; / and our little life / Is rounded with a sleep" (act 4, scene 1).

Works Cited

Bachelard, Gaston. *Water and Dreams. An Essay on the Imagination of Matter.* 1942. Trans. Edith Farrell. Dallas: Pegasus Foundation, 1983.

Bjerre, Thomas Ærvold. "'The Natural World Is the Most Universal Languages': An Interview with Ron Rash." *Appalachian Journal* 34 (2007): 216–27.

———. "Ron Rash: *One Foot in Eden.*" *Still in Print: The Southern Novel Today.* Ed. Jan Norby Gretlund. Columbia: University of South Carolina Press, 2010. 233–47.

Brown, Joyce Compton. "Ron Rash: The Power of Blood-Memory." *Appalachia and Beyond: Conversations with Writers from the Mountain South.* Ed. John Lang. Knoxville: University of Tennessee Press, 2006, 335–53.

Faulkner, William. *As I Lay Dying.* 1930. New York: Vintage International, 1990.

———. "Dry September." *Collected Stories.* New York: Vintage International, 1995. 169–83.

———. *The Wild Palms.* 1939. New York: Vintage Books, 1966.

Gay, William. *Provinces of Night.* London: Faber and Faber, 2001.

Higgins, Anna Dunlap. "'Anything but Surrender': Preserving Southern Appalachia in the Works of Ron Rash." *North Carolina Literary Review* 13 (2004): 49–58.

Jones, Madison. *A Buried Land.* 1964. New York: Permanent, 1987.

Kaufmann, Walter. *Ancient Philosophy.* Vol. 1. Upper Saddle River, N.J.: Prentice Hall, 2007.

Lane, John. "The Girl in the River: The Wild and Scenic Chattooga, Ron Rash's *Saints at the River,* and the Drowning of Rachel Trois." *South Carolina Review* 41.1 (Fall 2008): 162–67.

Muir, Edwin. *One Foot in Eden.* London: Faber and Faber, 1956.

Poe, Edgar Allan. *Poetry and Tales.* New York: Library of America, 1998.

Rash, Ron. *Nothing Gold Can Stay.* New York: HarperCollins, 2013.

———. "Irene [The Sleeper]." *The Edgar Allan Poe Society.* http://www.eapoe.org/works/poems/sleepera.htm. January 11, 2017.

———. *One Foot in Eden.* New York: Henry Holt, 2002.

———. *Raising the Dead.* Oak Ridge, Tenn.: Iris, 2002.

———. *Saints at the River.* New York: Henry Holt, 2004.

———. *Something Rich and Strange: New and Selected Stories.* New York: HarperCollins, 2014.

———. *Waking.* Spartanburg, S.C.: Hub City, 2011.

Shakespeare, William. *The Tempest.* Oxford: Oxford University Press, 2008.

Spill, Frédérique. "An Interview with Ron Rash." *Transatlantica* 1 (July 9, 2014). http://transatlantica.revues.org/6829. February 21, 2017.

Vernon, Zackary. "Commemorating vs. Commodifying: Ron Rash and the Search for an Appalachian Literary Identity." *Appalachian Journal* 41. 1–2 (Fall 2013/Winter 2014): 104–24.

Warren, Robert Penn. *Flood: A Romance of Our Time.* 1964. Baton Rouge: Louisiana State University Press, 2003.

Wilhelm, Randall. "Introduction: Blood Memory." *Ron Rash Reader.* Ed. Randall Wilhelm. Columbia: University of South Carolina Press, 2014. 1–32.

THE SINGLE EFFECT OF RON RASH'S ENVIRONMENTAL VISION

Brian Railsback

Early in the fall of 2012, not two months before his novel *The Cove* was published on November 6, Ron Rash sat in his cramped office at Western Carolina University and told me he thought he might give up novel writing altogether. He had struggled with *The Cove,* and although he conceded it was a good novel and he had worked hard on it, somehow he was not completely satisfied with the result. This is not an unusual feeling for writers: John Steinbeck, nearing the finish of *The Grapes of Wrath,* wrote that "it isn't the great book I had hoped it would be" and shortly thereafter decided to try his hand at forms other than the novel 90). Sitting in his office, long limbs gathered up almost spider-like on a chair among the usual piles of papers and books, Rash talked then of his fascination with the short story. He wanted to devote himself to the genre, perhaps be a part of its reinvigoration in American letters. Though an accomplished poet and novelist already, in 2012 Rash had published four collections of short stories, most recently, *Burning Bright* in 2010, which won the Frank O'Connor International Short Story Award. He spoke of his admiration for the efficiency of the short story, the surgical precision required of a writer to make so much happen in such a small space. In particular he mentioned his love of that moment in a short story where all its elements powerfully cohere for the reader by the end (Personal interview).

Rash's writing and work, which often captures the ills of twentieth- and twenty-first-century Appalachian life—from cotton lung to meth addiction—has deep roots in the writing of earlier centuries. It is not surprising that Rash has had Edgar Allan Poe in mind in thinking about short-story execution. When discussing his second short story, "Turtle Meat," about a man who ties a string to a big snapping turtle to find bodies lost in water, he acknowledged its early gothic roots in the work of Flannery O'Connor, William Faulkner, and Poe (Personal interview). Poe's famous discussion of the "single effect" in writing asserts that "in the whole composition there should be no word written, of which the tendency, direct or indirect, is not to the one pre-established design" (Poe 1026). The notions of single effect and pre-established design have much more import in the mature writing of Ron Rash: "I felt the more I understood the story I think I also understood how taut it really needs to be, how interwoven, and how every line has to, in a sense, almost set up a resonance that will come through again and again." Rash added, "You hope for that moment where suddenly [for the reader] it's as if you've got all these threads and suddenly it's almost like they're tied together" (Personal interview). Beyond matters of form, the "single effect" in theme, especially the complexities of environmental degradation, create a rich comprehensive approach to the land in Rash's fiction.

From Rash's 1994 short-story collection, *The Night the New Jesus Fell to Earth and Other Stories from Cliffside, North Carolina,* through to his 2015 novel, *Above the Waterfall,* the author has been honing his depiction of Appalachian cultural heritage, language, place, and spirituality. These elements cohere, like Poe's "single effect" theory, and create a distinctive and intentional environmental discourse. Where other American authors' writing might be found on a spectrum between ecophobia (antagonism toward nature) and biophilia (love of all living things), Rash's works seek to contain both ends and everything in between. In Rash's work the land and the people exist in a symbiotic and problematic relationship.

Keeping with his roots to the past, Rash's stylistic signature portrays Appalachians through language that connects to the land in an Emersonian ideal. If one can succinctly define Rash's theory of language, it does not stray far from Emerson's simple dictum in *Nature:* "1) Words are signs of natural facts; 2), Particular natural facts are symbols of particular spiritual Facts, and 3) Nature is the symbol of the spirit" (20). In Emerson's view the purist language words that are rich in meaning and true can be traced to nature. The ones closest to the original source of language are "Children and savages [who] use only nouns and names of things, which they continually convert into verbs, and apply to analogous mental facts" (20). Though certainly not the product of children and savages, Rash's narrative (and poetic) style achieves Emerson's ideal. In writing Rash has hewn closely to the natural artifact and rendered native dialect faithfully and poetically. Natural sounds and rhythms are important. He has weeded out passive verbs, as they drain energy from his prose. He has creatively bent nouns or adjectives into verbs: a character might say *I suspicioned,* rather than *I was suspicious.* "Verbs are so energetic that you got to use them to their maximum power," Rash noted of his own style; "you start making adjectives into nouns and verbs, using unusual words as verbs, but at the same time, that's something that Appalachian speech does do—I think that's one of the glories of its inventiveness" (Personal interview).

The result is a carefully wrought, uniquely Appalachian prose style with high verbal energy, precise rhythms, and vivid imagery; a voice that never lets a reader forget the distinct physical place of the story or novel. But underneath this intentional and cultural style lies the Emersonian notion of the spiritual aspect: words that adhere to the natural world are also closer to the purity of nature—the truth of it—as "every natural fact is a symbol of some spiritual fact" (Emerson 20). As generations move further away from the original source of language and speak in the words of the politician or professor in man-made chambers or classrooms, Emerson asserts not only that language is weakened but it becomes untrue: "The corruption of man is followed by the corruption of language" (22).

In much of Rash's fiction, artificial language caused by geographical distance from place, or the ambition to leave demonstrates Emerson's dynamic of the corrupt speaker revealing the corrupt soul. The walls left behind by people who use education to escape Appalachia or who are ignorant of its culture are built by words. In "Summer Work" this wall becomes clear when battle lines are drawn between a local landscaper, Cecil Ledbetter, and Ben Grier, a brilliant college student who wants out of Appalachia via medical school, during an explanation of how a weed eater works: "'That's the length you need,' Cecil looked up at us. 'Wait till you got it running full speed before you try to trim. You understand?' Ben smiled at him. 'Do you mean do we understand the concept of centrifugal force?' Ben said, still smiling. 'Yeah, I think we understand that, Cecil'" (*Casualties* 86). The narrator of the story, witnessing this exchange, realizes that "as soon as the words were out I knew Cecil Ledbetter would be a long time in forgiving Ben" (86). Eventually Cecil does forgive the words, but Ben nevertheless plays a prank that leaves Cecil permanently disabled. Worse, the narrator feels Ben has little remorse as the student goes on to become an M.D. in Boston.

The narrator in the short story "Honesty" is imprisoned in corrupted language, and he admits by the end of the story that his soul is lost. Seduced and subsequently tortured by his wife, Kelly, a heartless college administrator, the narrator is convinced by her to answer an ad written by "Hopelessly Lonely," a local woman named LeAnn McIntyre. Kelly urges him to answer the ad: "let's deconstruct this, darling. *Hopelessly Lonely.* Now would that be the signifier or the signified?" (*Chemistry and Other Stories* 95). Kelly understands that his ambition to be an author is as hopeless as his doomed book project, *The Myth of Robert Frost,* and has built for him a writer's study that is a mockery of his failure. The narrator describes himself as "an actor who mouthed the clichés and jargons of others because he has no words of his own" (97). At his wife's behest, the narrator takes LeAnn on a disastrous date, where she tells him, with blunt honesty, that she is the mother of three children by an ex-husband who is in prison and who vows to kill her as soon as he gets out. A man without words, with no longer anything to say, the narrator gives up lofty authorial ambitions and hands Kelly his mundane course syllabi for the fall; she cuts him by acknowledging, "You've finally found your voice" (106). Detached by false language from place and self, imprisoned by the empty academic language of his wife, the narrator cannot comfort nor comprehend the suffering woman who lives in a backwoods trailer and wants to believe there is some good left in him. The story ends with him assuring her that he is not a good man at all.

In one of Rash's most remarkable stories, "Their Ancient, Glittering Eyes," the contrast of an artificial language compared to that of those who are a part of the land is set up powerfully between the three wise old men of Jackson County, North Carolina, and a condescending game warden from Madison, Wisconsin. When the warden, Charles Meekins, explains to the old men that the large fish they claim to see in the river is merely a carp or trout (it proves to be a six-foot-long sturgeon), he speaks as if "his vocal cords had been pulled from his throat and reinstalled in his sinus cavity" (*Chemistry and Other Stories* 8). Aside from his voice, Meekins's disconnection from the land he is supposed to protect is notable as he listens to rock music rather than the people or nature around him, and he rarely gets out of his truck. As they seek to find and capture the big fish, Rash's story portrays the old men as "the long-ago warriors who once roamed these hills" (15). One of the three wise men, Rudisell, has a chance to gaff the sturgeon, but as he takes in its size, its scales (called scutes), and the rusted tackle in and around its mouth from earlier attempts by others, he lets it go. Rudisell summons more wisdom that Ahab when confronted with the ancient fish. The old boys have the last laugh on Meekins, noting the fish is "way bigger than you are" and prove its existence and his lack of faith by the scute Rudisell has retrieved. They walk away toward the sun, "much in the manner of old-world saints who have witnessed the blinding brilliance of the one true vision" (22). These good old boys are connected to something much bigger than the warden, for all his learning at a university a half continent away.

The separation from the land, signified by language in some of Rash's fiction, is more often underscored by physical or psychological distance. The degradation of the landscape, like the degradation of language, creates the danger of a decaying soul for many of Rash's characters. "Nature never became a toy to a wise spirit," Emerson wrote (9), but in stories like "Deep Gap" or "The Corpse Bird," unwise spirits have in their way obliterated much of nature for the characters in Rash's work (*Chemistry* and *Burning Bright*). Marshall Vaughn, the owner of a local hardware store in the small mountain village of Deep Gap, has been driven to near murder and suicide by the prevalence of crystal meth. In many tales, including the novels *The World Made Straight* and *Above the Waterfall*, Rash has examined the meth plague that has descended on the youth of

Appalachia. "Deep Gap" begins with Marshall recalling how he nearly murdered the drug-addled companions of his son, Brad, in a meth den in Charlotte as he tried to rescue his boy. Marshall believes at that time that he was separated from himself, wondering if "somehow his soul had indeed left his body the moment he'd stepped inside that apartment" (*Chemistry* 150). Once he retrieves his son and the young man's things from the apartment, Marshall dumps a lot of the stuff so he will "carry as little of Charlotte back to Deep Gap as possible" (151). Like a character out of an Emerson or Thoreau essay, Marshall longs to escape the corrupted environment of the big city and retreat to the natural simplicity of life in Deep Gap.

But Deep Gap itself has become a different place: the things of Charlotte have already arrived. The nearby town of Boone has become a city, complete with sprawl and traffic jams. On his way out of Boone one day, Marshall is haunted by a story on the radio about the disappearance of ancient peoples, either annihilated or assimilated. It is not long before he recalls Indian artifacts he found as a child or realizes he sees the last of the old farmers in overalls at his shop being replaced by customers who find his old hardware store "quaint": tourists who come by to check on such Mom and Pop operations before they are wiped off the Earth by Walmart, including a man from Ohio who informs Marshall that he is "a dying breed" (157). As his store slips away to big-box operations and he watches the old farms around his twelve-acre home become shopping centers and gated communities, his place seems "less a homestead than a shrinking island" (156). As drug dealers come to his store to harass him because Brad's checks keep bouncing, that island shrinks even further until all Marshall has is the store's back room—with its lingering smell of linseed oil and his father's and grandfather's pipe tobacco smoke—as the only place of refuge: "he looked around and realized the world he understood had been reduced to this one room" (160). In a final, desperate attempt to save his corrupted son from the taint of this new, encroaching world, he confronts Brad with a pistol and the idea of a murder-suicide to end their suffering. Like Abraham, Marshall is spared this choice; his son relents, but unlike the biblical father, Marshall may find himself in the same situation again as the new world squeezes out the old.

For Boyd Candler of "The Corpse Bird," the landscape has almost completely changed around him; he is among the few remaining unadulterated native Appalachians in the subdevelopment world. While Marshall recalled finding Indian artifacts as a child and feared as an adult that his people would go the same way, Candler lives in the aftermath of the dying breed. In this new world, his connection to the old ways and his latent belief in a lost spirituality reveal his complete isolation. Lying awake one night, unable to sleep because of engineering projects that seem to have little meaning to him beyond their tardiness and layoff implications, he hears an owl call from the branches of the last remaining ancient "scarlet oak" in a suburb built over a cotton field (*Chemistry and Other Stories* 166). He determines that the call is the sign of the corpse bird, and that if it remains in the tree to call on subsequent nights, the sickly girl in the house across the street, Jennifer Coleman, will die. Boyd, "who had grown up among people who believed the world could reveal all manner of things if you paid attention," remembered that his grandfather had died by the call of the corpse bird (166). Boyd had planned to be a farmer but gave it up when the family farm was erased; he went to college and tried to buy into the new world his teachers recommended to him: "a world where the sky did not matter, where land did not blacken your nails, cling to your boots, or callous your hands but was seen, if at all, through the glass windows of buildings and cars and planes" (169). Observing the neighborhood Halloween decorations, Boyd's anxiety about the corpse bird increases because he realizes "certain things shouldn't be mocked, that to do so might bring retribution" (171). He goes across the street to convince the Colemans to take Jennifer to the hospital, but though neighbors they are of the suburbs, where people wave occasionally but never share a meal together. His superstitions arouse concerns and suspicions of not only the Colemans but also his wife, Laura. Enraged at him for stirring up trouble, Laura chides him for being raised by people with superstitions, people who were "uneducated" (176). She tries to get him to relax and take an Ambien.

Desperate, Boyd finds his grandfather's old chainsaw and cuts the oak down. A spell is broken, for the corpse bird flies away "into the darkness it had been summoned from" (*Chemistry and Other Stories* 180). Boyd, exposed as some kind of "wild animal" in the neighborhood, is about to be led away by the police in handcuffs: "Boyd stood up and held his arms out before him, both palms upturned, like a man who's just set something free" (180). Like Christ, Boyd has saved the girl not by science but by the spirit, though he draws on old ways of the mountains that are more mysterious than Christianity. The cold irony is that the last vestiges of the old ways are the scarlet oak and Boyd; in order to save the girl, he destroys both and assures that the lives of the mountain folk who used to farm the land are now completely obliterated.

After the departure from the lighter stories of his first short-story collection, the arc of Rash's fiction from 2000 to 2014 is bleak, suggesting the physical, cultural, and spiritual degradation of the southern mountains. *One Foot in Eden* occurs during the period in which an entire Appalachian community is wiped out as water rises in a man-made reservoir, a cultural and environmental degradation as chilling as the impending destruction of the river in James Dickey's *Deliverance.* In *Serena* lumber barons George and Serena Pemberton come from Boston in 1929 and lay waste to the land and people in a horrific and ultimately self-immolating evil. In *Saints at the River,* a girl's drowning reveals a paralyzing debate between practical human interests (the retrieval of the girl's corpse) and stubborn environmentalists who fear the extraction will seriously damage the river. *The World Made Straight* illustrates the devastating plague of meth throughout the mountains. And where there is the possibility of love between an Appalachian girl and a German POW during WWI, it seems the land itself—intertwined with fate—dooms the couple in *The Cove.* Throughout so many of Rash's stories and novels, there is little room for hope. "One aspect of Appalachian life is a very dark, pessimistic view of the world," Rash has said, describing the influences of his heritage that feed into the bleak outlook of much of his fiction (Personal interview). The landscape directly plays a part in his outlook and those who live in the mountains: "I think that the sense of the mountains being so daunting, so intimidating, reminding us of our insignificance, I think all those things kind of affect mountain people" (Personal interview).

Yet, as it is in the mountains he inhabits, Rash's works contain descriptions of great, unspoiled beauty. At the beginning of *Saints at the River,* a twelve-year-old girl discovers the strange beauty—colors like the inside of a prism she saw at school—of the river in which she is presently drowning: "she is now inside that prism and knows something even the teacher does not know, that the prism's colors are voices, voices that swirl around her head like a crown, and at that moment her arms and legs she did not even know were flailing cease and she becomes part of the river" (5). Her moment of transcendence in the river is like the triumphant pilgrimage toward the sun that the three old fishermen make at the end of "Their Ancient, Glittering Eyes." In one of Rash's more recent stories, "Three A.M. and the Stars Were Out," (*Nothing Gold Can Stay* 227–39), Carson, a nearly retired veterinarian and his old friend and fellow Korean War veteran, Darnell Coe, struggle to deliver a calf at Coe's farm. They have both lost their wives and feel at the end of the line, but after the successful delivery of the calf, Carson and Darnell have a smoke in the darkness at the barn door, where they can see, as Carson puts it, stars that show better there than they do in town. In a moment so quiet they can hear the cow lick her newborn calf, the two men admit that the constellations they see whirling above were the very same that helped to keep them sane in the worst of the battle at Chosin Reservoir.

This current of hope, of the transforming power of nature despite the man-made ills of the twentieth and twenty-first centuries, culminates in Rash's novel *Above the Waterfall.* On one level, generally through the eyes of one of the novel's narrators, Les, a sheriff haunted by his wife's suicide attempt and the divorce that followed, Rash's novel revisits the Appalachia of earlier stories and novels: a land ravaged by meth addiction and environmental degradation. Les, three weeks away from retirement and soon to have more time to devote to painting watercolors, faces a final meth bust and the mystery of a massive fish kill in a developer's lake. His girlfriend Becky, however, is a state park superintendent who, despite a traumatizing childhood experience as a student survivor of a public school shooting, has found refuge in nature and its transformation through the art of poetry. While not firmly planted in the twenty-first century (the locals call her "a *bit quair,*" a phrase they use for Les as well, because of his introverted nature and interest in painting), she inhabits in her lonely work at the state park a nineteenth-century Romantic world informed by the work of Gerard Manley Hopkins (*Above the Waterfall* 8). The strange beauty that a dying girl finds in *Saints at the River* is fully understood by Becky. In her character, and in the conclusion of the novel for both characters, there is more hope for the world than found in all the rest of Rash's fiction. "I feel in many ways this is my most upbeat book," Rash noted in an interview with NPR the week *Above the Waterfall* was published (Interview). Despite his characters' troubled histories, Rash asserted that it is important to recognize that the novel is about "two people who are struggling toward some kind of redemption, and I think, to me, the most important thing about the book is I think in many ways they achieve it" (Interview).

The novel opens in Becky's voice, in a brief chapter that is a prose poem, as she sits at dusk in a fallow mountain field, in a moment diffused by time in her mind while she thinks of her grandfather's plowing there or the ancient cave painters at Lascaux in France. A phrase from Hopkins's "The Windhover" enters the narration as she contemplates the "*sillion shine*" left in the furrowed wake of her grandfather's old plow, now left to go with the field (*Above the Waterfall* 3; Hopkins 69). The one line that jars this chapter is her recollection that Les could not come, "claiming sheriff business to attend to" (*Above the Waterfall* 4). The banal present has no place during her reverie in the field. Becky is a practitioner of Hopkins's concept of *inscape;* she sees nature so intensely that the objects she apprehends send meaning back to her; as Robert Bernard Martin defines it, "what you look hard at seems to look hard at you. . . . When one understands a person, an object, or even an idea, through close study, that which is studied radiates back a meaning. . . . Inscape is that meaning, the inner coherence of the individual, distinguishing it from any other example" (205). "He's always been one of my favorite poets," Rash said of Hopkins, "and I've always admired the intensity of his vision" (Interview). As an artist in her own right, "Becky in many ways is trying to emulate his [Hopkins's] sense of language, the intensity of sounds. . . . [Hopkins] would be a poet that she would admire because in a sense he is seeing grace in the natural world" (Interview). Where Hopkins found grace in other places, such as the Bible, it is telling that for Becky and for Rash the place of grace is in the natural world of the mountains of western North Carolina. Becky has, as much as anyone can in Rash's world, both feet in Eden, and she wishes mightily to bring the sheriff there; in an e-mail she writes to him of the field: "I wish you could have seen the black-eyed susans. . . . They were transcendent, Les" (*Above the Waterfall* 7). The sheriff's narration opens with the image of a blue cell phone. He has a way to go.

Chapter 4 introduces Becky's protocol for survival. Leading a group of public school students on a nature walk in her park, she insists that the students and even the teacher leave behind cameras and cell phones. On her first day, she placed a brass plaque on the park bulletin board that is a quote from one of Hopkins's journal entries in which he explains the necessity of inscape: "How near at hand it was if they had eyes to see it" (*Above the Waterfall* 23). She takes the children through a dialogue designed to let them understand a bit about what was lost (the extinction of the Carolina Parakeet, also noted in Rash's novel *The Cove*) and to see more clearly what remains: a hummingbird's nest, the shell of a box turtle, a trout in the stream. Observing the trout, seeing it in yet another new way, she understands "Welsh notions Hopkins would have known" (24). The teacher notes the time on her watch, and the kids leave on the bus, but the image of the school bus leaving brings back Becky's school shooting memory, which "scalds" (25). Becky walks along a loop trail, immersing herself in the flowers and wildlife, trying to wash away the intrusive images of the shooting. By the end of the chapter her mind transcends the painful memories, and the narrative of the chapter itself dissolves into a prose poem, intense images of a five-lined skink, and Becky is free again: "The human in me unshackling" (26).

But such unshackling in the twenty-first century, even in Appalachia, is not easy. Les is confronted by wealthy developer, Howard Tucker, a local boy made good, who has developed a mountain resort complete with stocked trout and "No Trespassing" signs. Working public relations for Tucker is another local man, C. J. Gant, whose corruption—detachment from his land and people—is evident to Les as the sheriff notes early in the novel that Gant no longer calls native trout "speckled" but "brook" instead: "Something shed, same as his accent" (*Above the Waterfall* 17). Tucker wants to preserve the best fishing above the waterfall on his property for wealthy visitors and demands that the sheriff keep out local fisherman like Gerald Blackwelder; C. J. will lose his job if he cannot make Les do Tucker's bidding. Becky has been pulled from the other direction; her recent past includes a former boyfriend, extreme environmental activist Richard Pelfrey. Pelfrey organized a rally against strip mining at a coal company headquarters to remember the company's accidental killing of a toddler and the paltry $5,000 fine the owners paid for negligence. As the rally becomes violent, Pelfrey nearly beats a coal company executive to death; Richard's extremism appalls Becky, and despite her love for him she eventually leaves shortly before he is killed. The tension over who uses the land, in this case the developer who wants to exploit it for profit or the locals who want it to remain free for personal use, explodes for Les and Becky when Gerald Blackwelder is accused of dumping kerosene into the water above the waterfall and poisoning the fish on Tucker's property. It is left to Les to solve his last case.

Winding through the twenty-first-century mess that Rash's Appalachia has become is Becky's nineteenth-century solution. Throughout the novel Becky steps out of the present into something timeless, as when she avoids stepping on a copperhead: "Part of me not sight knew it was there. The atavistic like flint-rock sparked. Amazon tribes see Venus in the daylight. My grandfather needed no watch to tell time. What more might we recover if open to it? Perhaps even God" (*Above the Waterfall* 14). These moments are expressed in prose poem or, as in chapters 13, 20, 27, and 36, poems that Becky is consciously working out, which express in one way or another the transformative power of nature and inscape. Although not perfectly linear, as Becky's chapters progress through the novel, the narrative of the present dissolves into the timeless natural landscape expressed through her poetry. When Les is finally clear of the pettiness of solving his last whodunit, he finds Becky at Locust Creek Park, takes her hand, and together they walk across a bridge over a stream. They will not look back. More so than most Rash characters, they leave the page with hope and redemption from the corrupted world that almost brought both of them down.

As the novel began, it ends in a prose poem, but this one is completely detached from story and perhaps narrator; in the first edition it even appears in a smaller font so the last page is visually set apart. *Above the Waterfall* begins with images in Becky's head of the cave paintings at Lascaux and the "runic human handprint. Where less art's veil between us and the world?" (4). In the last page of the novel, we have a word painting much like the earlier description of Lascaux, but this one transcends time and crosses across North America. The first and last imprints in this image are not made by a human hand but rather a paw: "and now in this moment the front paw is lowered in the silence of fast-filling sand the first words and last words are printed. *I was here*" (253). The veil between us and the world has dropped away, and the imprints are older than humanity; here Rash has drawn on meaningful, nature-made imprints reminiscent of the words found under "the basement of time" at the end of Norman Maclean's *A River Runs through It* or the "vermiculate patterns that were maps of the world" on the backs of river trout described in the last paragraph of Cormac McCarthy's *The Road* (Maclean 104; McCarthy 241). As Becky knows through her study of Hopkins, if you look hard enough into nature the words are there. *Above the Waterfall* strongly suggests that she will help Les find them.

Regarding his approach to environmentalism in his writing, Rash stated, "I view my role as more witness. . . . I let the reader draw the conclusions" (Personal interview). He wants to bring the intensity of nature to the reader: "just showing it, describing it, the way a flower looks or describing the sound of a creek. I hope that I'm reminding the reader of that world. I hope in some ways maybe, and I mean it's up the reader to decide this, the wonder of it" (Personal interview). Throughout the body of his fiction, Rash has done much more than show it; like Hopkins's best poetry, Rash's fiction immerses the reader into a vision of the natural world. The consideration of language (pure or corrupted), the muscularity of Appalachian dialect, the native (mysterious) spirituality of Appalachian people, the ever-present considerations of what has been lost, and the heightened, poetic moments that instruct us about what remains all cohere in Rash's work toward a single effect for the reader: to inhabit what Rash refers to as "the wonder."

On July 10, 2015, Ron Rash gave a prepublication talk about and reading from *Above the Waterfall* for the Center for Life Enrichment in Highlands, North Carolina (I introduced him). As he spoke to the audience, he became particularly animated—his eyes literally lighting up—when he spoke about his new novel's emphasis on "the wonder." In postpublication interviews Rash made note of "the wonder" and in an e-mail to me defined it as the "overwhelming sense of a being"—using being as both noun and verb—"within all of the world's beauty and strangeness . . . what Becky calls invisioning" (Personal interview). In the Romantic tradition of Wordsworth, Emerson, or Poe, the best of Rash's characters apprehend the sublime beauty and strangeness of the world. Becky seeks the intensity of Hopkins's inscape and, as Romantic poets attempted to do nearly two centuries before, translates what meaning she finds through her art; she blazes a pathway toward redemption from a fallen world. Rash's environmental vision does not emphasize our typical binary approach to the land (exploit or preserve it) but rather invites us to experience what the author can show through his words, to understand that the sublime is still with us despite twenty-first-century environmental disasters, drug addictions, and false wonders such as cell phones or Twitter. The sustaining wonder is still around us; if we can disconnect and be open to it, our world may yet be made straight.

Works Cited

Dickey, James. *Deliverance.* Boston: Houghton Mifflin, 1970.

Emerson, Ralph Waldo. "Nature." *Ralph Waldo Emerson: Essays and Lectures.* New York: Library of America, 1983. 6–49.

Hopkins, Gerard Manley. *Poems of Gerard Manley Hopkins.* Ed. W. H. Gardner and N. H. MacKenzie. 4th ed. London: Oxford University Press, 1967. 69.

Maclean, Norman. *"A River Runs through It" and Other Stories.* Chicago: University of Chicago Press, 2001.

Martin, Robert Bernard. *Gerard Manley Hopkins: A Very Private Life.* New York: Putnam, 1991.

McCarthy, Cormac. *The Road.* New York: Knopf, 2006.

Poe, Edgar Allan. "Twice-Told Tales, by Nathaniel Hawthorne." Review. *Anthology of American Literature.* Ed. George McMichael et al. 4th ed. 2 vols. New York: Macmillan, 1989. 1024–27.

Rash, Ron. *Above the Waterfall.* New York: HarperCollins, 2015.

———. *Burning Bright.* New York: HarperCollins, 2010.

———. *Casualties.* Beaufort, S.C.: Bench, 2000.

———. *Chemistry and Other Stories.* New York: Henry Holt, 2007.

———. *The Cove.* New York: HarperCollins, 2012.

———. Interview by Robin Young. *Here and Now.* National Public Radio. WBUR, Boston, September 8, 2015. Radio.

———. *"The Night the New Jesus Fell to Earth" and Other Stories from Cliffside, North Carolina.* 1994. Columbia: University of South Carolina Press, 2014.

———. *Nothing Gold Can Stay.* New York: HarperCollins, 2013.

———. *One Foot in Eden.* New York: Henry Holt, 2002.

———. Personal interview. August 31, 2010.

———. "Re: The Wonder." Message to the author. October 6, 2015. E-mail.

———. *Saints at the River.* New York: Henry Holt, 2004.

———. *Serena.* New York: HarperCollins, 2008.

———. "Turtle Meat." *Reflections* 8 (1976): 103–7.

———. *The World Made Straight.* New York: Henry Holt, 2006.

Steinbeck, John. *Working Days: The Journals of* The Grapes of Wrath. Ed. Robert DeMott. New York: Viking, 1989.

FIERCE GHOSTS, STRANGE SHADOWS

Reading Ron Rash's Extinct and Endangered Species through Flannery O'Connor

Jimmy Dean Smith

In "Some Aspects of the Grotesque in Southern Fiction," Flannery O'Connor stipulates that her ideal writer would be grounded in both the specifics and the "mystery" of place: "Such a novelist . . . will have to descend far enough into himself to reach those underground springs that give life to big work. This descent into himself will, at the same time, be a descent into his region. . . . This is the beginning of vision" (*Collected Works* 821). To O'Connor, Ronald Emerick proposed, "mystery" means "the deeper realism and essential truths" (49) that the writer's descent reveals, a mixture of abstract "truths" and concrete "realism." It is rooted not only in place but in a *specific* place—the writer's ("his") own region. But southern writers, O'Connor observed in "The Fiction Writer and His Country," are often conceived "to be unhappy combinations of Poe and Erskine Caldwell" (*Collected Works* 802). O'Connor wrote John Hawkes, "I think I would admit to writing what Hawthorne called 'romances.' . . . Hawthorne interests me considerably. I feel more of a kinship with him than with any other American" (*Collected Works* 1156–57).

The addition of Hawthorne to this recipe opens up the region to an artist's moral vision. Robert Brinkmeyer wrote, "Like Hawthorne, O'Connor envisioned the writer as not being bound to the probable and the everyday, as free to rearrange aspects of the natural world—only after accurately describing them—to suggest the mysteries that lay beyond" (173). IIn "The Custom-House," which serves as an introduction to *The Scarlet Letter,* Hawthorne described the place of romance as "a neutral territory, somewhere between the real world and fairy-land, where the Actual and Imaginary may meet, and each imbue itself with the nature of the other" (35). Concrete place becomes liminal space, "a land suffused with truth *and* mystery" (Emerick 49, emphasis added). These "in-between" spaces are often represented as "clearings" in a landscape as in "Young Goodman Brown" where Brown sees the truth of the world unveiled or as "the middle of nowhere" in "A Good Man Is Hard To Find" where the grandmother and the Misfit debate ultimate wisdom.

Descent into region describes the process through which Ron Rash's work is most deeply indebted to O'Connor's fiction and ideas, and where he most nearly has gotten to the place—both physical and moral—where mystery reveals itself. O'Connor stressed the mythopoetic importance of place: "[Art] is something that one experiences . . . for the purpose of realizing in a fresh way, *through the senses,* the mystery of existence. . . . Fiction is the *concrete* expression of mystery—mystery that is *lived*" (*Collected Works* 988, emphasis added). As Rash's writing has progressed, the region he has referred to in interviews as his "spirit country"[1] has accrued both real and mythic resonance. It is not only an actual place (most often Madison and Watauga counties in western North Carolina, where he spent summers growing up learning the ways of woods and stream) that lifts up his spirit but also a place that feels alive with *literal* spirits, those of lives lost to time, illness, and violence. In *The World Made Straight,* Leonard Shuler tells young Travis Shelton, "You know a place is haunted when it feels more real than you are" (86). Leonard is referring to Shelton Laurel, a physical place with GPS coordinates, and which comes alive in the novel, through imagination, with the spirits of men and boys who were massacred there.

Rash's work also expresses the disturbing absence of nonhumans from this mysterious land. He has written of animals and birds William Bartram had seen and recorded in his journals and which Sheriff Alexander reads of in *One Foot in Eden;* rare plants André Michaux had illustrated and named like the (now) endangered *shortia galacafolia,* or Oconee Bell, as in the poem "Shee-Show" from *Raising the Dead;* predatory species like the mountain panther, or "cat-o-mount," once feared but now more recollection than threat. Even the jaguar that has been declared extinct reemerges and stakes its claim in an Appalachian creek bed that "*I was here*" in *Above the Waterfall* (*Above the Waterfall* 255). Rash's region is surely richly haunted as was O'Connor's, but "Ghosts can be very fierce and instructive. They cast strange shadows, particularly in our literature" (O'Connor, *Collected Works* 818).

While much of O'Connor's mythopoetic fiction takes place in cities and small towns and roadside cafés and doctors' offices, the mundane sites of modern life, perhaps her most distinctive location for invoking mystery is the southern woods. Significantly—and understandably, too, given her limited mobility during most of the years she was writing—the woods themselves are seldom entered into but rather seen at a distance: "A View of the Woods" is not only a title but also an O'Connor leitmotif. Thus, while "An Afternoon in the

Woods,"[2] "The River," and the terrifying "A Circle in the Fire," for instance, send characters—in all cases children—on troublesome hikes through the forest, O'Connor's work is far more likely to show us woods from a distance, landscapes weighted with mysterious importance.

This is evident in the ominous first sentence of "A Circle in the Fire": "Sometimes the last line of trees was a solid gray-blue wall a little darker than the sky but this afternoon it was almost black and behind it the sky was a livid glaring white" (*Collected Works* 232). (The portentous phrase *line of trees* is used three more times in this story: *Collected Works* 233, 247, 251.) Or in "A Good Man Is Hard to Find," where the massacre of a family takes place in woods that we, and the Grandmother, see from a distance: "Behind them the line of woods gaped like a dark open mouth" (*Collected Works* 146). Or in this, an apocalypse from O'Connor's "little morality play" (*Collected Works* 1009), "A View of the Woods": "The third time [Mr. Fortune] got up to look at the woods, it was almost six o'clock and the gaunt trunks appeared to be raised in a pool of red light that gushed from the almost hidden sun setting behind them. The old man stared for some time, as if for a prolonged instant he were caught up out of the rattle of everything that led to the future and were held there in the midst of an uncomfortable mystery that he had not apprehended before. He saw it, in his hallucination, as if someone were wounded behind the woods and the trees were bathed in blood. After a few minutes . . . [he] returned to his bed and shut his eyes and against the closed lids hellish red trunks rose up in a black wood" (*Collected Works* 150). The woods, O'Connor explained in a letter to her friend Betty Hester, "are the Christ symbol" of "A View of the Woods" (*Collected Works* 1014), citing further evidence from the story to bolster her reading. In the old man's time-stopping vision, the blood-drenched woods are imbued with the "uncomfortable mystery" and epiphanic terror of mythopoetic romance—from which Mr. Fortune, a modern pragmatic capitalist, recoils.

A central work in Rash's descent into region is "Last Rite," the third story in *Chemistry and Other Stories.* Based like so much of Rash's writing on family history and set on the preindustrial frontier of Watauga County, North Carolina, "Last Rite" depicts Sarah Hampton's quest to locate and name the *exact* site of her son Elijah's murder. The sheriff who reports the killing can do no better than to say the "back of beyond" and that "they don't even know what state that place is in, much less what county" (42). The place of death is known, that is—it is marked with a rusting skillet and a "swelling in the ground" (49)—but the family Bible, with a blank where "Place of Death" should be, demands more. The great mystery of Elijah's death may never be answered, for the plot is not a whodunit but a bereavement ritual to mark the space of Elijah's encounter with ultimacy. As O'Connor said, justifying the violence in her own stories, "I have found that violence is strangely capable of returning my characters to reality and preparing them to accept their moment of grace" (*Mystery* 112). But if Sarah has no way short of interrogating his killer to find out how well Elijah died, at least she can perform this one "last rite" and name the place.

As Sarah, her widowed daughter-in-law, Emily, and the surveyor she has hired to locate the dying place leave Boone, the land turns almost immediately "steeper, rockier," and more distinctly *physically present* as they initially ascend, before making the descent into mythopoetic space: "Sarvis and beard-tongue bloomed on the road's edge while dogwoods brightened the woods. . . . Outside of Silverstone the wagon road narrowed until it was no longer a road but a trail. The Stone Mountains loomed like thunderheads. . . . They traveled another hour before entering the gap, the mountains and woods closing around them, sunlight mere glances in the treetops. No birds sang and no deer or rabbit bolted into the undergrowth at their approach. The trees leaned over the trail as if listening" (47–49). At the end of the story, the *cartographical* mystery of Elijah's death is solved: "North Carolina, Watauga County," says the surveyor. But he continues: "Granite, yellow-jackets, snakes, and briars, that's all that mountain is" (50). As a smalltime scientist, an entrepreneur with precision instruments and no genuine feel for the landscape he measures out in spoonfuls of data, the surveyor represents modernity's urge to demystify. But he can get no further than dollars and data points: bare rock and noxious vermin are "all that mountain is" to him. But to Sarah, and to her son's widow, the woods are a grave before which they kneel, and, as in other Rash fiction,[3] they commune with their lost kin and their region by planting indigenous seeds into the earth.

Rash's description of the terrain—"No birds sang and no deer or rabbit bolted into the undergrowth at their approach. The trees leaned over the trail as if listening" (*Chemistry* 47–49)—builds suspense as the trio make their way into the wilderness. Are the assailants waiting to kill them as well? Even more important than building suspense, though, the description anthropomorphizes the woods as in O'Connor's fiction. Rash's woods "listen"; O'Connor's "gape . . . like a dark open mouth" (*Collected Works* 146), ready to devour an entire vacationing family (except for the cat) or perhaps to speak the mystery the woods contain which, in "A Good Man Is Hard to Find" is gunshots and screams and, worst of all, silence. In "Last Rite," though, the woods of Watauga County may be less immediately violent, but they are just as full of silence. The natural world can supply Sarah Hampton only so many facts about her son's death. Sarah—planting wildflower seeds that will bloom from her son's grave and wearily stretching out to sleep on the mound where Elijah died—imbues the witnessing woods with mythopoetic images of mother love and grace to counter the blunt horror of unexpected death.

While the story is impelled by a desire to fill in blank spaces—a line in the family Bible, coordinates on a rustic map—at its center is a great emptiness, a spiritual abyss that is only partially filled when the place of Elijah's death is settled. When Sarah, her duties done as best she can, lies down to sleep on the killing ground, her exhaustion reminds us of the *first* arduous task she made on her child's behalf many years ago. Over the last several months, the narrator tells us, between learning of Elijah's death and finally discovering his killing ground, Sarah had developed a pain in her stomach and "last week she'd coughed up a bright gout of blood" (*Chemistry* 49). She has worried that she will not finish her duty to her son before dying of her unnamed illness, but there is another reason her belly may ache. Sarah's name echoes the biblical Sarah, who called her son "Isaac" for the laughter he caused (Genesis 21),[4] but the irony is almost cruel for in Rash's story; Sarah Hampton has no cause to laugh. She aches in the hollowness of her womb, mourning the ghost to which she gave birth, an emptiness at the center of her body and in the back of beyond.

In *The Cove*[5] Laurel Shelton explicitly asks the question that lies behind much of the mystery of Rash's region: "Did a ghost even know it was a ghost? (19). In much of Rash's work but especially in *One Foot in Eden,* "Not Waving but Drowning," "Under Jocassee," and many of the poems in *Raising the Dead,* characters become aware that they are premature ghosts[6] haunting an impermanent landscape, in these cases vanishing not because of the NPS (National Park Service) or development but because of the South's need for power and thus for reservoirs that drown the backcountry. (Land that inspired Flannery O'Connor now lies beneath Georgia's Lake Sinclair.) With his marriage falling apart, Sheriff Will Alexander in *One Foot in Eden* thinks about the past when as newlyweds he and his wife, Janice, had made love: it was "like we'd stepped out of time into the sweet everlasting" (22–23). That lovely metaphor turns tragic as the marriage sours, and the sheriff meditates on the history and future of a valley that will soon fill with lake water. Nothing, it seems, is "everlasting"; temporariness is built into the temporal. In his next three paragraphs (23), Sheriff Alexander uses the words "vanish" three times and "disappear" twice more to suggest that impermanence is the natural state of things, that his region throngs with living ghosts and "once-presence[s]" ("The Vanquished," *Raising the Dead* 6). The romance ideology of the "sweet everlasting" betrays itself: it is not, as it first appears, so much a poeticism for sexual bliss as a reminder that eternity is timeless and that, euphemize as much as we like, dead is dead. Many of Rash's characters are the ghosts that haunt the region, some of them once-presences and some of them in transit.

One of Rash's most devastating fictions is his rewriting of the opening section of *Saints at the River* as the short story "Something Rich and Strange" in *Nothing*

Gold Can Stay. As in the 2004 novel, the passage is rife with border crossings, thresholds, and a mysterious liminality. The twelve-year-old Ruth Kowalsky of *Saints* becomes an unnamed pubescent girl who wades too far into the Tamassee river, which divides Georgia and South Carolina, and gets swept away by the fast rushing current. In a virtuoso sentence covering more than two hundred mostly one-syllable words, the story describes the young girl's drowning in a wild descent down the river and over a waterfall to her corpse's entrapment in a hydraulic. (She crosses another border, between life and death somewhere along the way.) The imagery is agonizingly concrete—"another rock smashes against her knee" (44)—and immediate until the sentence, which has operated with virtually no punctuation, climaxes with a mysterious calm signaled by the commas Rash has held in reserve: "[her] lungs explode in pain and then the pain is gone as bright colors shatter around her like glass shards, and she remembers her sixth-grade science class, the gurgle of the aquarium at the back of the room, the smell of chalk dust that morning the teacher held a prism out the window so it might fill with color, and she has a final, beautiful thought—that she is now inside the prism and knows something even the teacher does not know, that the prism's colors are voices, voices that swirl around her head like a crown, and at that moment her arms and legs she did not even know were flailing cease and she becomes part of the river" (*Nothing Gold Can Stay* 45).

The dying girl's revelation—her "final, beautiful thought"—is a synaesthetically poetic burst of voice and color, an almost sentimental rethinking of the last brutal paragraphs of O'Connor's "The River," in which another child drowns with the narrative focused fully on his dying thoughts and sensations.

In O'Connor's story five-year-old Harry Ashburn is an afterthought to his persistently hungover parents, who cannot remember to feed him and or provide him spiritual nourishment either. Their babysitter, Mrs. Connin, presumptuously takes Harry to a river baptism, where he christens himself "Bevel" and learns that he "counts" once he has been fully immersed "in the River of Life, in the River of Love, in the rich red river of Jesus' blood" (*Collected Works* 162). After a dreadful night at home, Bevel returns alone to the river to relive his experience of "counting," and story's point of view queasily narrows to Bevel's as he tries to go "under the river" (165) rather than return to his parents' apartment and its moral tawdriness. Furious that the river will not accept him, Bevel "hit[s] and splash[es] and kick[s] the filthy river" until, in a kind of happy ending, he "plunge[s] under . . . and . . . the waiting current [catches] him like a long gentle hand and pull[s] him swiftly forward and down" (171). The child relaxes since "he [is] moving swiftly and [knows] he [is] getting somewhere," and "all his fury and fear [leave] him" (171). The troubling conclusion of this story leaves us with many unanswered questions—is the child "saved" when he goes "under the river? Will his parents or the story's diabolical Mr. Paradise have their own epiphanies and receive grace? Readers are left pondering the encapsulation of mystery in the liminal spaces between life, death, and afterlife.

This story, as Sarah Gordon wrote, "embodies the idea of God's mysterious presence here on earth" (146). Bevel is saved, she asserts, because "the boy's faith has led him to God" (146), even more so because nature, so clearly a manifestation of "God's Grandeur," is central to the story's presentation. (After all, it is called "The River" and not, for example, "The Drowned Boy.") Gordon argued that G. M. Hopkins was very much on O'Connor's mind as she "devote[d] what is for her uncharacteristic time to the beauty of the natural world" (148), focusing especially on the visual imagery of the river. O'Connor referred to it as "a broad orange stream where the reflection of the sun was set like a diamond" (*Collected Works* 161) and to "the pieces of the white sun scattered in the river" (165). The sun-on-water imagery climaxes with (literally) brilliant synesthesia: "The air was so quiet he could hear the broken pieces of the sky knocking in the water" (165).

In "The River," wrote Gordon, O'Connor "emphasize[d] the reality of the incarnate God" (150). Ron Rash's beautiful prism image borrows its loveliness from O'Connor's diamond, but not the earlier writer's certainty of the child's spiritual destination. That is, while the drowning scene in "Something Rich and Strange" climaxes with prismatic light and a host of voices—a dazzling special effect for readers who make movies in their heads—Rash's story does not leave that image untroubled. First, the fractured light and host of voices the drowning girl experiences are demystified as the same sunlight-on-water image O'Connor captured. Second, Rash chose not to end his bravura sentence with that image of sentimental transcendence, and thus this story gains deeper connections with O'Connor's, which does not satisfy readers like Miles Orvell who saw the horror of the little boy's drowning and not little Bevel's ascent through childlike faith into heaven. Instead, with a brusque "and" to stop the poetic passage, Rash wrote, "she becomes part of the river," as if the drowning scene's *real* denouement is only a prosaic afterthought, an *oh-yeah* addendum to the sparkly gorgeousness. Dead, her corpse trapped in a hydraulic, the girl becomes a (some) thing,[7] a component of the landscape she and her vacationing family had scant moments before viewed from a distance. The remainder of the story develops this apparently unhappy premise into "something rich and strange." The girl is no longer *apart from nature;* she is *a part of nature.* Rash's work, as I have argued, embodies O'Connor's prescription for a writer who will descend into region to find the mysteries gathered therein; "Something Rich and Strange" takes the notion even further and becomes about *disintegration* into region.

While the girl's death-thoughts are presented in poetic and mystical language, invoking O'Connor's dictum that "violence is strangely capable of returning my characters to reality and preparing them to accept their moment of grace" (*Mystery* 112), to the neuroscientist those thoughts are mundane: the epiphany can be easily explained away. What Marshall Bruce Gentry asked about O'Connor might be adapted to Rash's story as well: "It is as if [Rash] is asking [himself] if revelations about the sacred ever come at too high a price" (64). Following the girl's death, "Something Rich and Strange" shifts its point of view to another character, an unnamed rescue diver who pulls bodies from the river. His pragmatic attitude is typified by the clunky tough-guy-ness of "[he] knew death punched no time clock" (*Nothing Gold Can Stay* 46). But rescue diving is the man's second job, one he performs for the community and law enforcement. His real job is teaching biology at the local high school working with students who would rather "talk . . . about prom instead of pupae and chrysalides" (48), the natural world's clues that this story is about transformation.

His first dive to recover the girl's body leads to a terrifying encounter "in the undercut behind the hydraulic," where "she had been upright, her head and back and legs pressed against a rock slab. Only the hair moved, its strands streaming upward. As the diver drifted closer, he saw that her eyes were open. Their faces were inches apart when he slipped an arm around her waist" ("Something Rich and Strange," *Nothing Gold Can Stay* 47). The girl is at the point of what-used-to-be-her-life when, like the diver's distracted students, she ought to be burbling on about prom and physically crossing the border from childhood into maturity, a stage in her own "pupation" that Rash emphasized with the clammy erotics of the scene. Faces close, the diver's arm around her waist—but then the current rips the mask from the biology teacher's face, and he has his own—terrifying—river vision, that "the girl's blue eyes had life in them [and he] could feel her heart beating against her chest and hear her whispering" (47). The girl has something she wants to tell him. What initially appears to be a weirdly sexualized encounter—an impression even more distinct in Rash's poem treating this same subject, "The Girl in the River" in *Waking* (41)—turns realistic and beautiful. The mystery of this girl's descent into the river—and Rash's simultaneous descent into his region, as the narrative follows both the girl and the diver down—is not orthodox, as it is in O'Connor's story of child drowning, nor is it postmodern filled with pixilated color and disembodied voices, nor heartlessly empirical either. The mystery of such vision is explained away as neuroscientific coldness.

In the story's remaining paragraphs, the girl tells the diver "something rich and strange," but nothing about prisms and a host of voices. Instead, once he overcomes his terror and goes back in for a second recovery attempt, she tells the river diver what it means to become part of a river; she reveals to the biology teacher what it means to be alive and then to be dead. Under the river's surface, the diver realizes, "all remained quiet and still, the girl's transformation unrushed, gentle. Crayfish and minnows unknitted flesh from bone, attentive to loosed threads" (49). In his own "beautiful vision" the little girl from Nebraska has become not some blossoming young woman to hold close at the prom but this: "She was less of what she had been, the blue rubbed from her eyes, flesh freed from the chandelier of bone. He touched what had once been a hand. The river whispered to him that it would not be long now" (49). The story ends with several sentences epitomizing the universal mystery of disintegration—or *re*integration?—into nature: "The midday sun leaned close and dazzling. Dogwoods bloomed small white stars. The diver knew in the coming days the petals would find their way into the river, drifting onto sandbars and gilding the backs of pools, and the diver knew some would drift over the falls into the hydraulic. They would furl among the last bones and like the last bones they would finally slip free" (50).

Some of the most distinctive mysteries inhabiting Rash's region are the species that science insists are extinct or nearly so. As plants and animals make their own way into the "sweet everlasting," they reappear as mysterious "relicts" in Rash's landscape. Throughout *Serena,* for example, we watch the title character wreak havoc like the chestnut blight (15–16), a human incarnation of an invasive species. In her attempt to bend the North Carolina ecosystem to her will, Serena destroys the weaker flora and fauna in her way (including her own husband), until finally the landscape appears as "what the end of the world will be like" (336). And yet, despite this environmental destruction the region harbors a cryptozoological wonder, the "extinct" panther that turns the tables on Pemberton, who had hitherto been hunting it (367). Similarly, in the poem "Catamount" a relict mountain lion appears, "a vision beyond human measure" (*Among the Believers* 69). "The Woman Who Believed in Jaguars" (*Burning Bright* 91–106) feints in the same direction, but the extinct species at its core is the Carolina parakeet (104–5). As John Lang notes (110), this story anticipates *The Cove,* in which the Carolina parakeet, thought extinct in the wild for more than a decade, is a leitmotif signifying the mystery living virtually undetected deep in the eponymical region.

The primary landscape of *The Cove* is "a place where only bad things happened" (1), a space "submerged in shadow even though it was midafternoon" (3). In the novel's preface, set in 1953, a TVA engineer explores the area, part of northern Madison County, which after damming will soon be deep underwater. He is trained in modern science but has a liking for myth as well. A native Kansan, he has collected mountain myths and knows what it means when he spots the remnants of a bottle tree scattered about with salt: a barrier to "keep evil from coming through" (2); the novel's heroine is reputed to be a witch, and locals strive to keep her magic locked up in the cove. Even in the weird landscape, however, he recollects that an "ornithologist claimed the area might hold the last Carolina parakeet" (3), an image that, in that "dark and silent"—and *temporary*—landscape, recalls the last line of the poem "Carolina Parakeet" and its tender depiction of fleeting absence, to "glimpse that bright vanishing" (*Raising the Dead* 62). Each section of *The Cove* is marked with a woodcut of a Carolina parakeet, the illustrations gradually fading away to signify the impermanence of earthly things.

In the novel's present time of 1918, the last year of World War I, Laurel Shelton goes looking for what she thinks might be a Carolina parakeet crying out from the cove and finds instead a haggard stranger (who is an escaped German POW from Hot Springs) playing a silver flute. This demystifying, however, is not the end of the bird's presence in the novel. Laurel remembers in disconcerting detail how her father, a farmer with a pragmatic need to rid his fields of two dozen Carolina parakeets, blasted away until all the birds lay dead, food for hogs (*The Cove* 76–77). For a moment, however, the birds had enlivened the cove with color and song. Before her father appeared with shotgun to protect the family's orchard, the birds' "bodies had knit together and lifted the whole cove skyward into the sun's full light" (76). As the novel's tragic love story develops, Rash identifies Laurel with the beautiful but doomed Carolina parakeets. When she is shot and killed, she is wearing a bright-green dress (216) that mirrors the plumage of the birds her father, among other practical-minded settlers of the region, wiped out. It is as if Laurel, in love, brings the "bright vanishing" back to the dark and foreboding place; she is the "vision" of Keatsian truth and beauty that Rash finds when he descends into the region.

O'Connor worried that Hawthornean romance could lead to aesthetic weakness: "Truth, Goodness and Beauty are abstractions and abstractions lead to thinness and allegory" (*Habit of Being* 520). *The Cove* flirts with such thinness because so much of it is indeed allegorical—and not just in the ways that Laurel Shelton equates to the Carolina parakeet and thus to a region whose deepest mystery is also its most fleeting. Laurel's birthmark (a reminder of the Hawthorne romance with a similar title) is purple like the butterfly that "[lights] on the stream edge to sip water" (11). Though it appalls the people of Mars Hill, who use it as evidence to claim that Laurel is marked as a witch, the birthmark "is a pretty hue" like "the bull thistle" (11). Laurel Shelton's name further reinforces the allegory. First, it links her with the mountain laurel growing in her region, and second, the sound *aura* in her name links the light seemingly denied the cove with supernatural light.

For Rash's readers Laurel Shelton's name is a particularly winsome reminder of how important place is in his writing. In Rash's "recycling" aesthetic, Laurel's name (in the world of this novel at least) reverses the hatred and violence of the place Shelton Laurel, also known as "Bloody Madison," holds in Rash's work, treated at length in *The World Made Straight.* Her name, that is, links her to the mysterious beauty of land and makes Laurel Shelton's fragility a comment on the place of place in Rash's writing. An image from the Shelton Laurel texts further connects Laurel, the Carolina parakeet, and her imperiled cove with vanishing species, in this case the speckled trout that is being fished out of Madison County's streams: "He remembered how you could not see the orange fins and red flank spots but only the dark backs in the rippling water. And how it was only when they lay gasping on the green bank moss that you realized how bright and pretty they were" (*The World Made Straight* 38). As Edwin Muir put it in the poem that gives Rash's first novel its name, "The world's great day is growing late," and "Time's handiworks by time are haunted"—or, as Frost said in the poem that gave Rash's fifth short-story collection its name, "Nothing gold can stay."

What these texts share is a belief in Eden—if not literally, then mythopoetically. "How far we have fallen' means the fall of Adam, the fall from innocence, from sanctifying grace" (*Habit of Being* 302), wrote O'Connor to her friend, Cecil Dawkins, an apprentice writer whose work she encouraged. Nearly twenty-five years later, Rash—not yet a professed acolyte of O'Connor—was in the early years of his own career when he wrote that "my kin have taught me . . . how to live with courage and dignity in a fallen world" ("Autobiographical Essay" 177), one where death and decay are the destiny of all creation. And yet, though the mythical Fall has resulted in, as O'Connor said, a concomitant "fall from sanctifying grace," neither O'Connor's nor Rash's work leaves one in despair. Hazel Motes, O'Connor's first rebel-saint, is a semiliterate product of enlightenment, refusing to believe in something as nebulous as grace, but even he thinks of Christ as a fierce real presence: "Later he saw Jesus move from tree to tree in the back of his mind, a wild ragged figure motioning him to turn around and come off into the dark where he was not sure of his footing" (*Collected Works* 11). That is, even though Christ is unwelcome in his thoughts, Hazel Motes cannot banish him entirely: Jesus remains "at the back of his mind," and the "wild" figure has a mystery to reveal to whoever follows along the slippery paths of that place.

"The artist penetrates the concrete world in order to find at its depths the image of its source, the image of ultimate reality," wrote O'Connor in "Novelist and Believer" (*Mystery* 157), "search[ing] desperately, feeling about in all experience for the *lost* God" (159, emphasis added), looking for a signifying emptiness, a meaningful void. A familiar passage from "Some Aspects of the Grotesque in Southern Fiction" amplifies this belief: "I think it is safe to say that while the South is hardly Christ-centered, it is most certainly Christ-haunted" (*Collected Works* 818). For this Catholic novelist, Christ is foremost among the "fierce and instructive" ghosts that haunt her region. If O'Connor's region is

"Christ-haunted," a place where "fierce and instructive" ghosts "cast strange shadows," then Rash's is haunted by lives that have disappeared—human and nonhuman—as well as those that are disappearing. Panther, Carolina parakeet, American chestnut, the life of a child, jaguar: these and other species are resurrected to haunt Rash's landscapes, demystified no more.

In *Saints at the River,* Rash took the story of the drowned girl from "Something Rich and Strange" in another direction. The photojournalist narrator, Maggie Glenn, recalls once seeing a rare Oconee Bell in the wild and feeling sure that the plant would survive human progress because its river habitat had been designated "Wild and Scenic" (162–63). She and her friends, she recounts, were environmentalists with a spiritual side, whom some local preacher had called "false prophets" because they "worshiped nature, not God, as though one were not part of the other" (165). What the region needs, implies the narrator, are *true* prophets who speak "a new language" like churchgoers who have "been possessed by the Holy Ghost and [speak] in tongues" (165)—"wild" prophets who descend into the region, listen to what the gaping mouth of the woods relates, and come back proclaiming the realness of mystery, the indisputable presence of what looked to be absence.

Notes

1. For more on Rash's comments and remembrances of his "spirit country," see my essay "Spirit Country," and Wilhelm, "Introduction" (2–5).

2. This story was initially proposed for inclusion in *A Good Man Is Hard to Find and Other Stories* but excluded to make room for "The Displaced Person" and also because O'Connor was "not wildly fond of" it (*Habit of Being* 73).

3. For other passages of "seeding the earth," see *Serena* (79) and "Into the Gorge" in *Burning Bright* (136, 138).

4. "Last Rite," published in *Casualties* in 2000 (and later reprinted in *Chemistry and Other Stories,* 2007), presages Rash's use of "the Isaac motif" in *One Foot in Eden* (2002), where similar irony is invoked, although in somewhat reverse fashion.

5. I am using the paperback edition of *The Cove* (2012), which differs both in pagination and in more significant ways from the hardback edition.

6. For more on the "ghosting" of characters in *Eureka Mill,* see Wilhelm, "Ghostly Bodies."

7. Daniel Cross Turner's work on "undead ecologies" promises new insights regarding ecotheory and the posthuman; see his "Undead Ecologies"; and for more on the posthuman in the work of Rash and other southern writers, see Anderson et al., *Undead Souths.*

Works Cited

Anderson, Gary, Taylor Hagood, and Daniel Cross Turner, eds. *Undead Souths: The Gothic and Beyond in Southern Literature and Culture.* Baton Rouge: Louisiana State University Press, 2015.

Brinkmeyer, Robert H. *The Art and Vision of Flannery O'Connor.* Baton Rouge: Louisiana State University Press, 1989.

Emerick, Ronald. "Hawthorne and O'Connor: A Literary Kinship." *Flannery O'Connor Bulletin* 18 (1989): 46–54.

Frost, Robert. "Nothing Gold Can Stay." *Collected Poems.* Ed. Edward Connery Lathem. New York: Henry Holt, 1969.

Gentry, Marshall Bruce. "How Sacred Is the Violence in 'A View of the Woods'?" *"On the Subject of the Feminist Business": Re-reading Flannery O'Connor.* Ed. Teresa Caruso. Washington, D.C.: Peter Lang, 2004. 64–73.

Gordon, Sarah. *Flannery O'Connor: The Obedient Imagination.* Athens: University of Georgia Press, 2000.

Hawthorne, Nathaniel. *The Scarlet Letter.* 1850. New York: Penguin, 2003.

Lang, John. *Understanding Ron Rash.* Columbia: University of South Carolina Press, 2014.

"The Last Carolina Parakeet." *Audubon: John James Audubon Center at Mill Grove.* National Audubon Society, 2015. Web. April 18, 2015.

Medina, Barbra, and Victor Medina. *Southern Appalachian Wildflowers.* Guilford, Conn.: Falcon, 2002.

Muir, Edwin. "One Foot in Eden." *Collected Poems.* London: Faber, 2003. 227.

O'Connor, Flannery. *Collected Works.* Ed. Sally Fitzgerald. New York: Library of America, 1988.

———. *The Habit of Being.* Ed. Sally Fitzgerald. New York: Farrar, 1979.

———. *Mystery and Manners: Occasional Prose.* Ed. Sally Fitzgerald and Robert Fitzgerald. New York: Farrar, 1969.

Orvell, Miles. *Invisible Parade: The Fiction of Flannery O'Connor.* Philadelphia: Temple University Press, 1972.

Rash, Ron. *Above the Waterfall.* New York: HarperCollins, 2015.

———. *Among the Believers.* Oak Ridge, Tenn.: Iris, 2000.

———. "Autobiographical Essay." *Southern Appalachian Poetry: An Anthology of Works by 37 Poets.* Ed. Marita Garin. Jefferson, N.C.: McFarland, 2008. 177–78.

———. *Burning Bright.* New York: HarperCollins, 2010.

———. *Chemistry and Other Stories.* New York: Henry Holt, 2007.

———. *Eureka Mill.* Spartanburg, S.C.: Hub City, 1998.

———. *The Cove.* New York: HarperCollins, 2012.

———. *Nothing Gold Can Stay.* New York: HarperCollins, 2013.

———. *One Foot in Eden.* New York: Henry Holt, 2002.

———. *Raising the Dead.* Oak Ridge, Tenn.: Iris, 2002.

———. *Saints at the River.* New York: Henry Holt, 2004.

———. *Serena.* New York: HarperCollins, 2008.

———. *Waking.* Spartanburg, S.C.: Hub City, 2011.

———. *The World Made Straight.* New York: Henry Holt, 2006.

Smith, Jimmy Dean. "Spirit Country: The Voice of the Earth and Ron Rash's Southern Appalachia." *North Carolina Literary Review* 23 (2011): 111–20.

Turner, Daniel Cross. "Undead Ecologies in James Dickey and Ron Rash." SAMLA, Atlanta, Georgia. October 2014. Conference Presentation.

Wilhelm, Randall. "Ghostly Bodies and Worker Voices: Power and Resistance in Ron Rash's *Eureka Mill.*" *South Carolina Review* 42.2 (2010): 25–36.

———. "Introduction: Blood Memory." *The Ron Rash Reader.* Ed. Randall Wilhelm. Columbia: University of South Carolina Press, 2014. 1–32.

"A COMFORT DURING A HARD TIME"

Food in Ron Rash's Poems, Short Stories, and Novels

Erica Abrams Locklear

In this day and age, one should not have to argue in defense of Appalachia. For decades scholars, activists, and community members have railed against long-standing stereotypes associated with the mountain South. They have explained the origins of commonly accepted ideas about Appalachia, discussed the rationale behind the creation of damaging stereotypes, and talked back to them.[1] Yet misunderstandings and exaggerations about the area persist. As American studies scholar Elizabeth Engelhardt explained, Appalachia "remains a region stuck in a vanished past, uniquely the repository of unassailable (white) poverty and inaccessible wilderness. Despite repeated attempts to articulate emotional backlash, thoughtful scholarship, and evidence countering and supporting these narratives, exotic Appalachia lingers" (77). Engelhardt has situated much of her work in the burgeoning field of foodways studies and has lamented the "excesses of southern food fetishism" (76). She has criticized the tendency to privilege some foods on the southern table over others, predicting that "Appalachia is poised to be the next big thing in food circles" (78). When coupled with already existing, deeply ingrained stereotypes about the region, Engelhardt worried that Appalachia could become a prime target for even more overgeneralizations. So she issued a call for us to "do it right" this time, because if we do, "Appalachian food studies can correct the excesses of southern food fetishism; open up fertile ground for a complicated story of race, class, gender, region and food; and tell a heck of a good story at the same time" (76). Considering the complexities of these stories encourages a nuanced portrait of a region that has never been monolithic.

One obvious way to begin constructing a more complete picture of Appalachia is by analyzing its literature. As this collection attests, Ron Rash is one of the region's most talented and prolific contemporary writers. For this reason his poems, short stories, and novels provide a captivating case study for doing precisely what Engelhardt recommended. Careful examination of food references throughout Rash's body of work reveal the difficult realities Appalachians—and western North Carolinians in particular—faced in the wake of the timber industry, the shift to large-scale production of tobacco, the migration of many mountain families to textile mills in the piedmont, and even the present-day problem of substance abuse in Appalachia. These themes permeate Rash's writing, and it is worth noting that food plays an integral role in his portrayal of these pivotal eras in Appalachian history. Foodways scholar Marcie Cohen Ferris wrote that "southern food has become untethered from the complex historical narrative responsible for this cuisine" (2). As a result consumers may indulge in heaping plates of fried chicken without considering the complex historical narrative that accompanies chicken in the South, particularly for African Americans.[2] Ferris insisted, "Food *is* history. Food *is* place. Food *is* power *and* disempowerment" (3). Each of these threads performs prominent roles in Rash's work: analyzing food in his writing teaches us much about Appalachian history, place, and power or lack thereof.

Historically speaking, Appalachia is inseparable from the Progressive Era.[3] Campaigns were designed to improve literacy rates, educate residents about sanitation, encourage patriotism and ideal citizenship, and teach mountain women "proper" cooking techniques. Within this context Appalachia has a long history of being viewed as inferior but redeemable.[4] Much of the possibility for redemption hinged on the perceived whiteness of Appalachia, a long-standing myth that undergirded most Progressive Era doctrine.[5] Its food traditions have a similar legacy. For instance, in a chapter entitled "Living Conditions and Health" in *The Southern Highlander and His Homeland,* John C. Campbell[6] wrote, "However philosophic the visitor may be as to matters of housing and sanitation, he is less apt to be indifferent to the question of food. No detail, probably, of the Highlander's living has been more severely criticized than his diet" (198). Local color writers, travel writers, and missionary workers began the trend of writing negatively about the region's food early in the twentieth century, and this tendency lingers today, ironically alongside the simultaneous movement to celebrate mountain food traditions including ramps, pickled watermelon, creasy greens, leather britches, poke sallet, apple stack cake, and more.

Meanwhile, other publications, like a 1927 *Mountain Life and Work* article by Floyd Bralliar, portrayed mountain people, not necessarily the food available, as the problem. Bralliar stated, "There is a feeling among the people that children at least must not be allowed to eat fruit" and goes on to cast Appalachians as ignorant of the health benefits of fruit consumption and the income potential associated with fruit sales, primarily strawberries, raspberries, peaches, cherries, grapes, and apples (17). The article makes valid points about the viability of earning an income from fruit in the mountains, but its advice also implies that either few had tried or were engaged in such ventures or did not understand how to cultivate fruits for home use or larger distribution. Bralliar seemed especially frustrated with "the average mountaineer," who according to Bralliar, "thinks his work is done when he has planted his trees" and "will tell you that, 'Peaches just natcherly don't do well here no more. The trees sorter peter out'" (18). Yet other accounts of Appalachian fruit availability in the 1920s overturn Bralliar's. Even Campbell, who was quick to criticize mountain diets, comments on the "abundant supply of wild blackberries" and noted that "apples are found more or less freely throughout the mountain region" (200). Like Bralliar, Campbell reported that "little or nothing is done in the way of spraying or pruning" yet "the trees bear abundantly unless caught by frost" (200). He even went on to comment: "The covered wagon with its load of crimson winesaps or big green 'horse apples' is a familiar sight in many a mountain metropolis" (200). Campbell also wrote about the "real attempt" that mountain people make to preserve fruits and vegetables for winter consumption, noting that "among the more prosperous families and even in the poorer homes, especially in the southern part of the mountains where fruit is more abundant and climatic conditions less severe, much is done in the preparing of jellies, apple-butter, and pickles" (200). Campbell's and Bralliar's ideas were contemporary with one another, while Rash entered the conversation decades later.

Even so, Rash's work functions as an important corrective to portrayals like Bralliar's. Although many present-day readers may not be familiar with articles from *Mountain Life and Work,* perceptions about Appalachian inferiority linger, and Rash's work responds to them. The speakers of many of Rash's poems clearly long for—and do not "severely criticize" as Campbell wrote—the food they consumed when living on the farm. Likewise Rash's short story "Where the Map Ends," in *Nothing Gold Can Stay,* depicts two runaway slaves who subsist on what food they can find in the North Carolina mountains, including "apples from orchards" (68). Early in the story the pair encounters an apple farmer who offers the fugitives not only apples, but also corn pone and sorghum (73, 74). Rash's depiction of the farmer functions in two important ways: in a story set during the Civil War it signals know-how concerning orchards long before the publication of articles like Bralliar's in 1927, and it also begins to overturn long-held assumptions about the "pure Anglo-Saxon stock" of Appalachia. As foodways scholar Fred W. Sauceman explained, "the most pervasive and lasting influences on the cooking of Appalachia . . . come from the practices of Native American populations" (18). Rash has added to that association by having a white farmer offer corn—a food long associated with Native Americans—to two African American fugitives. When considered in this way, it becomes clear that Rash not only has dispelled the idea that mountain people were ignorant concerning the cultivation of fruit, but he has also subtly eroded histories of

Appalachia that ignore the presence of Native and African Americans, as well as their food traditions. But perhaps the most recurring narrative Rash has constructed using food is one that explains the economic forces at play in the mountains that caused so many families to leave their farms and by extension, the foods those farms provided.

In some of Rash's work, the food supply available seems plentiful. In *Among the Believers,* Rash's second collection of poetry, the speaker of "In a Springhouse at Night" notes that canned vegetables and beans "fill the walls." Likewise, in "Abandoned Homestead in Watauga County," the speaker describes a cherry tree that "buckles in fruit." Notably there are no humans present to harvest the fruit. Instead that work is left to bees, birds, and the elements. And in a poem about blackberry picking from *Waking* that also takes place in Watauga County ("Watauga County: 1962"), the speaker's "pail / grows heavy" with the abundance of fruit, leaving his hands "stained like royalty." A few pages later, the speaker in "Raspberries" celebrates not only fresh raspberries but also the canned variety that was best enjoyed "when frost clouded window panes." References to a bounty of fruits that grow without human tending appear several times in Rash's work, as when mountain residents offer Serena, the titular character in Rash's fourth novel, "hats holding raspberries and blackberries, ferns twined around chewy combs of sourwood honey" during her pregnancy (200). These depictions suggest a food-productive landscape inhabited by people who know how to take advantage of foods that grow wild while also cultivating and preserving their yields, as the speaker in "Raspberries" suggests. Yet as literary critic John Lang pointed out, "Rash carefully avoids sentimentalizing or romanticizing agrarian life" (5).

Rash's first collection of poetry, *Eureka Mill,* illustrates Lang's point clearly. Featuring forty poems, the collection chronicles a family's move from an agrarian existence in the mountains to an industrial one in a textile mill town. The journey mirrors Rash's grandparents' move to Chester, South Carolina, but it also tells a story representative of thousands of mountain people who left home for the mills. Yet even in a collection that deeply criticizes mill life, in poems like "Drought" and "Spring Fever," Rash reminded readers that life on the farm was difficult too, especially in terms of food. In "Drought," when praying for rain proves unsuccessful and community members hang dead blacksnakes on fences to encourage rain, the plural first-person speakers compare their faithlessness to a "festering seed." Late summer brings only "cracked creekbeds" with rotting fish and "heat-killed hogs / and chickens." Relief eventually comes in the form of snow, but the speakers explain that many farms were mortgaged and "we listened in the barndark / to rats eating the grain." Neither adherence to Christian beliefs nor folklore about dead snakes brings rain when it is most needed. By killing the snakes in a desperate attempt to generate rain, the community inadvertently removes the rats' natural predator, making a difficult situation even worse. And in "Spring Fever" the speaker describes mill workers who long for life on the farm, especially during the spring planting season. But the speaker reasons that the men are "just remembering the best" and "It's easy to love a life / you only have to live the good parts of." Yet despite hailstorms, barns struck by lightning, and the loneliness of working on a farm, the poem emphasizes that the mill workers still long for that life and far prefer it over mill work.

Even so, Rash's writing never lets readers forget that food scarcity was a fact of life for many in the mountain South, especially during the Depression. In a poem called "Madison County: 1934" from *Raising the Dead,* Rash described a child so hungry that she steals eggs from a neighbor's chicken coop and eats them raw. The speaker is perplexed by the missing eggs and decides that the thief must be a chicken snake. To catch it he inserts a fish hook tied to a line in an egg but snares a girl instead of a snake, "the barb / unrelenting as hunger." Rash retold the incident in short-story form in *Burning Bright*'s opening story, "Hard Times." In it readers learn about two families living in Goshen Creek, Jacob and Edna and the Hartleys. Although the narrator explains that the Hartley family "is the poorest of them all," they are not known to steal and even kill their own dog to ensure that the animal was not taking Jacob and Edna's eggs (5, 8). The fact that one of the Hartley children is the culprit, and that she eats the eggs in secrecy, points to her dire situation. Perhaps even more telling is that Jacob warns the girl not to come back, telling her, "I'm going to put another hook in them eggs and this time there won't be no line on it. You'll swallow that hook and it'll tear your guts up" (17). Readers understand that Jacob's harsh warning will protect the girl from her father, who would severely punish her for stealing, but Rash also made clear that Jacob does not have eggs to spare, and the story provides no happy resolution for the hungry child.

When considered together Rash's body of work helps explain the problem of such food scarcity in the mountains. His poems, short stories, and novels demonstrate that economic forces—primarily the rise of the timber industry, large-scale tobacco production, textile mills in the piedmont, and increased substance abuse—encouraged (and still encourage) mountain residents to forsake cultivating their own foods in favor of working wage labor for cash. But in each case, the wages earned do not replace the food lost. Historically speaking and as Rash's portrayals explain, those involved in the timber industry experienced a gradual decline in farming know-how, even if timber workers were well fed in the camps, as they are in *Serena.* Tobacco farmers often found growing a lucrative cash crop more appealing than growing one's own food, which worked well until a crop failed. Textile workers living in a mill town had limited access to garden space and little time to cultivate the few crops one was able to plant. And finally, Rash portrays the increasing drug problem in the mountains as one that either replaces food entirely or decreases the quality of food options available. In other words Rash's work helps readers understand that despite what historical accounts of Appalachia may insist, the region's food scarcity was primarily the result of large-scale economic shifts determined by global markets rather than local residents.

Serena portrays the many changes the timber industry brought into the mountains. In particular the novel highlights the loss of land ownership to timber corporations and the resulting food consequences. As historian Ronald D. Eller explained, "By 1910 . . . in that portion of western North Carolina which later became the Great Smoky Mountains National Park, over 75 percent of the land came under the control of thirteen corporations, and one timber company alone owned over a third of the total acreage" (xxi). Rash's novel points out many disparities, including the kind and amount of food consumed, between those who own the timber corporations and those who work for them or who live in the vicinity but are not employed by the company. When Serena first arrives in the camp she has dinner with her husband, Pemberton, and his associates. A man named Wilkie apologizes to Serena that the dining room is "austere," yet "at seven o'clock, two kitchen workers set the table with Spode bone china and silver cutlery and linen napkins. They [leave] and [return] pushing a cart laden with wicker baskets of buttered biscuits and a silver platter draped with beef, large bowls of Steuben crystal brimming with potatoes and carrots and squash, various jams and relishes" (33, 36). Conversely the foods available and the space in which they are consumed are dramatically different for Widow Jenkins, a woman not involved in timbering. When one of the novel's main characters, Rachel, visits the widow, the narrator explains, "The greasy odor of fry pan lard filled the cabin, a scrim of smoke eddying around the room's borders" (40). In these examples not only are the foods consumed vastly different, but so too are the spaces in which consumption takes place. Widow Jenkins does not have a separate room for preparing her meals, so the scent of cooking lingers in the eating space. Yet Widow Jenkins, at least before her brutal murder, maintains independence and control over the food that she prepares.

Readers see a similar disparity in foods available for consumption between Serena, the timber owner and nonnative, and Rachel Harmon, the local woman who gives birth to Pemberton's child. One of Serena's first goals upon arriving to the camp involves training an eagle to catch snakes that threaten workers—and thus profits—in and around the timbering areas. After spending "two nights and a day" training the eagle, she feels weak from hunger, and Pemberton asks a man named Vaughn to bring her food. He appears "with a silver platter normally used to hold a ham or turkey. Heaped on it [are] thick slabs of beef and venison, green beans and squash and sweet potatoes drenched in butter. Buttermilk biscuits and a bowl of honey. A coffee pot and two cups" (89–90).

Just a few pages earlier, readers have learned that Rachel and her son, Jacob, are struggling to have enough to eat and Rachel must trap and kill a raccoon that has been stealing her eggs. Rachel does not want to kill the animal but thinks, "I don't even have a choice" (83). Like Widow Jenkins, Rachel still provides for herself, though she does work in the kitchen at the timber camp.

Conversely the men who work in the camps lose control over their own food and, what is perhaps more important, the land that was and could be used to produce food. Yet Rash was careful to underscore that foods available to those in the mountain South may not have always been plentiful or appetizing. In a scene portraying a group of timber workers who are amazed by Serena's eagle's abilities, Rash also described the food that they brought with them. While the men discuss how Serena feeds the eagle "prime-cut beef" for its training purposes, a character named Ross "unpack[s] his lunch and stare[s] dubiously at his sandwich. He slowly peel[s] back a soggy piece of white bread in the same manner he might a scab, revealing a gray slab of meat that appear[s] coated with mucus. For a few moments he simply stare[s] at the fatback" (106–7). He then tells another character, Dunbar, that he would "near about chase a dead snake around [his] ownself for a hunk of steak" (107). Dunbar replies: "Put it betwixt a big yallar-butter biscuit and I'd near give up the promise of heaven" (107). Certainly the food that the men are given in the camp is a significant improvement over slimy fatback. In the beginning of chapter 13, the narrator explains that the food "was brought forth from the yard-wide oven racks, ladled and poured from the five- and ten-gallon pots, slid and peeled off black skillets big around as harrow discs" (128). Providing enough food for the workers is clearly not an issue for the company. Moreover the variety of foods available to the workers is impressive: "Gallon bowls [are] filled with stewed apples and fried potatoes and grits and oatmeal, straw bread baskets stuffed with cat-head biscuits, heaped platters of hotcakes and fatback, saucers of butter and quart mason jars of blackberry jam. Last the coffee, the steaming pots set on plates, cups of cream and sugar as well though nearly all the men drank it black" (128). Yet the men have only fifteen minutes to eat, presumably because time spent eating is time not spent earning profit for the company. The narrator explains that when the work bell rings to return them to their duties, "the men [leave] so quickly their cast-down forks and spoons seem to retain a slight vibration, like pond water rippling after a splash" (128). Taken within this context of hurried eating and men who "raise their hands and point to empty bowls and platters, their mouths still working as they do," the portrayal of company-provided food takes a decidedly ominous tone (128).

As Eller explained, "For thousands of mountaineers, the coming timber industry not only meant the loss of valuable woodland, but it [also] meant the introduction of the first major form of nonagricultural work as well" (87). That work provided wage labor and a move away from an agrarian existence. Coupled with the mouth-watering meals for workers described in *Serena,* readers can understand why workers would choose a wage, as well as food provided for them, over the difficulties of farm life. But this choice was not without its consequences. Eller explained that "gradually, through the years, farm life had begun to deteriorate. Fields went uncultivated and grew up in weeds. Fences went down because the men were working at the lumber mills, and supplies, which before had been grown entirely on the farm, were now bought at the store or commissary" (123).

Rash's novel also demonstrates how the timber industry affected food options in other ways as well. In addition to the gradual loss of farming land and farming know-how, the devastation of the mountain landscape had equally dire consequences for the wild foods that the mountains once produced. Near the end of the novel Serena throws a birthday party for Pemberton. Notably the "supper fare was . . . austere, roast beef and potatoes, squash and bread" (340), a far cry from the luxurious meals described earlier in the text. The narrator also explains that Pemberton "had armed a crew with fishing poles that afternoon to catch trout for an hors d'oeuvre, but the men returned from the creeks fishless, claiming no trout remained in the valley or nearby ridges to catch" (340). Likewise in chapter 35 the narrator describes the cutting of the last tree, and when a worker named Stewart takes a drink from Rough Fork Creek, he spits it out, proclaiming that it "tastes like mud" (333). A man named Henryson says to Ross, who at this point would probably choose his fatback sandwich over his current situation, "Used to be thick with trout too, this here stream. There was many a day you and me took our supper from it. Now you'd not catch a knottyhead" (334). As these passages illustrate, Rash's depictions of food in *Serena* helped readers understand the food-related impact that the timber industry had on mountain people. Not only did it make a large majority of them dependent on it for food, but it also ravaged the landscape that could have previously helped sustain them after the collapse of the industry.

It is perhaps not surprising that extractive industry negatively impacted the food choices available to mountain people, but Rash's work also helps readers understand how agriculture that was focused primarily on one cash crop—in western North Carolina, tobacco—had a similar effect. Literary critics David A. Davis and Tara Powell have noted that "small farmers who depended on cotton and tobacco, inedible staple crops, for their income, could often not afford to raise enough of their own food for subsistence. Ironically, although the South had a primarily agricultural economy through the second half of the twentieth century, it imported a significant percentage of its food, and serious issues of food inequality reflect the region's troubling history of race and class divisions" (8). Certainly we can trace the "troubling history" of class divisions in Rash's work, though race divisions are not typically his focus.[7]

A poem called "Tobacco" appears in Rash's 1998 collection, *Eureka Mill,* and a slightly different version, one with stanza breaks and modified phrasing, appears in *Waking,* another poetry collection published in 2011. Despite the differences between the two versions, the main sentiment is the same. In the first line of the *Eureka Mill* version, the speaker calls tobacco a "dream" and laments that before its arrival, "we had thought our land generous enough, / the apple trees drooping their fruit to our hands, / the woods and streams thick with rabbit and trout." The speaker mentions the variety of crops planted, including oats, corn, wheat, and beans, noting that "the springhouse filled / with enough to carry us through the winter." But as the poem progresses, the speaker explains that because of rising taxes and fence laws, more cash was necessary to maintain the farm. So mountain people "bought those bitter seeds" and "broke / the best ground in our bottomlands." Instead of using that fertile soil to grow the abundance of crops noted earlier in the poem, farmers put all their resources into cultivating tobacco. The speaker laments, "We left the beans and corn unhoed" while weeds "strangle[d]" nearby fields and the apple orchards went unpruned "as we spent / the days kneeling to tobacco." But more often than not, "some blight or drought or sudden rain" would destroy the crop, and if not, then that just meant everyone had had a successful year, "so prices dropped." The poem ends with the speaker telling us, "Good harvest or bad we sank deeper in debt, / and planted more tobacco to get out, / and watched our dreams of fortune fade like smoke."

Even before the Burley tobacco boom, the crop was profitable in the mountains, demonstrating participation in a larger economy. Yet as Rash's poems demonstrate, growing and harvesting tobacco was incredibly labor intensive. Whether families were dependent on bright leaf tobacco or later, Burley tobacco, reliance on a single cash crop was a serious issue in terms of food production and availability. Writing about a similar situation in southeastern North Carolina, historian Adrienne Monteith Petty explained the "Live at Home" policy that North Carolina politicians advocated in the nineteen-teens. She cited county agent Robert J. Johnson, who in 1915 "encouraged farmers 'first of all to raise their home consumption and then all the cotton and tobacco they could'" (75). In other words farmers should raise enough food for home consumption in case their cash crops failed. That way they would not be completely reliant on cash generated from those crops to buy food. She elaborated: "agricultural experts, rural sociologists, politicians, and agricultural extension agents also promoted the "Live at Home" slogan to criticize farmers throughout North Carolina and the South for concentrating so heavily on cash-crop farming that they neglected production of food and feed crops. They chastised farmers for relying on food, flour, meat, and grain produced in the Midwest and often bought on credit" (75). As Petty pointed out, in the words of University of North Carolina–Chapel Hill rural sociologist Samuel Huntington Hobbs Jr., "you can't eat tobacco" (Petty 75). Petty also reminds us that "perhaps the most pressing need for cash derived from the need to pay off the mortgage on a farm" (89).

We see this trend dramatized in Rash's poem "Tobacco," where characters are caught in the cycle of needing to grow a cash crop to pay the mortgage necessary to own land on which they can grow food. The difficult reality of this situation makes the advice from O. Max Gardner, North Carolina's governor from 1929 until 1933, almost laughable: "I would recommend that each farmer, no matter how small his farm or family, raise at least $50 worth more food and feed stuffs and livestock products than he did last year. If he raised none of these last year, I would suggest that he plan to raise at least $100 worth this year" (qtd. in Petty 91). Yet as Petty explained, the program did have an impact, and "many small farmers reported increasing their corn production and raising winter vegetable crops for household needs" (94). Even so, as historian Tom Lee wrote: "Denied the cash that tobacco provided, without a viable crop to replace tobacco, and already attuned to the goods and luxuries that tobacco money bought, many mountain farmers faced a dismal outlook on the farm that pushed and pulled them toward public work, factory work, and life beyond the mountains" (176). This situation encouraged many families, like Rash's grandparents, to leave the mountains for the (often false) promise of prosperity in the textile mills. Lee asserted that "in the late nineteenth century, textile recruiters entered the mountains to secure labor, and families in southern Appalachia left by the hundreds and thousands" (199). Likewise Eller explains that "from 1900 to 1930, thousands of mountaineers left their farms for the mill districts" (125).

As previously mentioned the poems in Rash's *Eureka Mill* chronicle the experience of moving to and living in a textile mill town. At the same time that the collection contains poems like "Tobacco," that demonstrate the dangers of relying on a single, inedible cash crop, the collection also features poems like "County Fair" and "Brown Lung," both of which make grim commentary on the food-related consequences of the shift from an agrarian existence to an industrial one. In "County Fair" the speaker describes the highly processed foods available at the fair: "corn dogs, greasy french fries" and cotton candy, referencing the "week's pay" spent on "trinkets and souring stomachs." Yet the speaker explains that the men would always "end up / behind the livestock arena," men "whose best dreams" were of "the black dirt / of freshly-plowed fields." In the poem the men stand there, "in the cigarette dark," "just inhaling." Considered within the argumentative context this essay establishes, it seems painfully ironic that the men are inhaling tobacco smoke, since for so many mountain people, a too-heavy reliance on tobacco initiated the diaspora to mill towns, where workers struggle to earn cash spent on corn dogs, French fries, and cotton candy. In such situations it seems impossible to follow O. Max Gardner's advice to "Live at Home." Eller wrote that "most dreamed initially of returning to the land after a few years of public work, but the rising land values that accompanied industrial development soon pushed land ownership beyond the reach of the average miner or millhand" (xxii).

For this reason continued work in the textile mills became necessary for many mountain families. Working under the hazardous conditions present in most mills resulted in a plethora of health problems, including brown lung, a condition caused by inhalation of cotton dust in which airways narrow and sometimes fail. In a poem from *Eureka Mill* called "Brown Lung," the speaker describes lying awake at night "gasping for air," but when he dreams, he dreams of "bumper crops." If readers pause at this line they likely think of bumper crops of food, such as corn, tomatoes, or beans. Instead, in the next line the speaker finishes, "of Carolina cotton in my chest." Here the inedible cash crop of the mountains (tobacco) has been replaced by the inedible cash crop of the Deep South (cotton). In both cases bumper crops prove detrimental to the availability of edible foods and the ability to breathe life-sustaining air.

While Rash has commented on the food-related consequences of the timber industry, tobacco boom, and outmigration to textile mills, he has also treated the more contemporary issue of substance abuse in Appalachia and how that relates to food. According to a 2008 study commissioned by the Appalachian Regional Commission (ARC), "Appalachia suffers from disproportionately high rates of substance abuse and mental health disorders" ("ARC Study"). Rash confronted the rise of marijuana use in his short story "Speckled Trout," from *Chemistry and Other Stories,* and the resulting novel set in the 1970s, *The World Made Straight.* He did so in part through repeated references to food. In "Speckled Trout," when Lanny (Travis in the novel) finds Linwood (Carlton in the novel) Toomey's marijuana plants, the narrator describes them as being "staked like tomatoes and set in rows the same way as tobacco or corn" (212).[8] The narrator also comments that "he knew they were worth money, a lot of money" (212). In the same way that timber, tobacco, and textiles compromised the economic feasibility of growing enough food to sustain oneself, here Rash implied that the same phenomenon began occurring with the increase of marijuana production in Appalachia. Likewise, when Lanny (Travis) and his friend Shank visit Leonard, a drug dealer, Leonard offers them "two longneck Budweisers and a sandwich bag filled" not with a sandwich but instead "with pot and some rolling papers" (218). In this instance drugs have literally replaced food.

Rash has also portrayed how drugs, methamphetamine in particular, affect food availability in several of his short stories. Health researchers Michael S.

Dunn, Bruce A. Behringer, and Kristine Harper Bowers wrote that "methamphetamine (meth) is a large part of the substance abuse problem in Appalachia" (254). Certainly this problem is reflected in much of Rash's work, especially the stories in *Burning Bright* and *Nothing Gold Can Stay.* Both "Back of Beyond" and "The Ascent" from *Burning Bright* depict families ravaged by methamphetamine addiction, yet as critic John Lang pointed out, this issue "is scarcely a regional problem alone" but "has parallels to drug use in other parts of the United States and the world" (106). "Back of Beyond" describes parents whose son suffers from addiction, and because they are frightened of him and his friends, they sleep in an unheated trailer with "cereal boxes, some open, some not, a half-gallon milk container, its contents frozen solid" (28). In "The Ascent" the only food Jared's meth-addicted parents seem able to feed him is sugary cereal "with a green leprechaun on its front" (83). Neither story focuses on a move away from sustainable agriculture but instead both narrate how a reliance on the cash "crop" of drugs renders the purchase and preparation of healthy food nearly impossible. In each story characters seem to be doing the best they can, yet readers see clearly the impact of their addiction.

When considered together, the many food references in Rash's work demonstrate that while eating can be "a comfort during a hard time," as Rachel thinks in *Serena* when she and Jacob are trying to escape Galloway, it is also a human necessity directly impacted by economic forces. Since the late 1800s and the inception of the idea of Appalachia as distinctly "Other" from the rest of the nation, well-meaning and not-so-well-meaning people have tried to explain and remedy the so-called cultural deficiencies of the region and its people. Taken in their totality, the food references in Ron Rash's work not only begin to overturn long-held stereotypes about the mountains and its food, but they also historicize the plight of mountain people who long to grow their own food but have had a mighty hard time doing so.

Notes

1. The range of scholarship available on these topics is extensive. See especially Shapiro; Williams; Pudup; Harkins; and Billings, Norman, and Ledford.

2. For an excellent book-length treatment of this topic, see Williams-Forson.

3. The Progressive Era is most commonly dated between the 1890s and 1920s. It was a time of concerted social activism and political reform. In terms of national perceptions of Appalachia, it was a particularly formative time since many Progressive Era organizations, including missionary groups, targeted Appalachia for their reform efforts.

4. Many turn-of-the-twentieth-century publications tout this belief. For an especially overt example, see Frost.

5. For more about the perceived whiteness of Appalachia, see Semple; Green; and Satterwhite.

6. Although John C. Campbell is listed as the book's author, he died in 1919, and the

book was published in 1921. His second wife, Olive Dame Campbell, finished compiling his notes and completing the manuscript after his death, making authorship of particular passages difficult to determine.

7. As discussed earlier Rash's story "Where the Map Ends" in *Burning Bright* is an exception.

8. A similar reference occurs in chapter 1 of *The World Made Straight*, but in instances where the references occur in both genres, I quote from the short-story version.

Works Cited

"ARC Study: Disproportionately High Rates of Substance Abuse in Appalachia—Appalachian Regional Commission." N.p., n.d. Web. July 15, 2015.

Billings, Dwight B., Gurney Norman, and Katherine Ledford, eds. *Back Talk from Appalachia: Confronting Stereotypes.* Lexington: University Press of Kentucky, 2000.

Bralliar, Floyd. "Fruit on the Mountain Farm." *Mountain Life and Work* 3.1 (1927): 17–18, 25.

Campbell, John C. *The Southern Highlander and His Homeland.* 1921. Lexington: University Press of Kentucky, 1969.

Davis, David A., and Tara Powell, eds. *Writing in the Kitchen: Essays on Southern Literature and Foodways.* Jackson: University Press of Mississippi, 2014.

Dunn, Michael S., Bruce A. Behringer, and Kristine Harper Bowers. "Substance Abuse." *Appalachian Health and Well-Being.* Ed. Robert L. Ludke and Phillip J. Obermiller. Lexington: University Press of Kentucky, 2012. 251–74.

Eller, Ronald D. *Miners, Millhands, and Mountaineers: Industrialization of the Appalachian South, 1880–1930.* Knoxville: University of Tennessee Press, 1982.

Engelhardt, Elizabeth S. D. "Appalachian Chicken and Waffles: Countering Southern Food Fetishism." *Southern Cultures* 21.1 (2015): 73–83.

Ferris, Marcie Cohen. "History, Place, and Power: Studying Southern Food." *Southern Cultures* 21.1 (2015): 2–7.

Frost, William Goodell. "Our Contemporary Ancestors in the Southern Mountains." *Atlantic Monthly* 83.497 (1899): 311–20.

Green, Chris. *The Social Life of Poetry: Appalachia, Race, and Radical Modernism.* Palgrave Macmillan, 2009.

Harkins, Anthony. *Hillbilly: A Cultural History of an American Icon.* New York: Oxford University Press, 2004.

Lang, John. *Understanding Ron Rash.* Columbia: University of South Carolina Press, 2014.

Lee, Tom. "Southern Appalachia's Nineteenth-Century Bright Tobacco Boom: Industrialization, Urbanization, and the Culture of Tobacco." *Agricultural History* 88.2 (2014): 175–206.

Petty, Adrienne Monteith. *Standing Their Ground: Small Farmers in North Carolina since the Civil War.* New York: Oxford University Press, 2013.

Pudup, Mary Beth, Dwight B. Billings, and Altina L. Waller, eds. *Appalachia in the Making: The Mountain South in the Nineteenth Century.* Chapel Hill: University of North Carolina Press, 1995.

Rash, Ron. *Among the Believers.* Oak Ridge, Tenn.: Iris, 2000.

———. *Burning Bright.* New York: HarperCollins, 2010.

———. *Chemistry and Other Stories.* New York: Henry Holt, 2007.

———. *Eureka Mill.* Spartanburg, S.C.: Hub City, 1998.

———. *Nothing Gold Can Stay.* New York: HarperCollins, 2013.

———. *Raising the Dead.* Oak Ridge, Tenn.: Iris, 2002.

———. *Serena.* New York: HarperCollins, 2008.

———. *Waking.* Spartanburg, S.C.: Hub City, 2011.

———. *The World Made Straight.* New York: Henry Holt, 2006.

Satterwhite, Emily. *Dear Appalachia: Readers, Identity, and Popular Fiction since 1878.* Lexington: University Press of Kentucky, 2011.

Sauceman, Fred W. "Appalachian Foodways." *The New Encyclopedia of Southern Culture.* Vol. 7, *Foodways.* Ed. John T. Edge. Chapel Hill: University of North Carolina Press, 2007. 18–22.

Semple, Ellen Churchill. "The Anglo-Saxons of the Kentucky Mountains: A Study in Anthropogeography." 1901. *Appalachian Images in Folk and Popular Culture.* Knoxville: University of Tennessee Press, 1995. 146–74.

Shapiro, Henry D. *Appalachia on Our Mind: The Southern Mountains and Mountaineers in the American Consciousness, 1870–1920.* Chapel Hill: University of North Carolina Press, 1978.

Williams, Cratis D. "The Southern Mountaineer in Fact and Fiction: Part I–IV." *Appalachian Journal* 3.4 (1976): 334–92.

Williams-Forson, Psyche A. *Building Houses Out of Chicken Legs: Black Women, Food, and Power.* Chapel Hill: University of North Carolina Press, 2006.

Part II

INTERTEXTUAL STREAMS

"A BOXED AND STILLED FOREVER"

Vision, Death, and Affect in the Work of Ron Rash

Randall Wilhelm

"Vision is central to everything I do."
Ron Rash, personal interview

During the summer months of 2015, Ron Rash and I shared ideas about the visual nature of his novel *Above the Waterfall* while thumbing through art books on Edward Hopper. As devotees of Faulkner, we reveled in his ability to create pictures with words so intensely real they leapt off the page and lodged in our minds long after many of the narrative details slipped from memory. Not "trying to say" (as Benjy Compson would put it), but "trying to show" I suggested. "And with power," Rash replied. He was looking at a large color plate of Hopper's iconic painting *Nighthawks* and suddenly fell silent. Rash, who once told me he could look at the turning of a leaf in autumn for hours on end, was clearly focused on the emotional power of Hopper's image. He then began to tell how the painting had affected him when he first saw a large color reproduction in a gallery at Lenoir Rhyne College as a boy: "My father used to show me paintings from his collection of art books, but I had never seen one this big before. As soon as I entered the gallery it hit me. I don't know exactly what I did, but I remember standing there mesmerized by an overwhelming sense of loneliness. I couldn't put it into words; I mean, those three figures sitting in the diner so late at night, with the darkness all around. It haunted me. Still does."[1]

Hauntings are rife throughout Rash's work, and visual tropes express the undeadness of vision in a multitude of complex interactions. In Rash's memory-drenched and spirit-laden world, the past is never past, the (un)dead never dead. Rash has said that most of his work, particularly his novels, originate in mysterious visions that he must work to unveil.[2] A writer's writer with a keen eye for detail and scenic accuracy, Rash stated "vision is central to everything I do" (Personal interview). Even a cursory glance at his body of work bears witness to this fact. In a striking number of poems and stories, and in a gallery of finely rendered novelistic scenes, Rash has used fictional photographs and framed images that challenge readers to "picture this if you can." From his first stories and poems to his most recent novel, Rash has used textual imagery as sites of narrative visibility and affective vibrancy, a parallel discourse that evokes and challenges a host of figurative threads that weave narrative, thematic, and emotional meanings. In fact vision and visionary experiences are at the heart of Rash's aesthetics. Son of a sculptor, given the middle name "Vincent" for Van Gogh, Rash has imagined a world replete with fictional pictures, varieties of visual experience, and slippery oppositions between mechanical vision and human observation, spectatorship and insight, belief and knowledge.

Although the limited space of this essay prevents an extensive viewing of Rash's museum of words, I have chosen several representative works to examine how vision and visual tropes synergize, complicate, and represent aesthetic and affective readings of characters, actions, and objects. Rash was born with a compelling fascination for images as exemplified in his first viewing of Hopper's art and influenced heavily by visually charged writers such as Fyodor Dostoyevsky, Herman Melville, William Faulkner, Eudora Welty, Flannery O'Connor, and Cormac McCarthy, and his work is written with a camera eye that sees beyond mere description of narrative events and penetrates into the heart of mystery that fictional vision represents. Visual theorists have wrestled with oversimplification and emergent myths surrounding ekphrastic readings of verbal texts, but most agree there is a productive interdisciplinary turbulence in "painting with words," a tradition that looks backward to the classical philosophies of Plato and Aristotle.

W. J. T. Mitchell, for instance, acknowledged that the "wonders of visuality [and] practices of seeing the world and especially of seeing other people"—through human optics or in their fictional representations—"remain a mystery to be unraveled" (337). Textual visuality is "a problem of staging a paradox . . . that vision is itself invisible; that we cannot see what seeing is; that the eyeball (*pace* Emerson) is never transparent," so the question becomes how "to make seeing show itself" (Mitchell 337).

Recent studies that interrogate "fictional photographs" in literary texts offer a productive glimpse beyond this paradox. Katherine Henninger, for example, traced the visual legacy of the American South and the power of photography to "picture" women in culturally defined roles that reduce identity to stereotype. Fictional photographs that "do not physically exist outside the printed word . . . raise a host of questions about representation, reference, and ideologies of form. More readily than actual photographs, which work to naturalize a connection between 'the real' and the facades they represent, fictional photographs highlight their status as representations" and generate "anxiety about interpretive ambiguity and the process of representation itself" (Henninger 2, 4). While Henninger explored arenas of political visualization through codes of race, class, and gender, Rash's use of fictional photographs and "scenes of seeing" focus on aesthetic, ethical, and affective relations between text and image. Characters use pictures for personal, professional, and communal reasons. Rash's work stages vision through visual tropes for the display of characters' (dis)connections to the visible and invisible worlds that affect them most deeply. Fictional images and their framing by human desire birth a host of multilayered and ambiguous readings that question the veracity of narrative events and impinge on the surety of character interpretations of the actions, objects, and visions of the worlds in which they live.

Photographs of the Dead

Perhaps one of the more maudlin death rituals in Appalachia is the practice of families having photographs taken of their recently deceased. For the bereaved these images contain a mysterious and talismanic power that blurs the line between the living and the dead, as if the soul of the material corpse had been transferred through the photographic plate and into the image itself. As recent studies on the "undead" have argued,[3] these pictures of the dead are not merely images for remembrance and healing; they are disembodied energies that ghost the present in material form. *Undead Souths: The Gothic and Beyond in Southern Literature and Culture* explores an array of such energies, arguing that "undeadness speaks to a new understanding of human bodies as always contingent, transformative assemblages of human and nonhuman . . . living/dying/dead/undead" rage with affective power, with "the undead rarely mind[ing] their business but work[ing] hard to unsettle the livings' business as usual" (Anderson et al., Introduction 6–7). Existing in a vibrant space, undead images walk the borderlands between binary states of life and death and challenge anthropocentric notions of time and space. Photographs of the (un)dead create a double vortex of affective energies in Rash's work, inscribing memory and pain, hope and doubt for characters who witness the trauma and relive it through the crucible of time. Often these images of death undermine essentialist notions of presence and absence, materiality and spirit; characters often respond with neurotic confusion when death, mystery, and vibrancy converge.

Jane Bennett's work on "vibrant matters" explores the political economy of things, specifically nonhuman actants (electricity, chemicals, commodities, etc.) that impact human bodies and social structures "as quasi agents or forces . . . that run alongside and inside humans" (viii). Although Bennett eschewed discussions of subjectivity, her insights on the active force of "object-relations" allows for greater insight into the affective power of photographic productions, particularly ones that attempt visual representation of nonhuman forces located in death, absence, and memory. Gregory J. Seigworth and Melissa Gregg argued that "affect is in many ways synonymous with *force* or *forces of encounter* . . . born in *in-between-ness* and resid[ing] in as accumulative *beside-ness.* Affect can be understood then as a gradient of bodily capacity—a supple incrementalism of ever modulating force relations—that rises and falls not only along various rhythms and modalities of encounter but also through the troughs and sieves of sensation and sensibility" (2).

Rash's use of death photographs make visible the affective energies in the forces of encounter between the living and the dead. Rash's "Photograph of My Parents outside Eureka Cotton Mill. Dated June 1950," stages affective in-between-ness and modulating force relations through temporal and spatial disjunctions of trapped time and the doubled gazes of photographer and bereaved son. Rash's father, James Moody Rash, is shown with his wife, but the affective energies of the image focus on the father's left arm that "twists / like vine" and "sprouts a wire meshed fist" (*Eureka Mill* 58). His mother "cannot / guess what I will see, at least not yet, / in my father's odd pose, the fingerless / awkward clutch of metal, as if / caught in a sprung-steel grip" (58). Although Rash employed poetic license in the image of amputation (his father never suffered such an injury), the "odd pose," "clutch of metal," and "sprung-steel trap" shape a cluster of affective vibrancies the son—unborn in 1950—will live to see at age nineteen when his father dies in an automobile crash. The "clutch" of metal and "steel trap" evoke through displacement the suffering of the son years after the event, the force of encounter ever modulating between grief, disbelief, and acceptance of familial tragedy.

"Among the Believers," the titular poem of Rash's second volume of poetry, provides a paradigmatic example of affect and image making that pictures the death of an extended family member but complicates the mystery of undeadness that escapes its framing. The speaker, a nephew of his deceased great-aunt, has one foot in the moment of trauma and one in the decades-later present of remembrance. He struggles to understand the event to which he was eyewitness and to interpret the photograph a cousin took of her corpse, her stillborn child, and the "eternity" into which they presumably passed:

A cousin held
a camera above the open casket,
cast a shadow the camera raised
where flesh and wood and darkness met,
a photograph the husband claimed.
Nailed on the wall above his bed,
smudged and traced for five decades,

a cross of shadow shadowing death,
across an uncomprehending face"
(*Among the Believers* 70)

The poem's title sounds a note of certainty in the religious belief of an afterlife that the body of the poem complicates. Rash's chiasmatic wordplay in the final two lines ("a cross"/ "across" and "shadow"/"shadowing") creates monstrous reverberations of undeadness because of, even in spite of, the material coercion of human inscription and mechanical vision that attempts to picture what never can be seen by the human eye. In this photograph Rash saturated the death experience with affective vibrancy that also performs as specular consumption. The triad of photographer, subject, and audience grounds the scene of image making in literal context (perhaps a funeral home or another communal space of mourning); however, the cousin not only frames the image but also contaminates it with the intrusion of the camera's shadow. By the cousin's doing so, the medium of photography as "light writing" creates an opposite effect, what may be called "shadow writing," and blocks or mutates the intended image and collapses boundaries between subject and object, viewer and viewed.

In the logic of the poem the image is coerced and problematized in a trifecta of manipulation: first, by spatial defiguration (angle, framing, and exposure); second, by mechanical translation (aperture, shutter speed, and process development), and third, by human interpretation (the husband, and then the nephew, who presumably claims it for his own following his great-uncle's death). Despite the photograph's instability as reliable artifact, it shimmers with traces of emotional transfer and affect in visualizing human suffering and grief. Although from a professional's viewpoint the cousin botches the image in amateur fashion by introducing exterior elements inside the visual frame, the shadow of the camera activates subtle interchanges between the animate and the inanimate that operate in tension and conflict. In the attempt to capture life in death and inscribe death with life, the photograph makes visible the invisible act of seeing. The staging of paradox to which Mitchell alluded in "showing seeing" is pictured, ironically, by the cousin's amateur mistake. The camera's shadow invokes the material means of production and disrupts the surface of the death image, infusing it with the affective energies of animate and human forces that shape the photograph as consumption of loss and grief, hope and faith. If indeed "every picture tells a story," this photograph writes a book. In eight and a half lines, Rash created a fictional photograph that outstrips and complicates notions of photographic accuracy, artistic representation, and anthropocentric binaries of life and death, body and spirit.

Although Rash set the scene with descriptive details in the poem's first ten lines through the speaker's voice, it is significant that the photograph shrouds vision as a space "where flesh and wood and darkness met." In a testament to the complexity of Rash's visual aesthetics, the poem pictures seeing but refuses to picture death. Instead the fictional photograph posits a shadow land of mystery where death is "uncomprehending," a linguistic turn that exposes the affective energies of bereavement as untranslatable suffering. The placement of the photograph above the husband's bed suggests the image is not a memento mori but a haunting of absence and religious doubt. The "smudges" on the photograph's surface transfer the grit of human suffering onto the problematized image of death, the habitual tracing of the cross of shadow a visual illusion the husband neurotically repeats in desperation to maintain a faith the photograph's production belies.

But pictures of the living in Rash's work can be similarly myopic and obfuscating. In the dramatic monologue "A Preacher Who Takes Up Serpents Laments the Presence of Skeptics in His Church," Rash's fundamentalist character makes this point clear. In this poem the use of the camera performs as a device of spectacle and affective blindness. According to the preacher, his congregation sees Sunday mornings as exotic performance, the serpent handling an occasion for picture taking resembling something like a "Kodak moment." The preacher spares no time in ridiculing their spiritual blindness: "In the vanity of their unbelief / they will cover an eye with a camera / and believe it will make them see. / They see nothing" (*Among the Believers* 19). Although photographs fail to see anything in the poem, the speaker's dramatic account of his faith is on display through the actant energy coursing through the bodies of the snakes, transferring herpetological vibrancy into a physical emanation of the invisible. As in "Among the Believers," this poem pictures what cannot be seen—in this case "the presence of the Lord." The emphasis is on the failure of human vision, especially when mediated through a mechanical object whose "thingness" reveals nothing; its potential for the transfer of religious affect remains resolutely inert.

Framing Grief: "A boxed and stilled forever"

In *Saints at the River,* readers see the narrative events through the eyes of Maggie Glenn, staff photographer for the *State* newspaper in Columbia who returns to the "Dark Corner" in Oconee County on assignment to cover the drowning of a young girl in the wild Tamassee River. Maggie's venture into the backcountry of her youth is fraught with anxiety and disruption that she attempts to distance through the thin armor of her photographic lens. Through Maggie's character Rash staged a different visual encounter with death and suffering, one seen and developed through the mechanical vision of the camera but problematized by the viewpoint of the photographer. Rash critiqued the power of vision, especially when captured by a camera, through scenes of internet searches, references to war photographers' "picture books," and debates over the ethics of photography between Maggie and her partner, the award-winning journalist Allen Hemphill. In one scene Maggie attempts to understand Hemphill's interest in covering the story of the drowned girl trapped in an upstate mountain river when he had won acclaim for writing about global atrocities in Belfast, Kosovo, Cambodia, and Rwanda. On one website, Maggie reads an interview with Hemphill, who speaks about the "limitations of photography," a topic addressed by war photographers such as Matthew Brady and Frank Capa, among others, and by visual theorists such as Susan Sontag, whose study *On Photography* (1977) Hemphill has clearly read. In his interview Hemphill says, "There is always more that lies outside the camera's framed truth. . . . A photograph is voiceless. Neither its subject nor its producer can explain the suffering and injustice, give it context" (*Saints at the River* 73).

Rash's novel frames Maggie's struggles with objective journalism and personal affect through a series of photographic tropes that challenge and destabilize the camera's mechanical vision and critique the ethics of visual experience. Chapter 8 opens with an extended metaphor of the darkroom: "Under a darkroom safelight everything is gray. Your hands are drained of life. Stop bath settles in your nostrils and stomach like formaldehyde. Maybe that's the way it should be, because what a photograph does is embalm something or someone in *a boxed and stilled forever*" (131, emphasis added). Perhaps. But as Maggie continues, she enters into the "in-between-ness" of affect that arises "in the capacities to act or be acted upon . . . an impingement or extrusion of a momentary or sometimes more sustained state of relation *as well as* the passage . . . of forces or intensities [that resonate and] circulate about, between, and sometimes stick to bodies and worlds, *and* in the very passages or variations between these intensities and resonances themselves" (Seigworth 1). In other words the effect of shimmering affect is a force always in the process of becoming more or less intense but that tends to adhere to human emotional experience, even if one is not completely aware of the affect at any given time.

In developing her images, Maggie experiences this *in-between-ness* of affective forces, thinking a "darkroom is a place where your failures come to light, a wrong combination or f-stop and shutter speed, a misjudgment of depth of field or right exposure. Or you make new errors. You don't check the temperature of the chemicals; something spills; you turn the white light on too soon. *But sometimes, everything happens just as it should.* You rinse the print in the darkroom's gray light, and there in your hands is the photograph you hoped for" (131, emphasis added). Acted on by the stop-bath chemicals, the irradiated light, and the gentle turbulence of photographic paper in the process of imaging, Maggie's darkroom metaphor reveals a type of wonder—"*sometimes, everything happens just as it should*"—generated by the variations and intensities of affect, but it remains dubious that Maggie understands the transfer.

According to visual theorists such as Sontag, Barthes, and Henninger, the camera as object shapes the process and knowledge of "photography" and poses an unequal power play that raises questions about autonomy, representation, exploitation, and dominance. Photographic images seem more objective, more "real," offering the viewer a slice of life as it "truly" is (or has been through the lens of memory). And yet, this "blind" acceptance of constructed visuality provides the template for photography's exploitative power system. Sontag argued that "there is something predatory in the act of taking a picture. To photograph people is to violate them, by seeing them as they never see themselves, by having knowledge of them they can never have; it turns people into objects that can be symbolically possessed" (14). Rash framed this problem of representation in scenes of Maggie photographing the grieving Herb Kowalsky, who stares at the shimmering surface below which his daughter is held captive in a hydraulic, the wild river rushing unbridled in sheer affective force. "Get your camera out," Hemphill says; "You're about to get a chance at a really good photograph" (97). Raising her Nikon like a loaded gun, her intention is to "bring this instant in Herb Kowalsky's life into being. At that moment the part of me that aimed the lens cared nothing about Herb Kowalsky or his daughter or the river or federal law. I clicked the shutter again and again until my film ran out, then jammed in another roll. It's only about light and angle and texture, I told myself. Whatever these photos do for me or anyone else is not a motive. I'm just an observer, showing what's already there. Gnats circled Kowalsky's head and I saw him blink his right eye several times in quick succession. He raised his index finger to brush one of the insects from his eye, and I took a last photograph" (97–98).

Back in the darkroom Maggie lifts the print from the dryer and exults in wonder at the visible power of affect transfer. In a display of what Lauren Berlant called "cruel optimism,"[4] Maggie exults in this newly created object of desire: "I sat down at my desk to study the photograph more closely. Everything was right—light, shutter speed, symmetry" (132). But everything is emphatically *not* "right"—in the ethical and Sontagian sense—and Maggie knows this despite her attempt to delay and obfuscate her awareness. From a consumerist media profit angle, the picture may be "perfect"—a predatory untruth that others, including the staff in Columbia, praise enthusiastically—"This is one to nominate for awards" (132)—but this is clearly not the point Rash intended in this show of seeing.

The image seems to capture the unspoken pain of the suffering father, but even Maggie realizes the falsity of this vision: "Wolf Cliff Falls dominated the frame, the backdrop was all water and rock. Herb Kowalsky stood slightly to the right. No one else was in the photo. My shot angled upward out of the pool, ending not far from Kowalsky's head. Such a perspective usually makes a person seem larger than life, able to dominate a scene. But in this photograph the angle only emphasized Kowalsky's powerlessness, juxtaposed as he was next to the falls that held his daughter. You could make out that Kowalsky was staring into the water, and you could see the index finger raised *to brush away a tear that had not existed until this moment*" (132, emphasis added). Her reaction to this predatory act of "shooting" the father, of misrepresenting the truth for personal gain—the gnats are not visible in the final print—exposes Maggie's blindness to her own emotive and psychological reality. Her flippant comment about the image makes this clear: "'Of course, it's just a photograph,' I said teasingly. . . . 'There is always something more that lies outside the camera's framed, mechanical truth'" (133). A Sontagian proverb perhaps, but one she plays with in a curiously callous way.

Maggie's comment is doubly "blind" because she says this to Hemphill, who grimaces at the repetition of his own words that Maggie has read earlier during her Internet "background check" that showed photographs of Hemphill's deceased wife and daughter. Maggie cannot *see* that her co-option of Hemphill's language is a *blind* moral failure that turns his personal tragedy into a selfish, flirtatious comment. She is also blind to Sontag's message and curiously myopic if she is talking about the photograph itself. It is not what lies *beyond* the frame that makes this photograph disingenuous (in the aesthetic sense) but what is *inside* the frame that is left out, unpictured, unseeable—the gnats that prompt Kowalsky to make this action in the first place. What "lies" outside the frame is Maggie—photographer of deception and producer of cruel optimism. Her visual manipulation of Kowalsky's emotive vibrancy has deadly consequences for her cousin Randy Moseley, who later dives for the girl's body because of the media's demands[5]—activated by the photograph—to assuage the grieving father's "tears."

In Maggie's false picturing of Kowalsky's grief, she ironically produces a photograph of the dead. The undeadness of Ruth Kowalsky's drowned body emanating from beneath and through the rushing river finds expression in her father's vigilant posture at the site of her disappearance, and the vision Maggie "shoots" pictures the ensuing death of Moseley. In such an elaborate transfer of affective energies and causal effects, Rash's use of visual and photographic tropes display the ingenuity and complexity of his sense of the power of vision and the responsibility one has to see—and speak—honestly. For Rash vision performs as a sign of moral and ethical values, perhaps one of the few ways humans can interact genuinely with one another in a fallen world teeming with selfishness, equivocation, violence, and death.

Through the Lens Deathly

In *Serena* Rash continues the trope of photographic image making by using another photographer as a significant eye that pictures crucial thematic energies throbbing throughout the narrative. In the case of R. L. Frizzell, the staging of visual representation does not involve the ethics and framing of photographic images with which Maggie struggles in *Saints at the River.* Rather Frizzell's narrative purpose in *Serena* is triple visioned; he is recorder of death, imager of prophetic vision, and documentarian of environmental destruction. Frizzell's appearance in the text is seen through Pemberton's eyes and immediately evokes confusion and mystery. Only after Pemberton asks Galloway to interpret the scene does he begin to understand the photographer's presence in the lumber camp. "They're taking his picture for a remembering," Galloway says (124). "Pemberton understood then," the narration tells us, "another local custom that fascinated Buchanan—taking a picture of the deceased, the photograph a keepsake for the bereaved to place on a wall or fireboard" (124). The scene is a welter of gazes—human observation, mechanical vision, staged and framed images—that, like the photograph of the undead Holland Winchester in *One Foot in Eden,* sets the fulcrum of the narrative and pivots its direction toward its ultimate resolution.[6]

This is the first time in the narrative where Pemberton seems unsure (a feeling that will increase with rapidity), and it is significant that what disturbs his sense of self is a force that circulates *about* and *between* seer and seen. Frizzell's photograph of Ledbetter's corpse with his wife and children "sticks to" and penetrates Pemberton's adult self through affective transfer of a potent image cluster of death, wife, children, and logging that pictures his life as it has been and (unknown at the moment) is to come. The force of the encounter is brought to bear through the figure of the photographer. Frizzell's lurching gait in carrying the awkward tripod toward his second photographic subject further destabilizes Pemberton's assured stance in the camp as well as his emotional balance. Seeing Frizzell disappear under the black cloth, Pemberton becomes "fascinated"[7] with the image of the boy caught in the camera's lens. Rendered speechless by the realization that the boy is Rachel's son—and therefore *his* son too—Pemberton makes the first mistake that leads to his eventual demise: he pays for a print made from the negative so that he may see his disowned son.

Pemberton's experience in this scene is contemporaneous with discussions about "the irrational agency or action of The Photograph" regarding its essential duality by the mass observation (M-O) movement in British society of the 1930s (Lock 116). Photography's duality is expressed through what Andre Bazin and Roland Barthes call "absolute contingency," or "its total reliance on its referent (that to which is refers)," and to its "dumb indexicality (the fact that the photograph produces not a mere likeness, but a direct physical inscription of its subject matter)" (qtd. in Lock 116). Photographs such as Frizzell's image of Jacob that stuns Pemberton so much that he *must* have a copy (of a copy of a copy) shows the irrational power of photographs to reveal objective reality and the possibility of raising into consciousness vibrant energies that have remained repressed. It is in the "defamiliarized landscape—an 'exotic' vision of the everyday" (Lock 114) that makes possible "a kind of poetic (or pictorial) imagery at once irrational and objective" (Ray 178) and raises an essential "madness" that Barthes declares must be tamed by society. In the case of Pemberton's visual infidelity, of course, it is Serena who must tame Pemberton's irrational madness, for in the surreal world of the lumber camps—where women trump men, "widow-makers" attack loggers, and snakes fall from the sky—the only "madness" allowed is Serena's own will to power.

Pemberton's subversive act in procuring the photograph of Jacob punctures the façade of Serena's injunction to live only in the present.[8] Pemberton's visual dialogue with Rachel and Jacob—staged as a "stare down" in the middle of the camp—leads to one of his many (increasingly disturbing) dreams, the submerged irrationality breaking the surface of the unconscious and lodging firmly in his conscious mind: "That night Pemberton dreamed he and Serena had been hunting. . . . Something hidden in the far woods made a crying sound. Pemberton thought it was a panther, but Serena said no, that it was a baby. When Pemberton asked if they should go get it, Serena had smiled at him. That's Galloway's baby, not ours, she had said" (126).

Later Rash showed Pemberton's continued fascination with photographic images by pairing one of Pemberton as a two-year-old with the forbidden picture of Jacob. The scene not only "shows seeing," as Mitchell said, but also shows the literal *beside-ness* of affect, its "ever modulating force relations—that rises and falls . . . along various rhythms and modalities of encounter" and "through the troughs and sieves of sensation and sensibility" (Seigworth and Gregg 2). After dismissing Campbell, Pemberton takes the photograph of Jacob from the bottom drawer of his desk. Gazing on it Pemberton is transported into memory through the actants of the image and the fire in the hearth whose "rosy glow . . . spilled over the desk's surface" (172). The flames rise and fall, warming Pemberton in the act of looking and releasing childhood memories and emotive sensations long repressed that enclose "him like an invisible blanket" (172). To a much greater degree than Maggie's experience in the darkroom in *Saints at the River,* Pemberton's vibrant space opens the troughs and sieves of sensation that picture his recovery of emotive selfhood and compel him to open his family's leather worn photo album. It is significant that Pemberton feels "the sensation of entering an attic on a rainy day" (172) when turning the pages of the "desiccated" cardboard pages that release "the smell of things long stashed away" (172). Bennett's nonhuman actants are clearly acting on Pemberton. Memories and feelings rise to the surface of his conscious mind, revealing the web of cruelty into which he has been woven through his relationship with Serena. With

Jacob's photograph beside him, Pemberton peels through the memory book until "he [finds] a photograph of himself as a two-year-old and stop[s] turning" (172).

To foreground the transformative "beside-ness" of affect even further, Pemberton repeats this act again in a scene shortly later. Seeing the name "Jacob" in the camp's ledger, Pemberton muses on the visual characters in the word, thinking about "the way the raised *J* and *b* shaped the word to look like a bowl waiting to be filled" (216). The vision compels Pemberton to enact the irrational act once again: "for the first time since Serena's miscarriage, [he] took the photograph album from the bottom drawer. He set it *beside* the ledger and opened it to the last two pages. The photograph of himself as a two-year old was on the left, but it was the photograph on the opposite side that held his attention. Pemberton eased the ledger closer to *Jacob* and the child's photograph *lay side by side*" (216, emphasis added).

In Frizzell's final appearance in the novel he performs as imager of present ecological destruction and envisioner of human death to come. Even though Galloway's mother has garnered the attention as vessel for "second sight" and seer of the future, Rash invested Frizzell's photographs with a similar, perhaps even more prescient, visual power. Hired to document visually the stumps and slash of the desiccated valley in support of Secretary Albright's campaign for the creation of the Great Smokies National Park, Frizzell rises again from under his black shroud to picture death. Unlike Rachel's stilling of Jacob's movements for Frizzell's camera, this time the subjects refuse to be captured through the lens but instead shape the image themselves. Or, more accurately, Serena shapes the image, and for Pemberton it is not a pretty picture. Pemberton's desire for a connection with Jacob through the taboo photograph has been discovered by Serena and, in her mind, is visual evidence of Pemberton's disloyalty and weakness, traits that she cannot abide in a companion. In becoming a "negative" himself, Pemberton's fate is sealed.

Again confused by Frizzell's appearance in camp, Pemberton's authority is undercut repeatedly by Serena through both verbal and visual tropes. On seeing Frizzell's camera aimed at the ravaged landscape stretching below, Pemberton's first impulse is to censor the images. But Serena speaks to the photographer first, then questions Pemberton's fear of the visual: "Why not [allow him to take pictures]," she says. "I'm pleased with what we've done here. Aren't you?" (352). Acceding to the question, Pemberton pivots and demands Frizzell take their photograph, a suggestion upon which Serena frowns. "Not a portrait, *just* a photograph," Pemberton replies (352, emphasis added). "Indulge me this one time," he pleads. "We have no photograph of us together. Think of it as a last birthday present" (352). Serena agrees but controls this last image, forcing

Pemberton to accept the wasteland as background, a space the loggers describe as a graveyard and imagine "this is what the end of the world will be like" (336).

Significantly, after many detailed descriptions of photographs and paintings in the novel,[9] this last image is written with a glance. For a portrait Frizzell is puzzled why Serena will not dismount from her horse and warns her of its potential blurring. Of course Serena is not interested in photographic reproductions, but the picture that arises—Serena astride the white Arabian, with Pemberton on foot below her, in front of the slash and sprawl landscape of the background—is as much a picture of death as Frizzell's first photograph of Ledbetter in his coffin. Without knowing it Frizzell has captured the last visible trace of the couple's destroyed relationship, envisioning Pemberton's fate in the trap Serena has set for him. Her last words to her husband make this painfully clear: "You need to go" (353).

Although Pemberton dies shortly after, the photograph does not. Trapped in a "boxed and stilled forever," the image returns over forty years later in the novel's haunting coda as part of a series of photographs in a *Life* magazine spread featuring Serena as a wealthy timber baroness living in Sao Paulo, Brazil—but not for long. After four decades the photograph finds exposure through the lens of another camera: "*A nostalgic indulgence, she told her interviewer, quite out of character, but there it is. The photograph was of a young Serena Pemberton astride a huge white horse, an eagle on her right arm. Standing beside her was a tall, powerfully built man. In the background lay a wasteland of stumps and drowned limbs whose limits the frame could not encompass. The photograph's one flaw was Serena Pemberton's face, caught in motion and thus blurred to a gray featurelessness*" (370). The photograph is clearly an object of desire, both for Serena, whose "nostalgia" results from the transfer of affect, and for Jacob, who uses the information to track down Serena and enact vengeance onto and *into* the body of his father's murderer.

After-Effect

Rash's use of visual tropes charges his work with affective vibrancy and emotional transfer in a complex weave that attests to his deep awareness of the power of images to convey meaning in the lives of his characters. The young Rash's emotive reaction to the reproduction of Hopper's *Nighthawks* makes it clear that his interest in the visual is more than an aesthetic strategy for writing poetry and fiction. For Rash images—photographs, paintings, and visions—are vessels of memory, affect, and identity as well as tools for literary creation. Traces of Hopper's iconic painting appear in many of Rash's stories that evoke the loneliness of the human condition. Works such as "The Woman Who Believes in Jaguars," "Burning Bright," and "Hard Times" dramatize the desperation made flesh in many of Hopper's paintings. In *Saints at the River,* Rash wrote a café scene between Maggie and Hemphill that mirrors the figures in Hopper's famous late-night diner,[10] and in "Night Hawks" Rash made explicit his continued fascination with the painter. But Rash's interest in Hopper as "the great painter of human loneliness" ("Personal") is only one thread in the patchwork quilt of Rash's visual aesthetics. The haunting quality in Rash's work is seen through an abundance of photographs, paintings, photographers, and visual framers who attempt to picture what cannot be seen clearly. Rash's obsession with the Shelton Laurel Massacre in Madison County, North Carolina, and his compulsive rewriting of the event is a prime example of how vision affects his literary imagination. Lodged firmly in his mind, images poke and prod Rash's creative imagination with an unyielding demand to tell their stories. Through an aesthetic trove of visual tropes, Rash has pictured the pictures that see into the depths of the human condition and into the relentless pulsing of the human heart.

Notes

1. Rash and I spoke at length on the use of visual imagery in literature, particularly in his work, throughout the summer months of 2015.

2. Rash's working method almost always begins with an image. He has said he never outlines or plots his stories but develops a narrative out of a haunting image that he must follow to reveal its meaning. For instance *One Foot in Eden* began with Rash's vision of a farmer standing in his field with his back turned; *Serena* began with the image of a woman on horseback silhouetted against the sky; and *Above the Waterfall* began with a scene of an enormous fish kill despoiling a mountain stream.

3. For more on "undead" photographs, see Frye and Hutchinson, "What Remains Where."

4. For Berlant the "object of desire" is a cluster of promises that "allow us to encounter what is incoherent or enigmatic in our attachments" and is therefore "optimistic. . . . In optimism, the subject leans towards promises contained within the present moment of the encounter with their object" (93). In Maggie's case exposure to the "wonder" of the miraculous image creates and sustains her emotional identity as photographer from Columbia and not as Oconee County native, an affective distance she has maintained since leaving the area after graduating high school.

5. In what trauma theorists would call "the commodification of trauma," Maggie's photograph is a simplified and stereotypical image that transmits affective energies through the filtered archetype of the "Grieving Father." The media loves Maggie's photograph and prints it on the front page with the caption, *A father's grief,* accompanied by an article with the headline "Father Fights River and Law to Bring Daughter Home" (*Saints at the River* 154).

6. Mrs. Winchester points to Holland's photograph on the mantel and tells Isaac "You favor him, especially in the eyes." Isaac's recognition—"I looked up at the man in uniform. I studied his eyes and saw they were dark like mine, like hers" (*One Foot*

in Eden 165)—begins the unraveling of the murder mystery haunting the text from the beginning.

7. As scholars in text-image studies have argued, "fascination" occurs when viewing disturbing images of trauma, confusion, transgression, and upheaval. The tremendous affect of these visions conquers language and leaves viewers silent, mouths agape, frozen, unable to speak of the "unutterable sight" that has arrested them. Rash's story "Something Rich and Strange" is a prime example of fascination in his work (*Nothing Gold Can Stay* 43–50).

8. Serena's philosophy is captured in her comment to Pemberton: "This is what we want. . . . To be like this. No past or future, pure enough to live totally in the present" (87).

9. At George Vanderbilt's estate, for instance, Rash showed a host of visual art such as prints by Currier and Ives, a portrait of Cornelia Vanderbilt, and a painting by Renoir.

10. See pages 134–35.

Works Cited

Anderson, Eric Gary, Taylor Hagood, and Daniel Cross Turner. "Introduction." *Undead Souths: The Gothic and Beyond in Southern Literature and Culture.* Ed. Eric Gary Anderson, Taylor Hagood, and Daniel Cross Turner. Baton Rouge: Louisiana State University Press, 2015. 2–9.

Bennet, Jane. *Vibrant Matters: A Political Ecology of Things.* Durham: Duke University Press, 2010.

Berlant, Lauren. "Cruel Optimism." *The Affect Theory Reader.* Ed. Melissa Gregg and Gregory L. Seigworth. Durham: Duke University Press, 2010. 93–117.

Frye, Elizabeth Bradford, and Coleman Hutchinson. "What Remains Where: Civil War Poetry and Photography across 150 Years." *Undead Souths: The Gothic and Beyond in Southern Literature and Culture.* Ed. Eric Gary Anderson, Taylor Hagood, and Daniel Cross Turner. Baton Rouge: Louisiana State University Press, 2015. 36–51.

Henninger, Katherine. *Ordering the Façade: Photography and Contemporary Southern Women's Writing.* Chapel Hill: University of North Carolina Press, 2007.

Lock, Andy. "At Once Irrational and Objective: Photography's Construction of Place." *Affective Landscapes in Literature, Art, and Everyday Life: Memory, Place and the Senses.* Ed. Christine Berberich, Neil Campbell, and Robert Hudson. Surrey, U.K.: Ashgate, 2015. 113–30.

Mitchell, W. J. T. *What Do Pictures Want?* Chicago: University of Chicago Press, 2005.

Rash, Ron. *Above the Waterfall.* New York: HarperCollins, 2015.

———. *Among the Believers.* Oak Ridge, Tenn.: Iris, 2000.

———. *Eureka Mill.* Spartanburg, S.C.: Hub City, 1998.

———. "The Facts of Historical Fiction." *Publishers Weekly* April 10, 2006: 78.

———. *Nothing Gold Can Stay.* New York: HarperCollins, 2013.

———. *One Foot in Eden.* New York: Henry Holt, 2002.

———. Personal Interview. May–July 2015. Clemson, South Carolina.

———. *Saints at the River.* New York: Henry Holt, 2004.

———. *Serena.* New York: HarperCollins, 2008.

Ray, Paul C. *The Surrealist Movement in England.* London: Cornell University Press, 1971.

Seigworth, Gregory L., and Melissa Gregg. "An Inventory of Shimmers." *The Affect Theory Reader.* Ed. Melissa Gregg and Gregory L. Seigworth. Durham: Duke University Press, 2010. 1–25.

Sontag, Susan. *On Photography.* 1977. New York: Farrar, Straus, and Giroux, 2001.

"AWAKE IN THEIR WIDE PASTURE"

Formal Design in the Poems of Robert Morgan and Ron Rash

Jesse Graves

Ron Rash and Robert Morgan have become widely known as writers of narratives, of novels, poems, and short stories that invest deeply in the voices and experiences of their characters. Both writers have worked with themes specific to the culture of Appalachia, and both have used their home region almost exclusively as the setting for their works. Their writing imbues their native landscapes with a lyrical beauty, while never looking away from the hardships of life in remote and sometimes backward places. Embracing literary forms is a deeply personal choice for a writer, not unlike the choice to represent a region or way of life. Inherent abilities and tendencies, such as the kind of perfect-pitch ear for meter that some poets appear to possess, can account for significant influence in the engagement with formal techniques. An affinity with tradition, however, or an interest in the past that goes beyond recorded histories and into the shape of those assumed events, can also determine the modes and measures with which the poet elects to work. Poetic form is a part of literary history as well as cultural history, and many writers have viewed it as one of the beauties of nature and of human accomplishment, and as part of the inheritance of any poet. For Rash and Morgan, whose friendship stretches over three decades, their choices of form have involved employing traditional poetic structures with subtle variations. Both have sought an adaptable form, a means at home in the culture both poets represent in their work, and with the long traditions of poetic composition.

Since the publication in 1969 of Robert Morgan's first book of poetry, *Zirconia Poems,* and Fred Chappell's earliest collection of poems, *The World between the Eyes* in 1971, the genre of "Appalachian poetry" has experienced a renaissance unique in its history. Soon to follow were first full-length books by Jeff Daniel

Marion and George Ella Lyon. Within another decade early books by Maggie Anderson, Katherine Stripling Byer, and Michael McFee would help to carve out a significant corner of American poetry for a group of voices distinct from "southern literature" that found its roots and subject matter in the southern mountains. Formally, however, there was great diversity within this group of poets, with Morgan and Marion electing to write in the spare, often short-lined free verse driven by closely examined images and landscapes, and Chappell using a variety of forms and rhyme schemes, often to highlight his caustic wit and narrative sensibility. Increasingly, Appalachian poets have moved toward formal designs in their work, particularly including the more frequent use of syllabic verse (the controlled repetition of syllable counts within individual poetic lines, unaccompanied by metrical or rhyme patterns), which suggests an interesting case study as to the goals and outcomes of these recent formal directions.[1] Perhaps the only Appalachian poet who has been as widely regarded as Morgan and Rash over the past decade is Charles Wright,[2] who wrote, "In poems, all concerns are concerns of form" (3). The poems of Morgan and Rash present illustrative examples of why syllabics and other tendencies toward form have become important elements in the poetry of Appalachia, and they also serve as models by which to examine the impact of this movement.

Less than a decade separates Rash and Morgan in age, but Rash's first volume of poems *Eureka Mill,* appeared in 1998, while Morgan's first book, *Zirconia Poems,* came out in 1969, placing a full generation of readers between those debut books. One might call Ron Rash a member of the "second wave" of the Appalachian literary renaissance, because the surge that began in 1969 has not declined even momentarily in the thirty-nine years since, but has simply been followed by a younger group of writers of potentially equal ability. There are similarities between the two writers beyond their usage of formal poetic devices; both grew up among extended family in the western Carolinas (North for Morgan, North and South for Rash), and they have come from families that survived on rural farm work as well as labor in cotton-mill towns. Both have been better known as fiction writers, publishing novels and short-story collections, though each first gained wide recognition for poetry—the precedent for multigenre Appalachian writers traces back to the first generation of southern mountain poets who earned a national readership, including Jesse Stuart and James Still, both accomplished poets who have nevertheless been remembered best for their fiction. Both Morgan's and Rash's narrative poems also rely on one of the cornerstones of the lyric mode: an unswerving attention to the minutiae of particular moments in time to center the emotional resonance of their work.

Another common trait is that neither poet began his career writing syllabic verse. Morgan's first three books, *Zirconia Poems,* the chapbook *Life in the Crosshairs,* and *Red Owl,* present poems of such compressed lucidity that they seem to have been formed by underground pressures exactly as were the zircons dug from mines in Morgan's native Henderson County, North Carolina. Morgan's early poems were spare, tight, and primarily concerned with embodying the object in their crosshairs. In an unexpected turn, as Morgan's poems became more conversational, more about people and their stories, they also assumed more regular formal designs, countering the standard claim that free verse more closely resembles spoken language. Conversely Ron Rash began his career as a poet writing sustained narratives, as in his first book of poems, *Eureka Mill.* That collection tells about the lives the speaker's grandparents lived in a cotton-mill town, and like Morgan's work, Rash's is attuned to the details of natural environments and interior spaces in these early poems.

Among the several aesthetic reasons that two poets as remarkably gifted as Morgan and Rash would move toward formal structures in their poems, two motives emerge most convincingly. First, both poets have been invested in creating a sense of the living past, what Morgan called "a community across time."[3] Part of the living past of poetry is structural and aural regularity, the continuity of sound patterns and visual recognitions, which thus creates a bond and an agreement between the poet and the reader. In their recent work, Morgan and Rash have filled the worlds of their poems with voices of long-distant ancestors, memories of departed family members, and stories and myths from their home communities. Like so many Appalachian poets, Morgan and Rash have strived to evoke the sense of a continuous merging of past and present within worldly experience, while also establishing a note of particularity, a unique perspective through the pitch of their own poetic voices. This relates to the second compelling reason for a shift to more regular forms, which is to take a stance against prevailing cultural trends. American poetry since the 1960s has witnessed the rise of Beat poetry; the New York school and its stars, Frank O'Hara and John Ashbery; the black arts movement; the Black Mountain school; "disembodied poetics"; L=A=N=G=U=A=G=E poetry; and what Tony Hoagland recently called "the skittery poem of our moment."[4] Each of these movements takes a radical position in regard to verse form, all in favor of open forms, and all seemingly in competition to find the least historically derived version.

In lyric poetry a mastery of forms is secondary to the resonance of content, and it is notable that both Morgan and Rash also have written poems without syllable patterns, in standard free verse, and in other, often more complicated verse forms. In one of his signature poems, "Honey," from the 2000 collection *Topsoil Road,* Morgan revisited the image of the lattice[5] as a term of design, in this case to describe the hives of honey bees:

> a sealed relic of sun and time
> and roots of many acres fixed

in crystal-tight arrays, in rows
and lattices of sweeter latin
from scattered prose of meadow, woods. (53)

The first definition of "lattice" in *The American Heritage Dictionary* reflects the most familiar building-trade terminology: "An open framework made of strips of metal, wood, or similar material interwoven to form regular, patterned spaces." This is fitting as an image for the effect of writing syllabic lines, but there is also a third dictionary entry that applies to physics (a field Morgan has studied carefully and whose language he has brought to his poetry): "A regular, periodic configuration of points, particles, or objects throughout an area of space, especially the arrangement of ions or molecules in a crystalline solid." This breaking down of the line into its smallest particles deepens the metaphor of poetry as lattice work, without losing the freedom of the "open framework" so necessary to the poetics of Morgan and Rash. The pitfalls of working exclusively with a single syllabic count include the risk of sameness and predetermination, of limiting experience to representation on an artificially limited canvas, so Morgan and Rash have created frameworks for their poems with many different materials and textures.

The earliest instance of the eight-syllable line pattern in Morgan's work appears in his 1987 collection *At the Edge of the Orchard Country,* strikingly in the poem "Lightning Bug," and very subtly in several others. The opening lines of many of the book's most memorable poems, such as "Buffalo Trace," "Yellow," "The Gift of Tongues," and "Man and Machine," introduce the pattern but do not employ it throughout. Though lines such as "Sometimes in the winter mountains". and "The whole church got hot and vivid" are not metrically consistent, Morgan established a definite visual and aural echo effect that surfaces and resurfaces through the entire book, like a thread woven into an intricate design, barely visible in the fabric of the whole. In the poem "Lightning Bug," we see the emergence of the model Morgan would use more frequently in later work, in which the eight-syllable line is used for the entire poem. The content of "Lightning Bug," however, harkens back to Morgan's earliest "object" poems, with its close study of a thing existing in its element, a living thing in this case, though given the grandeur of permanence in the poem's beautiful opening line:

Carat of the first radiance.
You navigate like a creature
of the deep. I wish I could read
your morse across the night yard.
Your body is a piece of star
but your head is obscure. What small
photography! What instrument

panel is on? You are winnowed
through the hanging gardens of night.
Your noctilucent syllables
sing in the millennium of
the southern night with star-talking
dew, like the thinker sending nous
into the outerstillness from
the edge of the orchard country. (24)

An unassuming poem about one of the most common mysteries of summer, the luminescence of nocturnal flying insects, hardly nominates itself as a pivotal work, but it is perfectly characteristic of Morgan's method to submerge a crucial formal shift, the broad influence of which is still felt, within a poem about a humble subject. Morgan noted that he began writing this poem in 1969,[6] but was unable to complete it until he came upon the poem's concluding line, from which the collection takes its title, and which may have suggested the poem's rhythm.

Morgan mentioned the syllabic form as early as his 1983 essay "Good Measure" as it applies to the poem "Grandma's Bureau."[7] Morgan said, "'Grandma's Bureau' represents much of the work I have been doing recently. The versification is the simplest I know, an eight-syllable line with no regular meter, no counting of stresses. It is almost-free verse broken into an arbitrary length, based vaguely on four-beat common meter: a kind of humble blank verse. I like this form because it leaves the musical cadence almost entirely free to follow the content, the narrative line, the local dynamics of the sentence, yet has some of the surface tension of regularity, the expectation of repetition, with the fulfillment and surprises of advancement across an uneven terrain" (6). By the time of his 1990 collection, *Sigodlin,* Morgan had begun to work more rigorously with verse forms, including a highly successful pantoum ("Audubon's Flute"), and an equally striking anagram poem ("Mountain Graveyard"), as well as a number of poems with the eight-syllable line. In *Topsoil Road* the majority of poems use the eight-syllable line. Some of Morgan's most memorable poems appear in this volume, including "Topsoil Road," "Wild Peavines," "History's Madrigal," and two poems on the poet's father, "Mowing" and "Working in the Rain." "Mowing" presents an especially interesting case because we see Morgan taking on one of his central subjects, the nature of his father, and breaking with his signature syllabic form in doing so. A looser, more expansive line emerges, almost Whitman-esque, such as "Half-dancing and half-rowing into a weed bank," and "a wide wing of metal, tempered in Czechoslovakia." In a book filled with controlled line lengths, and regular syllable counts, the freedom these lines offer leaps off the page with the energy of the work they represent. They achieve the best kind of mimetic effect in which the form becomes a natural extension of its subject matter.

In his two most recent collections, *Terroir* (2011) and *Dark Energy* (2014), Morgan continued his work with the eight-syllable line, but in many poems he has also introduced a new formal development: the rhyming end couplet. The effect creates a dramatic sense of closure and offers an unexpected pleasure when no other rhymes have been established earlier in the poem. Take, for instance, the effect at the end of "October Crossing," a poem about "woolly bear" caterpillars, from the collection *Terroir:*

> However accurate the widths
> of colors on their prophet backs,
> or knowledge of their fate as moths,
> they seem intent on crossing this
> hard Styx or Jordan to the ditch,
> oblivious to the tires' high pitch. (3)

The conclusion of the poem, with its "ditch/pitch" end rhyme, elevates the seemingly unremarkable journey of the caterpillar to significant drama—a life-or-death situation. These caterpillars already have a cultural mythology associated with their appearance; they are supposed to predict the duration of winter by the width of the orange stripes on their backs, and in some Appalachian communities it is considered bad luck to have had one of these caterpillars see one's teeth.

Morgan employed the end rhyme in well over half of the poems in *Terroir* and in a similar number in *Dark Energy,* though the device hardly appears at all in his earlier work. Regarding the new technique, Morgan said, "I'm sure it was Shakespeare's use of the tag couplet in many of his soliloquies that inspired me to try tying off a poem with a rhyme."[8] In *Dark Energy* Morgan used an addendum to the end rhyme, with what could be considered a concept rhyme, as in the conclusion of the poem "Widdershins," in which the final two lines end with the words "said" and "heard" (77). The conceptual association between "said" and "heard" makes a kind of logical sense, even a kind of grammatical sense, as between verb and object. While the alliterative "d" that ends each word could make a case for these words as a slant rhyme, another example from the title poem, "Dark Energy," which concludes with lines ending in "zero" and "silence" (79), shows a clear relation between the meanings of the words. One end word answers the other and provides a context for interpreting the other, in Morgan's concept rhymes. Such poem endings include "birth" and "work" in "Big Talk," and "particles" and "fine rain" in "Rare." Almost all of Morgan's newer poems maintain the eight-syllable line, his "humble blank verse," while introducing further formal inventions.

Ron Rash has favored a tighter, more dramatic syllabic line than Morgan, working often with only seven syllables per line, calling back to the early Welsh meter *cywydd,* first made popular in the fourteenth century. Both poets have celebrated their Welsh ancestry in their work, and another interesting parallel between Morgan and Rash is that in the most influential essays written on each, and the ones that essentially served as their introductions to a general poetry-reading audience, commentators on their work mentioned the early Welsh alliterative method called *cynghanedd.*[9] The sound effect is similar to the Old English poetics found in *Beowulf,* though the repetitions are less ordered and can offer greater surprise for the reader and flexibility for the poet. Rash's poem "The Corpse Bird" illustrates the chiming and echoing of sounds, as well as demonstrates the seven-syllable verse line:

> Bed-sick she heard the bird's call
> fall soft as a pall that night
> quilts tightened around her throat,
> her gray eyes narrowed, their light
> gone as she saw what she'd heard
> waiting for her in the tree
> cut down at daybreak by kin
> to make the coffin, bury
> that perch around her so death
> might find one less place to rest.
> (*Among the Believers* 10)

The poem's opening line is a feast of sound chimes. Dividing the line into two measures, "Bed-sick she heard / the bird's call," one hears the echo of "b" of "bed" and "bird's," the "s" of "sick" and "she" picked up by "bird's," and then, in a perfect turn, a vowel chime with the internal rhyme of "heard" and "bird's." Anthony Hecht's glowing introduction to Rash's second poetry collection, *Among the Believers,* paid special attention to "The Corpse Bird": "What moves and impresses in these lines is related to a dramatic use of enjambment, to the poet's ability to force us beyond a point at which we had expected to rest in accepted resolution, and deliberately to confound a cluster of events; the fact of her "seeing" what she has heard as the light departs from her eyes (emphasized by the ambiguity of "narrowed," which can be read as either a verb or an adjective). . . . The lines, the small events, blend and flow together in a seamless utterance that is full of mystery and drama" (xii).

Many of the characteristics Hecht examined as the power of such concise and intricate poems emerge even more fully in Rash's third collection of poems, *Raising the Dead.* Two consecutive poems in this volume display Rash at his most masterful and deeply felt. "Watauga County, 1803" chronicles the drowning of a mountain family in a flood and begins with the powerful lines: "Night falling, river rising / into the cabin, a hound / howling on the porch, and then / an unbuckling from bank roots" (*Raising the Dead* 18). The drama of the scene wherein the cabin (which the speaker calls "covenant of that failed ark") slips into the flood waters surges on the sudden and tragic nature of the event described but also on the insistence of Rash's meter and rolling effect of catching the long "i" sound in the opening line and the "b" sound in the fourth line. "In Dismal Gorge," the poem that follows "Watauga County, 1803" in *Raising the Dead,* has a similarly tragic theme, as well as a similarly effective poetic design:

> The lost can stay lost down here,
> in laurel slicks, false-pathed caves.
> Too much too soon disappears.
>
> On creek banks clearings appear,
> once homesteads. Nothing remains.
> The lost can stay lost down here,
> like Tom Clark's child, our worst fears
> confirmed as we searched in vain.
> Too much too soon disappears.
>
> How often this is made clear
> where cliff shadows pall our days.
> The lost can stay lost down here,
>
> stones scattered like a river
> in drought, now twice-buried graves.
> Too much too soon disappears,
>
> lives slip away like water.
> We fill our Bibles with names.
> The lost can stay lost down here.
> Too much too soon disappears. (19)

The repetition of designated lines presents an apparent difficulty, but Rash has imposed the additional challenge of rhyme scheme, which is generally not a requirement of the villanelle. Rash has employed the poetic tools of a master builder, including slant rhyme and alliteration, and maintained his signature seven-syllable line. The forms are often invisible, or nearly so, in the poems of both Rash and Morgan, hidden by design, because both poets have showed the understanding that craft without substance is merely exercise, and skill on overt display diminishes the achievement.

One of Rash's finest poems is "Three A.M. and the Stars Were Out," from his 2011 collection, *Waking.* The poem recounts, in first person, the story of an aged veterinarian making a middle-of-the-night house call to a remote farm. Most of the action of the poem takes places inside the speaker's mind, as he makes the long drive to the farm, where he knows "what's to be done best done with / rifle or shotgun" (38–39). We are given access to his memories and speculations, as well as to his doubts and anxieties. It is also perhaps the most masterful display of technical facility, and of driving that facility to serve and enlarge the effect of a piece of writing, in all of Rash's work. Beyond the remarkable control of voice and tone, Rash's command of syntax and sentence structure distinguishes this poem. The most startling formal detail is that the first sixty-four lines are one single sentence. This dramatic technique creates a propulsive, rambling sensation about what the speaker reveals of his many years of experiences traveling country back roads. That long, musing, associative opening is followed by a one-line sentence: "Though sometimes it all works out" (65). The startling juxtaposition of those two sentences is eye-opening and generates a heightened sense of gravity around the one-line sentence.

"Three A.M. and the Stars Were Out" reads like a Shakespearean soliloquy, except there is no reason to assume that the words in the car have been spoken aloud. No specific implied listener to what the speaker has to say is identified, so the piece is not quite a dramatic monologue (though the tone and situation could easily be imagined in a Robert Browning poem), but more of an interior monologue, in which the thoughts of the speaker are uninterrupted by a narrator. This is a form of stream-of-consciousness writing, a once-experimental modernist technique that now feels as familiar as third-person, omniscient narration, because all readers understand the design and the purpose of entering into the stream of a character's thoughts. Readers understand what is being revealed, and why it has taken a form: the thought process itself made visible, generally associated with the way characters think out loud in plays.

Rash has addressed poetic form, and literary inheritance, most directly in "Dylan Thomas," also from his collection *Waking:*

> Scawmy, gray-souled November
> blinds the whale-road, pall draper
> over this ship bearing one
> whose name means *of the ocean*
> in a language he denied
> allegiance to, though his lines
> rang with *cynghanedd*—English
> reined in by Celtic music,
> stitched tight as the coracle
> that wombed Taliesin—tribal
> rain-downs of sounds, not enough:

a small people lose their tongue
one poet at a time. Talent—squanderer, fraud, miscreant,
apt sobriquets for a life
lived badly between the lines.
The coast recedes. Last gulls cry.
Down in the hold his drunk wife
smokes and flirts with the seamen
who play cards on his coffin. (51)

Rash's poem rebukes Thomas for abandoning, even denying, the language of his people, even though the key characteristics of the language do not leave him. Rash has found a way to acknowledge poetic tradition, and to recognize how it emanates from poetry even when it has been openly rejected. Through his own destructive choices, Thomas wasted his opportunity to be the great poet of the Welsh tongue, and the final humiliation is that his poorly chosen wife does not even mourn him after his death. Interestingly a recent poem of Morgan's also redresses Dylan Thomas, and his most famous poem, "Do Not Go Gentle into That Good Night." In his response poem, "Go Gentle," from *Terroir,* Morgan asserted that Thomas could not understand the affective energies that surround the end of a parent's life, and that no one except the speaker in Thomas's poem would want "a loved / one angry and in fear scream out" instead of gently passing "to that night" (45).

Rash has varied his formal approaches throughout his work, as has Morgan, but the use of the seven-syllable pattern persists in nearly all of Rash's poetry. In "Good Friday, 2006: Shelton Laurel," a poem from *Waking,* the pattern contains and unspools the actant energies in the landscape, its history of violence and the irrevocable human print on the natural world: "Below the knoll a man kneels. / Face close to the earth, he works / soil like a potter works clay, / kneading and shaping until / hands slowly open, reveal / a single green stalk" (60). But after this bucolic scene in the present, the past emerges as a swarm of shades, the victims of the Shelton Laurel Massacre, whose undeadness trembles "where oak trees knit tight shadows / across the marble" of their mass grave (60). Compression of form melds with intensity of emotion, fusing the syllabic form with a lyrical dynamism that moves effortlessly in and between time, states of being, human and natural worlds. For Rash the form *is* the land, packed with brutality, death, and acts of violence that fuse human action through layers of history. The poem's final lines dramatize the landscape as container of natural process, agricultural tradition, and traumatic witness: "Wind lifts / the leaves, grow still. A man sows / his field the old way. The land / unscrolls like a palimpsest" (60).

In a technological society, ways of doing things change rapidly—new means replace old means—but in Appalachia entire ways of life have changed in three generations. This is not to say that Appalachia was ever a nontechnological society, but simply that in this region the means and the ends of survival were often indistinguishable, that a life on the land is synchronous with a livelihood drawn from the land. In urban settings people commute to work rather than walk; they cook on a gas or electric stove rather than coal; they work on a laptop rather than a typewriter; in these instances the means change but ends remain the same. As the economy of operating a small farm becomes unviable, both the means and the ends of the lives it has supported must change. Robert Morgan's and Ron Rash's work represents that of a generation of Appalachian writers who witnessed firsthand, mostly in the lives of their parents, the shift away from a primarily agricultural livelihood. These poets have recorded not only the work and ways of living; they have also recorded the change itself and its attendant losses. One could call their work commemorative, and as memory is mother of the muses, that would be an accurate claim, but in another sense, these writers, and so many others in the region, have given history a second life. Morgan and Rash have taken Eliot's claim about "the historical sense"[10] seriously, and by embracing certain aspects of poetry's long tradition, such as syllabic verse forms, their work invokes the past as a deeper layer, a substrata, of life in the continuously evolving present moment.

Notes

1. A notable example of this trend toward formal design among Appalachian poets can be found in Yale Younger Poet's Prize winner Maurice Manning's 2007 collection *Bucolics,* which employs a consistent syllabic structure throughout. Manning has measured the voice of a farmworker speaking in heavy rural dialect into regular syllabic lines, all the while maintaining the naturalness of the narrator's speech.

2. Charles Wright was born in Tennessee in 1935 and taught for many years at the University of Virginia. He has been named United States poet laureate; has won the Pulitzer Prize and the National Book Award; and is generally considered a strong candidate for the permanent canon of American poetry.

3. Robert Morgan has used this phrase in interviews, including on *The Oprah Winfrey Show,* but I first heard it when he visited a class I was teaching at Cornell. The phrase so resonated with my students that several included it in their final papers.

4. Tony Hoagland's essay "Fear of Narrative and the Skittery Poem of Our Moment," a critique of the state of contemporary American poetry, first appeared in *Poetry* in March 2006.

5. Morgan also used this term in his prose piece "Mica: Reflective Bits from a Notebooks" (*Good Measure* 123).

6. In his essay "The Cubist of Memory," Morgan said, "Finally the phrase . . . came to me this year [1983]. It suggested redolence, proximity and distance, a projecting of attention out to the horizon of trees and stars. Suddenly the poem felt complete, and I could let it rest" (*Good Measure* 11).

7. The poem mentioned, "Grandma's Bureau," was collected later in the 1990 volume *Sigodlin* though was not re-collected in either *Green River* (1991) or *The Strange Attractor* (2004), Morgan's two "new and selected" volumes.

8. E-mail to the author, September 6, 2015.

9. See Hecht and Harmon.

10. In "Tradition and the Individual Talent," T. S. Eliot declared the necessity of a poet developing what he called "the historical sense" if the poet was to mature as an artist (*Selected Prose* 38).

Works Cited

The American Heritage Dictionary. 5th ed. New York: Dell, 2012.

Eliot, T. S. *Selected Prose.* Ed. Frank Kermode. New York: Harcourt Brace Jovanovich, 1975.

Harmon, William. "Robert Morgan's Pelagian Georgics." *Parnassus: Poetry in Review* 9.2 (1981): 5–30.

Hecht, Anthony. "A Gift Matched with Skills of the First Order." *Among the Believers.* By Ron Rash. Oak Ridge, Tenn.: Iris, 2000: xi–xv.

Hoagland, Tony. "Fear of Narrative and the Skittery Poem of Our Moment." *Poetry* March 2006. https://www.poetryfoundation.org/poetrymagazine/articles/detail/68489. July 25, 2015.

Manning, Maurice. *Bucolics.* New York: Houghton Mifflin Harcourt, 2007.

Morgan, Robert. *At the Edge of the Orchard Country.* 1987. Winston-Salem, N.C.: Press 53, 2014.

———. *Dark Energy.* New York: Penguin, 2015.

———. *Good Measure.* Baton Rouge: Louisiana State University Press, 1993.

———. *Sigodlin.* 1990. Winston-Salem, N.C.: Press 53, 2015.

———. *Terroir.* New York: Penguin, 2011.

———. *Topsoil Road.* Baton Rouge: Louisiana State University Press, 2000.

Rash, Ron. *Among the Believers.* Oak Ridge, Tenn.: Iris, 2000.

———. *Raising the Dead.* Oak Ridge, Tenn.: Iris, 2002.

———. *Serena.* New York: HarperCollins, 2008.

———. *Waking.* Spartanburg, S.C.: Hub City, 2011.

Wright, Charles. *Halflife.* Ann Arbor: University of Michigan Press, 1988.

RON RASH AND EUDORA WELTY

Walking the Same Worn Path

Mae Miller Claxton

In her address to the Society for the Study of Southern Literature in 2012, entitled "New Landscapes of Southern Literary Studies," Barbara Ladd charted the trajectory of southern literature from its perceived "aristocratic" roots, to the educated middle- and upper-class southern writers of the Renascence, such as Faulkner, O'Connor, and Welty, to more recent trends. Ladd recounted Louis D. Rubin Jr.'s attempt in the 1950s to find a director at Johns Hopkins for his proposed dissertation on Thomas Wolfe. One professor whom he approached stated that Wolfe did not really fit into the mold of the southern writer because he was not a "gentleman" and his work does not reflect an "aristocratic ideal" (Ladd 1). Rubin chose another dissertation director and continued along his academic path in another direction. Rubin's experience illustrates a southern preoccupation with class that has more recently reentered the conversation about southern studies. Thomas Wolfe hailed from Asheville, in Appalachia, with working-class parents who clawed their way into the middle class. Rubin and his fellow scholars went on to remove any further perceptions of southern literature as "aristocratic." Writers such as Faulkner, Welty, Wolfe, and others emerged from the middle class, but most of their families, like Wolfe's, had working-class roots. In her address Ladd noted a resurgent interest in class in more recent southern literature: "we have witnessed the flourishing of a powerful working class and poor white literature—I'm thinking here of writers like Harry Crews, Dorothy Allison, Jim Grimsley, and Larry Brown" (2). This new literature, according to Ladd, has not received as much scholarly attention, especially as it connects to southern studies. She continued, "we have yet to see a well-developed narrative of 'class' in southern literary and cultural studies, specifically one that accounts, in any truly historicized way, for the poor South and, even more specifically, for the poor white South" (2). With the shift of focus to class, new themes emerge. Race becomes complicated, as writers have focused more on multiethnic populations at the margins. Native American writers have take on a new importance as they confronted issues of extreme poverty and racism. Ecocriticism becomes part of the conversation, since the removal and pollution of natural resources most often affects the segments of population without power in society.

Those of us who study and teach Appalachian literature find that the books in our courses connect closely with this "rough South" or "grit lit" genre. In his preface to *Grit Lit: A Rough South Reader,* Tom Franklin had some trouble defining "grit lit," although he knew what it is not. He wrote, "So what's Grit Lit? It's the dirty South seen without romanticism or the false nostalgia of *Gone with the Wind* fans. People who are interested in the South as it really is, not moonlight and magnolia but grit in your workboots, especially if it's a steeltoe with the leather so worn at the toe that the metal shows" (viii). Appalachian literature has long been relegated to a subgenre of southern literature and subjected to stereotyping and patronizing discussion, if it is mentioned at all. In *Inhabiting Contemporary Southern and Appalachian Literature,* Casey Clabough noted that the "new" southern studies emphasizes the South's connection to other "global" spaces, for example the Caribbean or South Africa, but seldom mentions southern Appalachia. Clabough comments that "the South's Appalachian region, the communities that exist along and within thousands of square miles of hills, hollows, and mountains, is mentioned but once and only in passing" (16). Clabough claims that scholars who focus on Appalachian studies have successfully established themselves "almost entirely independent of those scholars who purport to explicate the South as a whole. Theirs is the excitement of a dynamic and promising field still in the process of establishing itself" (16).

Arguably the best writing coming out of the South at this time is coming from the "mountain South," "upper South," or "southern Appalachia." While Appalachian studies may be doing fine on its own, as Clabough maintains, I believe it is worthwhile to connect writers of Appalachian literature with other writers of the South who are similarly exploring issues of marginality and class. To make this point, I look at two writers in this context. One is Mississippi writer Eudora Welty, an established member of the Southern Renascence, and the other is Ron Rash, a card-carrying member of the contemporary "grit lit" genre[1] who has been receiving increasing attention nationally. While both of these writers grew up largely in middle-class families, their work devotes considerable attention to lower-class issues in their fiction, and a comparative study can deepen our understanding of both writers' exploration of class and provide a broader picture of new directions in southern studies. Beginning with Welty's well-known story "A Worn Path" and moving to three of Rash's works, the focus will be on privileged knowledge; class; racism; poverty; and history's impact on the present—all issues that have long preoccupied both of these writers.

Even well-known scholars of southern literature have sometimes characterized Eudora Welty as "Miss Welty," the polite spinster who wrote her sharply tuned fiction in the upstairs bedroom of her parents' Tudor home in a comfortable Jackson, Mississippi suburb.[2] One might even think that Eudora Welty and Ron Rash might have little in common. It is indeed difficult to imagine Rash sipping a mint julep in a seersucker suit in Welty's garden. On the other hand, Rash has quoted Eudora Welty's well-known essay "Place in Fiction" at almost every one of his readings—"One place comprehended can make us understand other places better" (Welty, *Stories* 792)—and has stated repeatedly his great admiration for her writing. If not mint juleps in the garden, I can certainly imagine Rash and Welty drinking Maker's Mark (her preferred drink, according to biographer Suzanne Marrs) on her porch.[3]

Despite her "southern lady" reputation, Welty demonstrated her acute awareness of both sides of the proverbial railroad tracks in her fiction. As a young woman from a comfortable middle-class background, equipped with "a good liberal arts education," Welty traveled around Mississippi for the WPA writing and photographing the Depression-era South (Welty, preface). Her first stories emerged from the hardscrabble people, rural areas, and extreme poverty she encountered in her home state. Welty commented in the preface to *One Time One Place,* "of the ways of life in the world I knew absolutely nothing at all. I didn't even know this. My complete innocence was the last thing I would have suspected of myself. Anyway, I was fit to be amazed" (11). In the 1940s the impact of World War II strongly influenced Welty's fiction, as Suzanne Marrs and other scholars have shown. With her two brothers and intimate friends facing danger, Welty turned her gaze outward to the global theater. The 1960s brought other revelations to Welty as she witnessed the turbulence of the civil rights movement. After Medgar Evers was assassinated on June 12, 1963, Welty quickly wrote a searing story, "Where Is the Voice Coming From?," through the perspective of his white killer and published it in the *New Yorker* on July 6, 1963. She and the editors worked on the story over the phone, removing names of actual people or places that might create legal difficulties (Marrs 303–4). In the 1970s Welty again documented poverty, hardship, and environmental devastation in her upper South novel *Losing Battles.* She wrote in her memoir *One Writer's Beginnings,* "As you have seen, I am a writer who came of a sheltered life. A sheltered life can be a daring life as well. For all serious daring starts from within" (*Stories* 948). While it might be tempting to separate southern writers into groups based on class, I believe that such groups tend to overlap as often as they diverge.

In Welty's "A Worn Path," an often-anthologized story, readers and scholars have largely focused on Phoenix's adventures on the path and not on Welty's more deeply intertwined narratives of race, poverty, violence, and oppression.

In an essay entitled "'Is Phoenix Jackson's Grandson Really Dead?,'" Welty described the story as "a day's journey an old woman makes on foot from deep in the country into town and into a doctor's office on behalf of her little grandson; he is at home, periodically ill, and periodically she comes for his medicine; they give it to her as usual, she receives it and starts the journey back" (*Stories* 815). Welty's accretion of phrases in this passage suggests Phoenix's long journey, the "habit of love" that sends her out on the path time and again (817). It is clearly a story about a personal relationship, but Welty did not ignore the historical and societal forces that impact Phoenix as a poor African American woman living in rural Mississippi. Phoenix walks through a landscape and encounters people who remind readers of alternative stories of oppression and tragedy.

Written in 1940, "A Worn Path" reminds readers that slavery is not far removed from the present as Phoenix walks along a storied path, the Natchez Trace, where many slaves traveled from "the Forks of the Road," a well-known slave market near Natchez, into the interior of the country. Phoenix states that she was born a slave. As a black woman in Mississippi, she would have been subjected to segregation, racial oppression, and lack of opportunity. She tells the nurse in the doctor's office, "I never did go to school, I was too old at the Surrender. . . . I'm an old woman without an education" (*Stories* 178). Since she lives in the country, she has little need for money, but in this story she is heading into town and must resort to subterfuge in order to get a few coins to buy her grandson a "little windmill" (179). Although Welty portrayed Phoenix not as a victim but as a woman well able to persevere even with these liabilities, she clearly showed Phoenix's challenges with no education and a lack of easily accessible health care.

Welty also depicted the physical danger that Phoenix faces. On her path she sees something "tall, black and skinny there moving before her. At first she took it for a man" (*Stories* 173). Although Phoenix has encountered a scarecrow, the reference to lynching is unmistakable. African American men and women both were still being lynched during this time period. Later in the story, she encounters a white hunter who points a gun at her, just to see her reaction: "'Doesn't the gun scare you?' he said, still pointing it. 'No, sir, I seen plenty go off closer by, in my day, and for less than what I done,' she said, holding utterly still" (176). Phoenix has clearly encountered violence and danger before, and they do not scare her now.

Welty also sharply contrasted Phoenix's knowledge with the privileged knowledge possessed by the white people in the story. The hunter opens his bag to show her the birds he has shot. Phoenix's relationship with the natural world she encounters along the path has been very different. Rather than killing the animals, Phoenix talks to them as participants in her journey: "Out of my way, all you foxes, owls, beetles, jack rabbits, coons and wild animals! . . . Keep out from under these feet, little bob-whites. . . . Keep the big wild hogs out of my path. Don't let none of those come running my direction. I got a long way" (*Stories* 171). She seeks a kind of safe passage from the species that would naturally inhabit the piney woods she travels through in contrast to dangerous human-introduced species such as wild hogs. The woods are also Phoenix's natural habitat. She walks through this environment with an understanding and knowledge of the plants and animals she encounters.

It is only when she comes to town that she gets confused and must ask for assistance from others: "In the paved city it was Christmas time. There were red and green electric lights strung and crisscrossed everywhere, and all turned on in the daytime. Old Phoenix would have been lost if she had not distrusted her eyesight and depended on her feet to know where to take her" (*Stories* 176). Confused by the trappings of modern society, Phoenix must trust her previous knowledge of the path in order to reach her destination, the doctor's office. In this professional setting, she is categorized as a "charity case," and the diploma hanging up in the doctor's office, a piece of paper defining power and authority, symbolizes knowledge. While society has denied Phoenix a similar document, Welty privileged Phoenix's close, personal knowledge of the natural world and the love that propels her out onto that path.

At times in the story, Phoenix trusts senses other than her eyesight. When she crosses a log, she "shut her eyes. Lifting her skirt, leveling her cane fiercely before her, like a festival figure in some parade, she began to march across. Then she opened her eyes and she was safe on the other side" (*Stories* 172). Welty suggested a deeper kind of knowledge in this passage, achieved by Phoenix's senses and by instinct. Soon after, Phoenix sees a little boy with a slice of marble cake on a plate, but when she tries to take it there is just air (172). On a previous trip, she remembers, she saw a two-headed snake that blocked her path (173). Later she sees a black dog that frightens her, sending her into the ditch "like a little puff of milkweed" (174). There she stays in a kind of dream until the hunter comes along with his dog "on a chain" and pulls her out. These encounters add a mythical, dreamlike quality to Phoenix's walk through the winter woods. Elaine Orr noted the pre-Christian, old European symbolism in "A Worn Path," citing Marija Gimbutas's description of the Regeneratrix or witch, an old woman who represents death and regeneration (59). This goddess is associated with birds, snakes, and dogs, all animals that appear in Welty's stories (60). She is also a "seer, she 'knows'" (59), and is closely" associated with the winter solstice, the same time period of Welty's story set in December at Christmas time (59).

In his story "Their Ancient, Glittering Eyes" from his collection *Chemistry and Other Stories* (2007), Rash created characters who have much in common with Phoenix. Octogenarians Rudisell and Campbell, along with their friend Creech, "a mere seventy-six," embark on a quest to capture an ancient, mythical being, a giant water monster. They are not as oppressed as Phoenix but still encounter bias, ridicule, and disrespect. Rash contrasted the experiential knowledge of region and place possessed by these men with the scientific classroom knowledge of Charles Meekins, the county's game warden. Even though he has been in Jackson County, North Carolina, for just four years, Meekins believes that his education and government credentials carry more weight than the octogenarians' accumulated years of life experience in this particular place.

Like Welty, Rash cast doubt on eyesight as a way to obtain knowledge in his story, leading his readers to seek a deeper, more complex vision. The two boys who first see the monster fish, for example, are not taken seriously, even by the older men: "'Flouridated water,' Rudisell wheezed. 'Makes them see things'" (*Chemistry and Other Stories* 3). When the three men see the monster fish for themselves, others make fun of them, and the game warden does not believe them: "'When you're looking into water you can't really judge the size of something,' Meekins said. He looked at some of the younger men and winked. 'Especially if your vision isn't all that good to begin with'" (8). Bearing the authority of his title as a spokesman for the government, Meekins refuses to find their story credible, causing the men to reach into their resources of experience and wisdom to catch the fish. They also use a book they obtained from the library to identify their water monster, which turns out to be a sturgeon. When they are faced with the real possibility of catching the sturgeon with a snake and bearing their evidence to the "smart-ass game warden," Rudisell purposefully snaps the line, and the sturgeon sinks slowly back into the water. At first Creech and Campbell are angry, but they quickly understand why Rudisell let the big fish go. Creech remarks, "You done the right thing. I didn't *see* that at first, but I *see* it now" (20, emphasis added). In the end no one can take away their own wisdom and experience, their hard-won knowledge of life. But Meekins does not see and does not believe their fish story: "Must be nice to have nothing better to do than make up stories, but this is getting old real quick" (21). In a kind of "slow, dignified procession," Campbell follows Rudisell with the fishing equipment, and Creech follows him with the book. In the end Rash privileged his elderly protagonists' view of the world and their respectful acknowledgement of the sturgeon's place in it.

While Welty included pre-Christian, old European imagery in "A Worn Path," Rash's story similarly depicts a landscape of myth and ancient mystery. His work, however, suggests Cherokee tales of water monsters in the rivers of western North Carolina, the uktena, dragon-like creatures that inhabit deep pools in rivers. James Mooney described the uktena as "a great snake, as large around as a tree trunk, with horns on its head, and a bright, blazing crest like a diamond upon its forehead, and scales glittering like sparks of fire." The person who can obtain the diamond, Ulûñsû'tî or "Transparent," will possess great power, but it will be a dangerous power: "Whoever owns the Ulûñsû'tî is sure of success in hunting, love, rainmaking, and every other business, but its great use is in life prophecy. When it is consulted for this purpose the future is seen mirrored in the clear crystal as a tree is reflected in the quiet stream below, and the conjurer knows whether the sick man will recover, whether the warrior will return from battle, or whether the youth will live to be old" (Mooney, "Uktena"). Both the Cherokees and Celtic people believed that water could be a conduit to another world.[4] Mooney wrote, "There is another world under this, and it is like ours in everything—animals, plants, and people—save that the seasons are different. The streams that come down from the mountains are the trails by which we reach this underworld, and the springs at their heads are the doorways by which we enter" ("How the World Was Made"). Both Welty's and Rash's works tap into an ancient knowledge that can be acquired not through books but through oral narratives preceding written language, knowledge closely connected to the natural world.

Rash's third novel, *The World Made Straight,* details a journey undertaken by another marginalized character, a teenage boy. It is a coming-of-age story in which Travis Shelton, the son of an unsuccessful tobacco farmer, encounters increasing danger and violence in his unrelenting search for knowledge. While Phoenix is impacted by the tragedy of slavery and oppression, Travis is weighted down by class, by a violent family history, and by stifling restrictions placed on him by society. Travis's experience of education came from his teachers in high school "who used sentences with big words against him when he gave them trouble, trying to tangle him up in a laurel slick of language. Figuring he hadn't read nothing but what they made him read, never used a dictionary to look up a word he didn't know" (21). Leonard Shuler, who acts as a kind of surrogate father, teacher, and mentor for Travis, opens a door, guiding him to explore the world at his own pace. Leonard provides books but does not force words on Travis, understanding the frustration he is experiencing. Rash wrote, "*Landscape as destiny.* Leonard had carried that phrase in his head for years, though he could not remember the context or where it came from. But he knew what it meant here, the sense of being closed in, of human limitation" (156–57). Shuler knew that this landscape had impacted his own destiny. His ex-wife Kera had accused him of always living in "the passive voice," letting others make choices so if things went wrong he didn't have to bear the blame" (54).

Leonard helps Travis to see the world differently. When Travis finds a pair of eyeglasses at the site of the Shelton Laurel Massacre, he imagines how thirteen-year-old David Shelton might have felt that day when he was killed by Confederate soldiers for being suspected of sympathizing with the Union. Travis's vision through the glasses may be blurry, but his understanding of the past has become clearer. Like Phoenix in "A Worn Path" and the characters in "Their Ancient,

Glittering Eyes," Travis obtains a knowledge that goes beyond what he can see. Unfortunately knowledge can be dangerous, and when Travis learns about the massacre of his family members at Shelton Laurel, he sees vividly how history impacts the present. Rash left his readers to question whether art and writing can make the world straight. He suggested hope when Travis thinks to himself after putting money in an envelope to Dena, a woman even more down and out than him: "One thing done right, maybe even a kind of beginning, he told himself" (*World Made Straight* 288). The book ends with the image of Travis climbing as he drives up the ascent to Antioch, smelling the newly plowed earth as the road gently straightens out (289). With an education denied to him because of his class and familiar circumstances, Travis seizes power through his own experiential pursuit of knowledge that was birthed by his educational father figure, Leonard.

The most direct connection of "A Worn Path" to Rash's works comes in *Serena*—a novel very much about class and those who exploit the resources of the poor, particularly natural resources. In the opening paragraphs of the book, Rash described the young, pregnant Rachel Harmon and her father, dressed in "his shabby frock coat" at the train station prepared to meet Pemberton and his new wife (3). Abe Harmon displays a bowie knife, prepared to defend his daughter's honor. Buchanan and Wilkie, the other owners of the company, are also waiting on the train platform. Rash sharply contrasts them with Rachel and her father: "Buchanan, ever the dandy, had waxed his moustache and oiled his hair. His polished bluchers gleamed, the white cotton dress shirt fresh-pressed. Wilkie wore a gray fedora, as he often did to protect his bald pate from the sun. A Princeton Phi Beta Kappa key glinted on the older man's watch job; a blue silk handkerchief tucked in his breast pocket" (3–4). Rachel's father is a poor farmer while Pemberton, Serena, Buchanan, and Wilkie are clearly well educated and wealthy. Pemberton has sexually exploited Rachel, who is a young mountain girl without much formal education and with very little money, and in this scene he kills Rachel's father, even though Mr. Harmon is clearly drunk and ill equipped to fight the well-trained, epee-wielding younger Pemberton.

In the opening chapter of the book, Rachel loses her father and appears weak, unable to fight against the superior power of the Pembertons, but throughout the novel, she slowly but steadily gains strength. Her father may not be well trained in combat with a knife, but he has passed on important knowledge to Rachel about how to run a house and farm. She repairs the roof of her cabin, admiring her father's careful craftsmanship; gathers ginseng and replants the berries; and kills a raccoon that has been eating her eggs. She knows the place where she has grown up and understands how to use its resources respectfully. According to Rash the scene of Rachel embarking on a long journey of healing for her young son, who is desperately ill, was based on Rash's reading of Welty's story.[5] Barefoot and sick herself, Rachel walks into town carrying her son, encountering a variety of mythical beings that attempt to impede her errand. Hallucinating three wild dogs that block her way on a bridge, Rachel feels the planks of the bridge under her feet and thinks, "Them dogs ain't real but this is, and it will get me and this young one to town" (*Serena* 96). When the doctor comments on her trip—"I don't know how you did it. You must love that child dear as life"—Rachel replies, "I tried not to . . . I just couldn't find a way to stop myself" (97). Rachel obtains a kind of healing for herself as well as her son as she acknowledges her great love for him and her willingness to sacrifice on his behalf. The event is a turning point as Rachel achieves an insurmountable power through the love of her son. At the end of the novel, like Phoenix, Rachel proves that she can survive in the modern world away from the natural world she understands. She uses trains to escape from the Pembertons and travels as far away as Seattle, where she gets a job washing dishes in a café. Her journey to find healing and safety for her son requires a much further journey than the visit to the doctor, but the goal was the same: the survival of a child.

Like Welty's writing, Rash's writing deals with the human condition with a complexity that rewards close reading and analysis. In "What Will Survive of Us," a short piece Rash wrote about "A Worn Path" and William Gay's story "What Will You Do When Your Skin Cannot Contain You," Rash wrote that Phoenix has lost much: "Eyesight, memory, vigor, family—all have been taken from her. Even the grandchild, whose medicine is the reason for her journey, is possibly dead." What remains is familial love: "All that survives is Phoenix's love for her grandchild, and that love is honored each time she walks the worn path toward town, toward the hospital where she demands the medicine that she believes might heal him." Welty tells a family story in her memoir *One Writer's Beginnings* about a dramatic journey her own West Virginia mother took with her father, Welty's grandfather, who had developed appendicitis and had to be transported across an icy river by raft to flag down a train to take them to a hospital in Baltimore (*Stories* 893). Welty's mother had to return by herself since her father died of a ruptured appendix on the operating table at Johns Hopkins. Unlike in "A Worn Path," Welty's real-life story of her mother and grandfather did not end with healing, but the journey was the same, undertaken with love, no matter the outcome.

In the end Rash and Welty would have had much to talk about on the porch sipping their whiskey.[6] Both had Appalachian roots, and both wrote with a rooted sense of place, often with characters on the margins that possess wisdom and knowledge that others fail to see. Rash ended "Their Ancient, Glittering Eyes" with the image of his character Rudisell holding up a scale in front of the game warden Charles Meekins's face "as if were a silty monocle they both might peer through" (*Chemistry and Other Stories* 21). While Meekins fails to understand what he sees, the reader does. The quest is completed. In a Flannery O'Connor–like ending, Rash wrote, "They walked westward toward the store, the late-afternoon sun burnishing their cracked and wasted faces. Coming out of the shadows, they blinked their eyes as if dazzled, much in the manner of old-world saints who have witnessed the blinding brilliance of the one true vision" (22). I maintain in this essay that comparing Rash's and Welty's writing helps us see each writer's vision more clearly. In addition Rash's works and his appreciation of Welty as a writer remind readers that a close reading of Welty's works quickly evaporates any notions of the writer as sheltered, privileged, and ignorant of the classist, racist, oppressive society in which she lived. From that upstairs bedroom in the brick Tudor home in the suburbs of Jackson, Welty saw clearly. At the end of her essay "'Is Phoenix Jackson's Grandson Really Dead?,'" Welty compared the "worn path" of her story to the "worn path" of the writer: "The way to get there is the all-important, all-absorbing problem, and this problem is your reason for undertaking the story. Your only guide, too, is your sureness about your subject, about what the subject is. . . . And finally too, like Phoenix, you have to assume that what you are working in aid of is life, not death. But you would make the trip anyway—wouldn't you?—just on hope" (*Stories* 818). I contend that the "worn path" of southern literary studies has room for more writers, specifically those like Rash and other "grit lit" writers who have much to teach us about class, race, oppression, and poverty. Far from being the proverbial railroad track that separates classes and races within a single town, this path connects all southern writers.

Notes

1. Rash, for example, is included in Franklin's collection *Grit Lit: A Rough South Reader.*

2. See Pierpont.

3. See Wallace.

4. The transformative power of water is a common theme for Rash. For more on the role of early Irish mythology and the natural world, particularly the creation myth of the formation of Lough Neagh, see Baldwin, who also quotes Luke Miller in Rash's *Saints at the River:* "That's what the Celts believed—that water was a conduit to the next world" (Baldwin 64; Rash, *Saints* 45).

5. Rash mentioned this to me in conversation one day at Western Carolina University.

6. Ron Rash visited the Eudora Welty House Museum for a reading on November 21, 2014. The Facebook posting states, "We thoroughly enjoyed having author Ron Rash here Friday night to sign his latest short story collection *Something Rich and Strange.* He spoke of his appreciation and adoration of Eudora Welty. Thanks, Lemuria Bookstore, for making it possible to host a master of the short story!"

Works Cited

Baldwin, Kara. "'Incredible Eloquence': How Ron Rash's Novels Keep the Celtic Literary Tradition Alive." *South Carolina Review* 39.1 (Fall) 2006: 37–46.

Clabough, Casey. *Inhabiting Contemporary Southern and Appalachian Literature: Region and Place in the Twenty-First Century.* Gainesville: University Press of Florida, 2012.

Earley, Tony. "Mephisto Tennessee Waltz." *New York Times on the Web.* New York Times Company. November 21, 1999. Web. June 18, 2015.

"The Forks of the Road Slave Market at Natchez." *Mississippi History Now.* Mississippi Historical Society, 2015. Web. May 21, 2015.

Franklin, Tom. "Preface: What's Grit Lit?" *Grit Lit: A Rough South Reader.* Ed. Brian Carpenter and Tom Franklin. Columbia: University of South Carolina Press, 2012. xii–viii.

Ladd, Barbara. "New Landscapes of Southern Literary Studies." Society for the Study of Southern Literature. Nashville, Tenn. Plenary Address. March 29, 2012.

Marrs, Suzanne. *Eudora Welty: A Biography.* New York: Harcourt, 2005.

Mooney, James. "How the World Was Made." *Myths of the Cherokee.* John Bruno Hare, 2010. Web. July 2, 2015.

———. "The Uktena and the Ulûñsû'tï." *Myths of the Cherokee.* John Bruno Hare, 2010. Web. May 21, 2015.

Orr, Elaine. "'Unsettling Every Definition of Otherness': Another Reading of Eudora Welty's 'A Worn Path.'" *South Atlantic Review* 57.2 (1992): 57–72. Web. May 21, 2015.

Pierpont, Claudia Roth. "A Perfect Lady." *New Yorker* October 5, 1998: 94–104.

Rash, Ron. *Chemistry and Other Stories.* New York: Henry Holt, 2007.

———. "The Importance of Place." *Marly Rusoff Literary Agency.* 2014. Web. August 15, 2014.

———. *Saints at the River.* New York: Henry Holt, 2004.

———. *Serena.* New York: HarperCollins, 2008.

———. "What Will Survive of Us." *Short Fiction: Stories Worth Reading.* Ed. Andre DuBus III. New York: Pearson, 2017. 35–45.

———. *The World Made Straight.* New York: Henry Holt, 2006.

Wallace, Emily. "Eudora Welty's Christmas Eggnog." *Garden and Gun.* 2015. Web. December 12, 2014.

Welty, Eudora. Preface. *One Time One Place: Mississippi in the Depression.* Jackson: University Press of Mississippi, 1996. 7–12.

———. *Stories, Essays, and Memoir.* New York: Library of America, 1998.

———. "Where Is the Voice Coming From?" *New Yorker* July 6, 1963.

THE CHRIST-ABANDONED LANDSCAPE OF RASH'S *NOTHING GOLD CAN STAY*

Martha Greene Eads

What close reader of Ron Rash's fiction could begin to question Flannery O'Connor's deep and abiding influence on his work? Praising Rash's "fierce intellig[ence]," Silas House offered as an example of this influence in Rash's ability "to recite entire . . . passages from the writing of Flannery O'Connor" (13). Rash himself, describing the delight he has taken in being surprised by his own work, referred to O'Connor's account of writing her wickedly funny seduction story "Good Country People." He marveled that although the story's "shocking ending seems inevitable, . . . O'Connor said that while writing, she didn't know the leg would be stolen until the moment it was" ("In the Beginning"). Rash also claimed that "A Good Man Is Hard to Find" is "as perfect as any story I know" (Charney). In a 2009 interview, he revealed to Randall Wilhelm and Jesse Graves that O'Connor "glower[s] down" at him from a photo on his office wall as he writes (6). The degree to which much of Rash's short fiction resembles O'Connor's is striking. Beyond their births and experiences as southerners and their artistic decisions to write about hardscrabble rural settings—hers in Georgia and his in North Carolina—Rash's and O'Connor's work share a twisted sense of humor, and each writer has delighted in giving smart-alecky characters their comeuppances. Like O'Connor, Rash has also demonstrated a keen awareness of the religious influences on his characters, but Christianity does little or nothing in either writer's stories to shield those characters from violence and suffering.

O'Connor, of course, is famous for her frequent use of violence to awaken her characters to their inadequate spiritual condition. An assault in a doctor's office launches Ruby Turpin on a surprising interior quest in "Revelation"; Sheppard's young son's suicide forces him to face his own internal poverty in "The Lame Shall Enter First"; being fatally gored by a bull enables the hard-hearted Mrs. May finally to glimpse grace in "Greenleaf." O'Connor explained her artistic strategy in her essay "On Her Own Work": "I have found that violence is strangely capable of returning my characters to reality and preparing them to accept their moment of grace. Their heads are so hard that almost nothing else will do the work" (*Mystery and Manners* 112). Elsewhere she confessed, "It seems to me that all good stories are about conversion, about a character's changing" (*Habit of Being* 275). More often than not, O'Connor's characters' conversions result directly from their encounters with violence.

For O'Connor's characters, violent suffering and even humiliation are harbingers of hope. As a devout Roman Catholic struggling to communicate the Gospel to an audience she perceived to be increasingly secular, O'Connor hoped the bizarre elements in her fiction would awaken her readers to the need they share with her characters for spiritual deliverance. She discussed this intention in "The Fiction Writer and His Country":

> The novelist with Christian concerns will find in modern life distortions which are repugnant to him, and his problem will be to make these appear as distortions to an audience which is used to seeing them as natural; and he may well be forced to take ever more violent means to get his vision across to this hostile audience. When you can assume that your audience holds the same beliefs you do, you can relax a little and use more normal means of talking to it; when you have to assume that it does not, then you have to make your vision apparent by shock—to the hard of hearing you shout, and for the almost-blind you draw large and startling figures. (*Mystery and Manners* 33–34)

The "Christian concerns" to which O'Connor referred include the recognition of both humanity's sinful condition and the atonement for and deliverance from sin available through Jesus Christ. Contemporary readers' senses are dulled, she suggested elsewhere, by exposure to increasing levels of nihilistic thinking: "If you live today, you breathe in nihilism. In or out of the Church, it's the gas you breathe" (*Habit of Being* 97). Repeatedly O'Connor showed that even those in the South she famously described as "Christ-haunted" are suffering nihilism's effects.

Also writing in the "Christ-haunted" South, Rash has shared O'Connor's concern about sin and its effects. Some readers might argue that this central, shared concern confirms Rash's status as O'Connor's literary and even theological descendent. The difference in their handling of this concern, however, serves as a reminder that no writer springs, Athena-like, from another's head. If O'Connor is—arguably—Ron Rash's literary and theological mother, then a literary-philosophical paternity test would likely point to William James. John Lang, in discussing Rash's novel *Saints at the River,* explained the significance of Rash's having used an epigraph from William James's chapter on saintliness in *The Varieties of Religious Experience: A Study in Human Nature.* In *Varieties,* based on the Gifford Lectures he delivered at the University of Edinburgh in 1901 and 1902, James explored commonalities among individuals from various traditions and thus called into question Christianity's uniqueness.

In describing Rash's religious perspective, Lang quoted from James's description of ascetics of all faiths who believe "that there is an element of real wrongness in the world, which is neither to be ignored nor evaded, but which must be squarely met and overcome by an appeal to the soul's heroic resources, and neutralized and cleansed by suffering" (Lang 70; James 362). Lang asserted that "James's view of asceticism parallels in significant ways Rash's sense of Appalachian stoicism and of the world as decidedly postlapsarian" (70). The stoic element Lang identified is the point at which Rash's fiction diverges most sharply from O'Connor's. Both writers have recognized humanity's sin-wracked condition, and their stories call for repentance and atonement. In Rash's fiction, however, the Christ to whom O'Connor directs her characters (and her readers) for salvation is conspicuously absent.

Roger Lundin's discussion of William James's impact on American religious life offers clues about this absence. In *Believing Again: Doubt and Faith in a Secular Age,* Lundin looked to James, Charles Darwin, and Aldous Huxley as the sources of a nineteenth-century "materialist narrative [that] swept over the landscape of modern culture and into every corner of human life, including religious experience" (7). Such a narrative made "open unbelief . . . for the first time an intellectually viable and socially acceptable option in the countries of the North Atlantic" (104). Drawing from Richard Rorty's *Consequences of Pragmatism,* Lundin asserted that James, like Friedrich Nietzsche, "abandoned the 'notion of *discovering the truth,*' which is the foundation of theology and science, and embraced the imaginative power to create the truth, which is the cornerstone of poetry and the arts" (85). Lundin argued that many writers, including Emily Dickinson, Herman Melville, and Robert Frost, "have wrestled with belief and unbelief for the past two centuries, and they will no doubt continue to do so in the decades to come" (103). Rash's persistence in considering O'Connor's themes yet resistance to drawing conclusions similar to hers reveals the degree to which his work stands in the intellectual line Lundin traced, at least in part, of William James's. Although Lundin included O'Connor among those who wrestle with faith, it is her *characters* rather than herself who illustrate the struggle. Readers may mistake her as "a hillbilly nihilist," she observed in a 1955 letter to Robie Macauley, but she described herself instead as "a hillbilly Thomist" (*Habit of Being* 81). Consistently she points to Christ's church as the site of deliverance.

In contrast Rash's 2013 collection *Nothing Gold Can Stay* (the title of which comes from a poem by Robert Frost about the Fall) offers hope not in the form of conventional Christianity but instead in examples of the Jamesian ascetic's capacity to meet the world's wrongness with heroic inner resources. Rash's commentary on National Public Radio's call-in show *On Point* in January 2015 reveals a strikingly similar aesthetic. Noting his long-standing interest in "the hard considerations of the poor," Rash continued: "Very often what I think makes . . . stories work is when you have characters who are in such tough situations that the veneer falls away, and they reveal who they are, sometimes to themselves. And I think that's very rich, as far as literature, . . . those moments." Several stories in *Nothing Gold Can Stay* illustrate such self-revelation of the soul's resources. Three striking examples are "The Trusty," which opens the volume; "Those Who Are Dead Are Only Now Forgiven," which concludes the second of the book's three sections; and the "The Dowry," the second story in section 3.

In "The Trusty" Rash reenvisioned O'Connor's "Good Country People." In O'Connor's story, published in her 1948 collection *A Good Man Is Hard to Find,* a thirty-year-old philosophy Ph.D. named Joy Hopewell has moved back home, changing her name to "Hulga" to spite the mother off whom she is sponging. Undoubtedly Hulga has rejected along with her name any early Christian formation she has received, having replaced it with an intellectual naturalist view that, as Lundin wrote, "[traces] the origins of religious belief to the shadowy regions of human need, and [dismisses] out of hand the possibility that religious claims might actually be true" (116). Ralph Wood, in *Flannery O'Connor and the Christ-Haunted South,* claimed that Hulga is O'Connor's "nihilist philosopher" (181). When a boyish-looking Bible peddler named Manley Pointer shows up at her family farm, Hulga resolves to relieve him of his religious illusions by seducing him. Failing to note the significance of either his false name or the lightness of his valise when he returns to the farm for a picnic with her, Hulga leads him to the barn loft, where she tells him, "We are all damned, . . . but some of us have taken off our blindfolds and see that there's nothing to see. It's a kind of salvation" (O'Connor, "Good Country People" 191). When Pointer coaxes her to remove the prosthetic leg she has worn since a childhood accident, the tables turn. He reveals that his valise contains only two Bibles, one of them hollowed out to accommodate a flask, a package of condoms, and a deck of pornographic playing cards.

Hulga has no resources for responding to such a surprise. O'Connor wrote, "Her voice when she spoke had an almost pleading sound. 'Aren't you,' she murmured, 'aren't you just good country people?'" (195). Disgusted with Hulga's failure to show him the good time he had expected, Manley Pointer places her prosthesis in his valise and heads down the loft ladder, telling her derisively, "you ain't so smart. I been believing in nothing ever since I was born!" O'Connor recounted, "The girl was left sitting on the straw in the dusty sunlight. When she turned her churning face toward the opening, she saw his blue figure struggling successfully over the green speckled lake" (195). The Heideggerian Hulga finds herself out-nihiled by a huckster. In the story's two remaining paragraphs, O'Connor undercut the devastation in which she left her protagonist. Spotting Manley Pointer from the garden as he crosses the meadow, Hulga's mother observes to her hired help, Mrs. Freeman, "He was so simple . . . but I guess the world would be better off if we were all that simple." Mrs. Freeman replies, "Some can't be that simple. . . . I know I never could" (195). Any sympathy the reader might feel for the unfortunate but unsympathetic Hulga fades as the irony swells.

Rash employed irony in a similar way throughout "The Trusty." As in "Good Country People," a character who sets out to seduce another gets taken. Sinkler is a grifter on a prison work detail who has been entrusted with hauling water from local farms several times a day. When a plain young woman named Lucy Sorrels begrudgingly agrees to let him draw from her well, Sinkler decides she will do "to quench another kind of thirst" (*Nothing Gold Can Stay* 4). Over the next few days, Sinkler flirts with Lucy, erroneously concluding that she is as desperate to escape her life as he is his. Lucy eventually tells him that her much older husband "cusses me every day and won't let me go nowhere. When he's drunk, he fetches his rifle and swears he's going to shoot me" (15). Before long they have plans to flee together. Kissing Sinkler, Lucy tells him, "I been thirsting for that all last night and this morning. . . . That's what it's like—a thirsting. Chet ain't never been able to stanch it, but you can" (15). Now infatuated, Sinkler claims to have money saved for travel, and Lucy says she knows a footpath through the mountains to Asheville, where they can catch a train. When she suggests they can hock the silver locket her mother left her, Sinkler says, "And all this time I thought you had a heart of gold, Lucy Sorrels. . . . No, darling. You keep it around your pretty neck. I got plenty for tickets, and maybe something extra for a shiny bracelet to go with that necklace" (18). And when she tells him she dreams of California, he replies, "That's just where an angel like you belongs" (19).

This angel, however, is flying too close to the ground, and as the story collection's title warns, nothing *gold* can stay. Lucy leads Sinkler in circles around the farm, and he consistently fails to begin connecting the dots of her betrayal. Even when he hears Lucy's husband digging a grave, he remains oblivious, thinking simply that he and Lucy are emerging into a populated area near Asheville. Not until he kneels by a spring to drink and recognizes his handprint from an earlier stop does he realize what lies ahead for him: "He stared at the two star-shaped indentations, water slowly filling the new one. No one would hear the shot, he knew. . . . Leaves rustled as someone approached. The footsteps paused, and Sinkler heard the soft click of a rifle's safety being released. The leaves rustled again, but he was too worn out to run. They would want the clothes as well as the money, he told himself, and there was no reason to prolong any of it. His trembling fingers clasped the shirt's top button, pushed it through the slit in the chambray" (26). The humor in the story gives way to horror, and the fine-grained detail of the final image manages to stir sympathy and even a kind of admiration for a character who initially evokes suspicion and disdain along with amusement. The different outcomes of these two reverse-seduction stories exemplify the difference between O'Connor's and Rash's worldviews. In "Good Country People," Hulga's self-absorption and sense of superiority have cut her off not only from her mother and their neighbors but also from God. While the Bible salesman's betrayal has devastated her, it may prompt her to face the limits of her nihilistic view and her need for redemption. Wood discussed this possibility, writing:

> We last glimpse [Hulga] as she lies stranded in the hayloft, her churning face and bewildered eyes squinting after Pointer as he flees across the field. In her blinded vision, he appears to be a water-walking Christ: "She saw his blue figure struggling successfully across the green speckled lake. . . . Pointer is, in fact, [Hulga] Hopewell's unintentional savior, having stolen not so much her wooden leg as her false faith. . . . Having neither church nor creed to give her life moral formation and thus communal shape, Hulga has descended into an uglifying solipsism. Now at last she has the chance to become what she and all others are called to be, a creature utterly unlike her sinful self. She has suffered a blessed loss, a saving devastation, a deflowering not of her sexual virginity but of her virginal nihilism. If only by the negation of her Nothingness, she has been potentially freed for a positive life of communion with God and her mother—and perhaps even with the small-minded Mrs. Freeman. (208–9)

While O'Connor declined to assure us of Hulga's salvation, she leaves her, like so many of her other characters, in a position to receive grace—indeed in a position desperate for grace.

Many of these characters are autobiographical, as O'Connor biographers and critics have regularly observed. Undoubtedly aware of the materialist narrative's origins, O'Connor wrote to Father John McCown in 1962, "I have [James's] Gifford lecture, which meant a lot to me at one time" (*Habit of Being* 463). Although James was not himself a nihilist, Lundin demonstrated the way in which his pragmatism contributed to certain forms of nihilism, which O'Connor was ever ready to reject—perhaps most humorously in the letter to Robie Macauley cited earlier, where she frames herself as "a hillbilly Thomist" (*Habit of Being* 81). The humor with which O'Connor wrote that letter appears also in the ironically comic conclusion of "Good Country People," which leaves readers, as soon as they stop wincing at Hulga's plight, grinning over the exchange between her mother and Mrs. Freeman. The story—particularly when set alongside O'Connor's other short fiction, essays, and letters—dares readers to "hope well" that on the other side of her humiliation, Hulga will somehow find joy.

Rash made no such move in "The Trusty." Instead, in his story's final paragraph, he ennobled the despicable Sinkler by endowing him with a stoic response to his fate. Rash characterized Sinkler throughout the story as lazy, dishonest, manipulative, and even potentially murderous, only in the end to align him with that Jamesian description of a religious ascetic who recognizes "that there is an element of real wrongness in the world, which is neither to be ignored nor evaded, but which must be squarely met and overcome by an appeal to the soul's heroic resources, and neutralized and cleansed by suffering" (James 362). Readers might argue that Sinkler is merely resigning himself to his fate, but another interpretation is that he is meeting his final challenge with a surprising measure of existential courage.

Moreover, while Hulga's conversion brings her to the threshold of human and spiritual community, Sinkler's leaves him existentially alone. "No one would hear the shot," he realizes, "and, in a few weeks, when autumn came and the trees started to shed, the upturned earth would be completely obscured" (26). No one, aside from the marveling reader, benefits from his final surge of courage. In "Those Who Are Dead Are Only Now Forgiven," however, Rash depicted a far more admirable protagonist, whose final courageous act thrusts him squarely into community but nevertheless invites readers' horror and despair. Jody, returning to isolated Canton, North Carolina, after his first year at N.C. State, discovers that his girlfriend, Lauren, is cooking meth and living with two of their high school classmates, Katie Lynn and Billy Rankin, the bully who had tormented Jody for academically outperforming him and others in his social class. Rash described Jody's response to a humiliating incident in the cafeteria during their freshman year of high school: "Billy outweighed him by fifty pounds and Jody would have done nothing if Lauren hadn't been with him. He went after Billy, driving onto the linoleum, praying a teacher would break it up quick. But it was Lauren who got to them first. By the time a teacher intervened, Lauren had broken off two fingernails shredding Billy's left cheek" (*Nothing Gold Can Stay* 129).

Having been Jody's ally against Billy as well as against poverty and social stigmatization, Lauren had also spurred Jody on to academic excellence. When she decided inexplicably to stay home after graduation instead of going to college, Jody had assured her that he would earn enough as an engineer to make a good life for both of them. But within months of his departure for college, their long-distance relationship had faltered. By Christmas Lauren was using drugs; by spring break her mother and brother had had to find the money to put her in rehab. By the end of Jody's school year, Lauren is so relapsed that her brother has given up on her. When Jody returns home and finally sees her in the light of day, he observes that "Lauren's jeans hung loose on her hips, her teeth nubbed and discolored as Indian corn. Jody imagined a breed of meth heads evolving to veins and nose and mouth, just enough flesh on bone to keep the passageways open" (132–33). Still he loves her.

Failing to convince Lauren to leave Katie and Billy, he spends another night at his mother's shabby house, remembering his guidance counselor's advice: "Lauren has let both of us down, . . . but don't let that keep you from achieving what you want in life" (142). As Rash described that long night, including Jody's staring at Internet images of meth addicts in decline and subsequently packing a suitcase, readers anticipate Jody's return to college. As the story draws to a close, however, Jody goes back to the meth house, urging Lauren to leave, telling her that he will not ask her again. "I can't, baby," Lauren replies. "I just can't." His loyalty overcoming his good judgment, Jody retrieves his suitcase from the car to cast his lot with Lauren. The story's final paragraph, briefer than "The Trusty's," is equally devastating: "Turn on the fire, Billy," Katie Lynn said as she filled the [meth] pipe. "This boy's been a long time out in the cold" (143). The imagery is apt. Jody's self-sacrificing love may remind readers of Christ's, but his descent into hell will not end on a third day.

Again Rash has demonstrated his keen awareness of humanity's fallen condition, but in this story he also showed how aspects of the Christian tradition—or at least a certain form of Christian religiosity—leave Lauren hopeless. When Jody first urges her to go home with him, she says, "Haven't you heard? Bad girls don't get to go home. They don't even get prayed for, at least that's what [my brother] says" (132). She tells him that she has what she needs—meth—where she is. "The Lord provides," she taunts him. "Isn't that what we learned in church? Has being around all those atheist professors caused you to lose your faith, Jody, like Reverend Wilkinson's wife warned us about in Sunday school?" (133–34). It is no coincidence, of course, that at the center of the meth house living room is a "felt-lined collection plate on the floor, among its sparse coins and bills a glass pipe and baggie" (131). Jody's final act in the story, upon returning to the house with his suitcase, is to take "the money from his pocket and place it in the collection plate" (143). Clearly, Christian faith as these characters have encountered it is inadequate to exorcise them of the demons of poverty, broken family systems, and drug addiction.

Carmen Rueda overoptimistically called Jody's "transformative experience" an "epiphany—a revealing moment of change in which the protagonist suddenly understands what is really important for him. Over the brief promise of personal triumph away from the mountains thanks to college education, Jody chooses love and loyalty, as he refuses to suppress his emotions and values to reach success" (86). Although she did not join John Lang in looking to William

James for insight into Rash's work, Rueda's characterization of Jody as a sort of existential hero is reminiscent of James's description of the saintly (Christian or otherwise) ascetic's response to evil. While some individuals, James wrote, "by fortunate health and circumstances, [escape personal] suffering of any great amount of evil [and] endeavor to ignore its existence in the wider universe," the ascetic regards

> such optimism . . . a shallow dodge or mean evasion. It accepts, in lieu of a real deliverance, what is a lucky personal accident merely, a cranny to escape by. It leaves the general world unhelped and still in the clutch of Satan. . . . If one has ever taken the fact of the prevalence of tragic death in this world's history fairly into his mind,—freezing, drowning, entombment alive, wild beasts, worse men, and hideous diseases,—he can with difficulty, it seems to me, continue his own career with worldly prosperity without suspecting that he may all the while not be really inside the game, that he may lack the great initiation.
>
> Well, this is exactly what asceticism thinks; and it voluntarily takes the initiation. (362–63)

Jody's guidance counselor's advice—not to let Lauren's self-destructive choice prevent him from making his own escape—cannot counter his internal call to enter into suffering with her. Love has prompted him to take up a cross, the significance of which James acknowledges: "The folly of the cross, so inexplicable by the intellect, has yet its indestructible vital meaning" (364). James, in offering his account of religious experience that extends beyond traditional Christianity, thus provided Rash's readers with a framework for acknowledging Jody's sacrifice as religious without making him a conventional literary Christ figure.

Looking for such a Christ figure in "The Dowry," Rueda described the protagonist of that story, Pastor Boone, as "the sacrificial lamb that takes away the world's sin" and a characterization of Appalachia as "a region that has often been sacrificed for the benefit of the rest of America" (87). Certainly the story focuses on sin, and much of Rash's work reveals his concern—even his outrage—about the rape of Appalachia. "The Dowry," however, is not a story of redemption in any Christian sense but instead an illustration of the modern decline of faith Roger Lundin described, a decline that extends far beyond Appalachia.

In the story's opening image and conversation, Rash signaled that "The Dowry" depicts a world in which traditional Christian faith falters. "The garden angel's wings were submerged," Pastor Boone observes through his window, "the redbud's dark branches damasked white" (*Nothing Gold Can Stay* 173). As he braces himself to make a pastoral call in the bitter weather, his housekeeper warns him about catching "the ague" and threatens that "instead of hearing yourself read the Good Book, you'll be hearing it read over your coffin." Teasing her gently about her eschatological interpretation, he sets forth in his buggy. Declining the driving assistance of her husband (whose Sabbath observance is apparently more worthy of preserving than the housekeeper's own), Pastor Boone begins planning the next week's sermon. "Instead of a chapter of Acts on mercy, he pondered the opening verse in Obadiah, *The pride of thine own heart hath deceived thee,*" Rash wrote (178).

The first five pages invite readers to interpret Boone's change of plan as a rebuke of the man he is preparing to visit, Leland Davidson. Davidson, a Confederate veteran, lost a hand in battle and has refused to let his daughter Helen marry Union veteran Ethan Burke unless Burke will amputate his own hand. Pastor Boone makes his way to talk sense into Davidson—to secure permission for his star-crossed parishioner-sweethearts to marry. In a battle of the Bible in the Davidson parlor, Pastor Boone and Colonel Davidson each reach for scriptural support:

> "Colossians says *Forgive as the Lord forgave you.*"
>
> "So you have come to bandy verses," the Colonel said, tugging back the sleeve so firelight reddened the stubbed wrist. "*Life shall go for life, eye for eye, tooth for tooth,* thus hand for hand."
>
> "Luke says *love your enemies, do good to them.*"
>
> "Leviticus says to chase our enemies," Colonel Davidson countered, "*and they shall Fall before you by the sword.*"
>
> "You quote overly from the Old Testament," Pastor Boone said, "Therein lies more retribution than forgiveness."
>
> "Yet they are cleaved together as one book," Colonel Davidson answered. "Thus we choose which answers to live by." (181)

Certainly their debate illustrates the struggle to reconcile the apparent conflict between the Old Testament's emphasis on justice and the New Testament's elevation of mercy. Rash was, however, going beyond illustrating this tension to point out another: the modern tension between belief and unbelief that developed in response to what Lundin called the "materialist narrative," a tension that Pastor Boone embodies (Ludlin 7). The story's postbellum timing is right; Lundin observed that "the trauma of the Civil War" and "the shock of the Darwinian revolution" presented a double assault on traditional Christian belief in the United States (78).

Appropriately Rash places the writings of Darwin and Thomas Huxley at least on the periphery if not at the center of Pastor Boone's consciousness. After his biblical sparring match with Colonel Davidson, Pastor Boone turns to his physician-friend Noah Andrews, whose office "served as a salon for the best-educated men in Marshall to discuss everything from literature and politics to science and religion" (184). On Andrews's office shelves, *Man's Place in Nature* and *On the Origin of the Species* rest alongside works by Shakespeare, Scott, and Thackeray. "An oil lamp . . . its flame alive" illuminates this temple of learning, and "a lacquered darkness gave the office the aura of a confessional booth, which, like the room's seeming immutability, no doubt made it easier to speak of fears too often confirmed" (185). Responding to Pastor Boone's observations that Dr. Andrews's imported pipe did not take long to arrive, the latter responds, "I only wish ideas could cross the ocean as quickly" (187). When Pastor Boone convinces Dr. Andrews to satisfy Colonel Davidson's bloody demand by performing a surgical amputation, the physician fumes, "I can't believe I've allowed you to talk me into this barbarism, and for no other reason than some bundles of papyrus written thousands of years ago. We may as well be living in mud huts, grinding rocks to make fire. Huxley and his X Club will soon end such nonsense in England, but in this country we still believe the recidivists not the innovators bring advancement in human endeavors" (190). As the surgical procedure begins, Dr. Andrews takes up the subject Mrs. Newell had broached as the story opens: the resurrection of the dead. Clearly he is more skeptical than she about its historicity.

Whether the dead—Christ specifically—can be raised is central to this story's conflict. Passages about mercy in the New Testament book of Acts—one of which Pastor Boone has rejected for his next week's sermon—follow closely on assertions about Christ's resurrection. Acts opens with a description of Christ's ascension forty days after His resurrection, and the next chapter recounts Peter's Pentecost sermon, in which he identifies Christ as not only as King David's descendent ("Davidson?") but also the fulfillment of David's prophetic vision of a messianic resurrection. Those who heard this sermon and subsequently trusted in Christ were baptized, witnessed, and performed miracles, subsequently establishing a radically joyful, hospitable, and merciful community (Acts 2:41–47). Biblical scholar N. T. Wright asserted in *Acts For Everyone* that "the good news, the great news, of Jesus is that with his resurrection it becomes clear not only that he is Messiah and Lord, but that in his death he has dealt evil itself a blow from which, though it still retains some power, it will never recover" (39).

Roger Lundin asserted that this good news of Christian faith was no longer a surety for many educated people by the mid-nineteenth century. Quoting from James Turner's *Without God, Without Creed: The Origins of Unbelief in America* (1985), Lundin asserted that religious doubt gave rise to agnosticism, a belief system that "entailed both a 'permanent suspension of belief in God' and a stubborn inability to rest in the reality of God." Noting that Thomas Huxley coined the term "agnostism" in 1869, Lundin argued that it "quickly 'became the distinctively modern unbelief' and established itself as a 'self-sustaining phenomenon'" in the decades after the American Civil War (104). In "The Dowry" Doctor Andrews exemplifies this postbellum agnosticism.

His friend Pastor Boone, although a clergyman, is not immune to agnosticism. His shift in sermon text from Acts is the evidence. Of course Obadiah is a judgment passage, and Davidson certainly deserves to be judged. Rash made clear, however, that Pastor Boone reads Obadiah as a judgment of his own life rather than of Davidson's. Rash wrote, "To hold together what frayed benevolence remained in the church, a pastor need appear neutral. . . . Yet there were times, he suspected his silence [about his Union sympathies] had been mere cowardice" (175). A few pages later, he reflects, "Even in the war's brutal last winter, he had never lacked firewood and food, and, childless, no son to fear for. No outliers had abused him. Almost alone in that dark time, he, Christ's shepherd, had been blessed" (177). It is glimpsing the prints of young Ethan's poorly repaired boots in the snow from his own relatively luxurious buggy, not a direct encounter with the cruel Davidson, that prompts Pastor Boone's consideration of Obadiah 1:3: "The pride of thine heart hath deceived thee" (178). The rest of the verse, which Rash omitted, reads, "thou that dwellest in the clefts of the rock, whose habitation is high; that saith in his heart, Who shall bring me down to the ground?" Pastor Boone is the character guilty of having taken refuge in his own "high habitation" during the war, and he knows that he must pay for his sin.

Thus Pastor Boone determines, when Davidson will not agree to lift his hand-for-a-hand demand, to sacrifice his own hand—not only as a dowry but as a payment for his own wartime forms of idolatry: congregational conflict avoidance and material comfort. He exemplifies William James's observation in *Varieties of Religious Experience* that "the desire to gain wealth and the fear to lose it are our chief breeders of cowardice and propagators of corruption," and he despises himself for doing so (308). Confronted with the suffering resulting from the Civil War, including the suffering Colonel Davidson is inflicting on Helen and Ethan, and deprived of the spiritual resources a more robust Christian faith might have offered him, Pastor Boone has no choice but, in Jamesian terms, to "voluntarily [take] the initiation" into suffering. When Dr. Andrews observes that "it always comes down to guilt, does it not, that and somebody's blood. Your religion, I mean," Pastor Boone replies, "I suppose, though I would add that hope is also a factor" (190). He himself, however, must undergo amputation to extend hope to Helen and Ethan and to claim it for himself. If Christ's crucifixion has not resulted in a sure triumph over evil and death through resurrection, the saintly ascetic must embrace some sort of salvific sacrifice of his own.

Rash's decision to focus on the sacrifice of a hand has biblical resonance, of course; many readers of "The Dowry" will remember both the Old Testament eye-for-an-eye passage Colonel Davidson cites and Jesus's provocative challenge to radical obedience in Matthew 5 and Mark 9. Fewer, perhaps, are aware of another striking literary connection, to Emily Dickinson's "Those—dying then."

Lundin asserted that her 1882 poem describes the spiritual loss many have experienced with the rise of unbelief:

> Those—dying then,
> Knew where they went—
> They went to God's Right Hand—
> That Hand is amputated now
> And God cannot be found—
>
> The abdication of Belief
> Makes the Behavior small—
> Better an ignis fatuus
> Than no illume at all—(1069)

Lundin explained, "Dickinson here refuses to place the blame for the loss of belief. She renders the amputation of God's hand in the passive voice, and with the word 'abdication' she leaves it unclear whether God's disappearance is a result of divine self-mutilation or a parricidal act of human aggression. What is clear is that belief's abdication has created a void in the lives of many who had once rested in its assurances" (114). Whether or not Rash had Dickinson's poem in mind when he wrote "The Dowry," the two works function similarly to illustrate unbelief's tightening grasp since the U.S. Civil War.

For Dickinson, Lundin pointed out, as for many other modern poets, novelists, and dramatists, unbelief became a way station within belief. He quoted a line from a letter she wrote around the same time as "Those—dying then": "On subjects, of which we know nothing, or should I say *Beings*—we both believe, and disbelieve a hundred times an Hour, which keeps Believing nimble" (Ludlin 115). Like Dickinson, Pastor Boone likely moves back and forth from belief to unbelief. He, however, like Jody and Sinkler, comes to the limits of his wisdom, ability, and strength in the face of evil. Rash used all three characters to suggest, at least obliquely, in *Nothing Gold Can Stay* that the hope Christian faith once offered cannot meet the demands suffering makes on modern women and men shaped by the materialist narrative. O'Connor recognized this difficulty, but her "hillbilly Thomism" enables her to counter it by directing her agnostic characters through their encounters with violence to Christ's cross and subsequently to the church. For Rash, as for William James, the cross offers no surety, no uniquely salvific power. *Nothing Gold Can Stay* echoes James's advice in "The Value of Saintliness":

> In a general way, then, and "on the whole," our abandonment of theological criteria, and our testing of religion by practical common sense and the empirical method, leave it in possession of its towering place in history.

> Economically, the saintly group of qualities is indispensable to the world's welfare. The great saints are immediate successes; the smaller ones are at least heralds and harbingers, and they may be leavens also, of a better mundane order. Let us be saints, then, if we can, whether or not we succeed visibly and temporally. But in our Father's house are many mansions, and each of us must discover for himself the kind of religion and the amount of saintship which best comports with what he believes to be his powers and feels to be his truest mission and vocation. There are no successes to be guaranteed and no set orders to be given to individuals, so long as we follow the methods of empirical philosophy. (377)

Rash accepted the label "a religious man" in an interview with Thomas Ærvold Bjerre (222), and Anna Dunlap Higgins noted that his "own particular background, passed down to him via his mother's line, was Southern Baptist, although not the staid version one might imagine." Higgins asserted that "the poet is a deeply spiritual man, believing in the grace of second birth" (53). The nature of such birth, however, at least as it appears in *Nothing Gold Can Stay,* is uncertain. It is certainly less overtly Christian than O'Connor's. While she stripped away her characters' phony virtues entirely, offering them Christ's grace instead, Rash's characters find no help from God but discover their own capacity to respond with human grace to suffering. When I asked Rash directly about this matter during the call-in segment of his January *On Point* interview, he was elusive. Noting his short fiction's similarities to and differences from Flannery O'Connor's, I asked him if he believes that the Christ who died for sins in O'Connor's twentieth-century fiction has abandoned the South in the twenty-first. Chuckling a bit, he replied: "That's a tough one. . . . That's a very interesting idea; I hadn't thought of it that way, but I think very often what I am interested in very often is putting people in my stories, sometimes my novels, who are willing to sacrifice themselves for others. O'Connor remains one of my favorite writers, I would say that, but in some ways—important ways—I think we're very different, and I think what [you're] talking about is part of that." *Nothing Gold Can Stay* reveals that difference to be the intellectual patrimony Rash received from William James.

Works Cited

Bjerre, Thomas Ærvold. "'The Natural World Is the Most Universal of Languages': An Interview with Ron Rash." *Appalachian Journal* 34 (2007): 216–27.

Charney, Noah. "Ron Rash: How I Write." *Daily Beast.* February 27, 2013. Web.

Dickinson, Emily. *The Poems of Emily Dickinson.* Ed. Thomas H. Johnson. 3 vols. Cambridge, Mass.: Harvard University Press, 1955.

Higgins, Anna Dunlap. "Anything but Surrender: Preserving Southern Appalachia in the Works of Ron Rash." *North Carolina Literary Review* 13 (2004): 49–58.

House, Silas. "Making Himself Heard." *Appalachian Heritage* 30.4 (Fall 2002): 11–14.

James, William. "The Value of Saintliness." *The Varieties of Religious Experience: A Study in Human Nature.* 1902. Middlesex, England: Penguin, 1985. 221–51.

Lang, John. *Understanding Ron Rash.* Columbia: University of South Carolina Press, 2014.

Lundin, Roger. *Believing Again: Doubt and Faith in a Secular Age.* Grand Rapids: Eerdmans, 2009.

O'Connor, Flannery. "Good Country People." *A Good Man Is Hard to Find and Other Stories.* 1948. San Diego: Harvest/Harcourt Brace Jovanovich, 1983. 169–96.

———. *The Habit of Being: Letters Edited and with an Introduction by Sally Fitzgerald.* New York: Farrar, Straus and Giroux, 1979.

———. *Mystery and Manners: Occasional Prose Selected and Edited by Sally and Robert Fitzgerald.* New York: Farrar, Straus and Giroux, 1962.

Rash, Ron. "In the Beginning." *Wall Street Journal* March 9, 2013: C12.

———. Interview with Tom Graham. "On Point." *NPR.org.* NPR. January 22, 2015. Web. March 24, 2015.

———. *The Night the New Jesus Fell to Earth and Other Stories from Cliffside, North Carolina.* 1994. Columbia: University of South Carolina Press, 2015.

———. *Nothing Gold Can Stay.* New York: HarperCollins, 2013.

Rueda, Carmen. "Transience and Change in Appalachia: Ron Rash's *Nothing Gold Can* Stay." *Appalachian Journal* 42.1–2 (Fall 2014/Winter 2015): 82–89.

Wilhelm, Randall, and Jesse Graves. "An Interview with Ron Rash." In "P.S.: Insights, Interviews and More." *Serena.* By Ron Rash. New York: HarperCollins, 2009. 3–8.

Wood, Ralph. *Flannery O'Connor and the Christ-Haunted South.* Grand Rapids: Eerdmans, 2004.

Wright, N. T. *Acts for Everyone. Part One: Chapters 1–12.* Louisville: Westminster John Knox, 2008.

"BEYOND GENDER"

Subversion and the Creation of Chaos in *Serena* and *Macbeth*

Barbara Bennett

When Ron Rash's *Serena* was published in 2008, the *New York Times* noted about the book's title character that her "inability to sleep well is not this book's only intimation of Lady Macbeth. In a novel punctuated by monstrous logging accidents . . . she schemes and thrives" (Maslin). More can be found in the parallels between Lady Macbeth and Serena, however, than just insomnia and their propensity to scheme and thrive. Both women subvert female gender expectations and, by doing so, disrupt a balance of order in nature, in the community, and in the universe. Serena's subversion of traditional gender roles parallels the disruption of the logging camp and its surrounding environs, much like Macbeth and Lady Macbeth challenge the natural order and societal conventions in their own world, suggesting in both cases that when order is disrupted, lives are ruined and lost, and chaos reigns until order is restored.

Most contemporary scholars see gender as a cultural construct rather than a biological fact. Judith Butler, for one, asked if "being female constitute[s] a 'natural fact' or a cultural performance" (xxxi), and Simone de Beauvoir asserted, "One is not born a woman, but rather becomes one" (249). If these writers are correct, Lady Macbeth and Serena are simply refusing to play the role assigned to them by society, instead choosing their actions consciously to move beyond expectations of female behavior. By refusing to live by traditional gender roles, though, the two female characters vilify themselves in the eyes of men, while at the same time raising themselves to an almost supernatural level through intimidation of men who fear the unknowable female. Men in Shakespeare's play and Rash's novel simply do not know what to do with seemingly "masculinized" women. These male characters have been taught that women behave a certain way, and when they are faced with a woman who subverts those expectations, they are stumped into inaction.

Consider for example the physical descriptions of Serena. In the opening chapter of Rash's novel, Serena's physicality is given a large amount of attention. Rash described her as tall—taller than both her husband's partners, Wilkie and Buchanan—and she dresses in men's clothing. When she steps from the train to the planks of the station, even though there is a two-foot gap between them, she "did not reach for [her husband's] hand" (5). As soon as she meets Buchanan, she berates him for an inadequate handshake—we must assume he gives her a soft hand because she is a woman. In contrast, Rash wrote, Buchanan's and Wilkie's wives are distinctly feminine and avoid altogether the logging camp, which they see as too rough and uncivilized. Later on we learn Serena is not shy about her body, as most women are in her husband's experience (20); she rides a horse like a man, straddling its back (21), and she seems "the equal of any man" (22).

Emotionally, too, she breaks gender stereotypes. Pembroke, her husband, tells the sheriff, "It's not her nature to make outward shows of emotion" (149). She is ambitious and loves power; she is dominant and even pitiless. In an early scene, she quotes Medea, another woman well known for thwarting gender expectations by killing her own children, when Serena says, "*Myself will grip the sword—yea, though I die*" (18). Yet Serena refuses to acknowledge her behavior as unusual and adamantly defends herself. To Cheney, who makes a snide comment about women lacking analytical skills, she answers, "Obviously, your views on my sex were formed by the slatterns you grew up with [in the mountains], but I assure you the natures of women are more various than your limited experience allows" (34).

Men in Shakespeare's drama make the same mistake of assuming Lady Macbeth is as frail as other women around her. When Macduff is forced to tell Lady Macbeth that the king has been murdered, he says, "O gentle lady, / 'Tis not for you to hear what I can speak: / The repetition, as in a woman's ear, / Would murder as it fell" (2.3.85–88), having no idea, of course, that she is behind the murder. Most telling, though, is of course Lady Macbeth's soliloquy in which she beseeches the spirits to separate her from any "feminine" weaknesses that she might have and replace them with powerful and violent "masculine" strengths:

> Come, you spirits
> That tend on mortal thoughts, unsex me here,
> And fill me, from the crown to the toe, top-full
> Of direst cruelty! Make thick my blood,
> Stop up th' access and passage to remorse,
> That no compunctious visitings of nature
> Shake my fell purpose, not keep peace between

Th' effect and it! Come to my woman's breasts,
And take my milk for gall, you murd'ring ministers,
Wherever in your sightless substances
You wait on nature's mischief! Come, thick night,
And pall thee in the dunnest smoke of hell,
That my keen knife see not the wound it makes,
Nor heaven peep through the blanket of the dark,
To cry, 'Hold, hold!' (1.5. 41–55)

This speech illustrates Lady Macbeth's belief that gender roles can be put on and taken off like an article of clothing. Judy Celine A. Ick explained, "Unlike Macbeth for whom identity is circumscribed, [Lady Macbeth] displays a sense of the possibility of unlimited identities. Her 'unsex me here' speech suggests the perception that her body is a mere vessel for roles" (89). In fact, she goes on, "in *Macbeth,* all significant female characters display an awareness if not a masterful exploitation of the idea that things need not be as they seem, that meaning is arbitrary" (84). An instance of this is the "doubling confusion of the witches' language [that] springs from the manipulation of the division between appearances and the underlying realities"—when, for example, Lady Macbeth tells her husband, "look like th'innocent flower, But be the serpent under't" (1.5.66–68). What one looks like may have little to do with a person's essential self.

Like Pemberton, Macbeth sees, understands, and perhaps fears the masculine in his wife. He recognizes that her power lies in her ability to deny gendered behavior and take on instead traditional traits of men. He also fears what that deviation might do to others and the community in which they live. Macbeth goes as far as to warn his wife to give birth to boys only, that her influence might corrupt young girls: "Bring forth men-children only; / For thy undaunted mettle should compose / Nothing but males" (1.7.73–75). Both Pemberton and Macbeth need their wives to be fearless and strong, but both seem to sense the possible consequences for the denial of the feminine.

At the beginning of the novel, Pemberton is very comfortable with his own masculinity and seems to feel no fear of his wife usurping his power. Because he wields such domination over his workers and the natural environment, he feels secure; as Michael Kimmel noted in "Masculinity as Homophobia," "we equate manhood with being strong, successful, capable, reliable, in control" (125), and at the start of the novel, Pemberton is all these things. His wife's power in public is tempered by her submission to him in private—sexually, as well as when he sees her weak when she is training her eagle. As Rachel Willis pointed out in "Masculinities and Murder: George Pemberton in Ron Rash's *Serena,*" women work as a kind of currency men use to "improve their ranking on the masculine social scale" (quoting Kimmel 129), and thus "Serena's public dominance enhances Pemberton's masculine identity by making others believe Pemberton is unconcerned about asserting his own power" (Willis 19). It is only when Pemberton's manhood is challenged—when Galloway begins serving Serena, doing things she does not trust to her husband—that he falls in status and eventually fails as a man. In the end, as he is dying, he yearns to make it back to camp, "not so much to survive as prove to Serena he was strong enough after all, worthy of her" (Rash 366–67).

Both Serena and Lady Macbeth use their power to manipulate their husbands into murder, the women being more ambitious than their mates. Serena tells Pemberton that she will commit the murder herself if necessary (141), and Lady Macbeth goads Macbeth into action by questioning his manhood; when Macbeth says, "I dare do all that may become a man," Lady Macbeth answers, "What beast was't then / that made you break . . . Be so much more the man" (1.7.46–47), and she later questions him with "Are you a man? (3.4.59), concluding, "What, quite unmanned in folly" (3.4.73). Moreover both men, before their first kills, have to talk themselves into the deed. Macbeth debates the act in his soliloquy that begins with "Is this a dagger which I see before me / The handle toward my hand?" (2.1.32–33), and Pemberton thinks, "*Do this one thing,* he told himself, reciting the words like a mantra, as he'd done since he'd awakened at first light" (146). Once the murders are complete, both men are satisfied, but their wives see the first death only as a beginning. When Pemberton says, "It's over and done with and we've got all we wanted," Serena answers, "At least for today. . . . A start, a true beginning" (152).

In a powerful connection between Serena and Lady Macbeth, both women are childless, (although Lady Macbeth claims she has "given suck" [1.7.54], it appears that no child survives), as if their denial of the feminine has made them expressly unsuitable to be mothers. Additionally both stories contain foils for the women, females with strong maternal abilities that make their counterparts more masculine by comparison. Ick described Lady Macduff "as the ideal mother who functions to make starkly horrible the role that Lady Macbeth has so unnaturally perverted" (73). In addition Ick claimed that in contrast to Lady Macbeth's rejection of her gender's behavior, critics have pointed out that Duncan has maternal qualities and serves as both father and mother to the kingdom. Finally, as a specific example of Lady Macbeth's unnatural inclinations, she admits to being willing to "dash out her baby's brains" to get what she wants (Ick 78).

Serena, in comparison, is able to conceive but unable to carry the baby to term. When she decides, however, that it is time to become pregnant, she does so within a more masculine framework of violence and blood. As she tells Pemberton that "it's time to make our heir" (153), her abdomen is smeared with Buchanan's blood, and she refuses to wash it off. It may be that her inability to give birth to a live child is related to her focus on the present rather than the future. She cannot sacrifice her own goals and aspirations for wealth and power for a child and its future. In one conversation with Kephart—during which he remarks that he is working on the national park "for the future"—Serena says, "What future? Where is it? . . . All I see is the here and now" (136).

In contrast to Serena's lack of maternal instincts, Rash offered Rachel, Pemberton's premarriage dalliance. Rachel becomes pregnant easily—too easily, perhaps, for the time and place—but she takes to it naturally and, unlike Serena, is willing to sacrifice everything to secure the safety of and future for her son, Jacob. When she and her baby both become ill, she walks a mile barefoot while feverish and delirious to get help for him. Her sacrifice for her child only reinforces her role as maternal ideal, in contrast to Serena, who seemingly refuses to sacrifice anything for anyone but herself. And while Serena destroys nature deliberately and systematically—such as when she suggests the rattlesnakes should all be killed off, despite the role they play in keeping the rodent population in check—Rachel is nurturing, preserving the forest for the future while gathering ginseng, digging "a good six inches around the ginseng plant to insure she didn't cut the root" by mistake, then she "separated the berries from the ginseng plants and placed them in the broken soil," presumably so she would have a crop the next year (79). Her focus is always on the future. She grew up in harmony with nature, learning from the land the lessons it had to teach (50). The adherence to the "natural" order of a woman's role in this era is a direct affront to Serena, and attempting to kill Rachel and her baby is the only response that nonmaternal Serena can muster, especially in conjunction with her rage that Rachel has given Pemberton what she has not be able to.

The gender upheaval in each female character is paralleled by an upheaval in nature. In *Macbeth* this is illustrated with the "weird sisters." While assuming that witches are female, Banquo is nonetheless put off by their masculine appearance. He says, "You should be women, / And yet your beards forbid me to interpret / That you are so" (1.3.45–47). Shakespeare connected the witches to Lady Macbeth in several ways, one of which is their denial of traditional female behavior. Ick claimed that Lady Macbeth's power—like that of the witches—"is both demonized and valorized. Women in power are aligned with villains or the supernatural" (33). And like the witches, Lady Macbeth is "stripped" of her power rather swiftly (Ick 75), something that happens to Serena only in her death.

Serena, like Lady Macbeth and the witches, is also aligned with the supernatural. Riding on the white Arabian horse, Serena blends into the snow so "she appeared to ride the air itself," and the men who observe this phenomenon exaggerate her abilities in their minds: they "ascribed all sorts of powers to Serena, some bordering on the otherworldly" (68). For example they believe that Serena takes the rattlesnakes her eagle hunts and milks them, "coating her tongue with the poison" (102). Even more than the supernatural, she borders on the mythical: "At a distance, horse, eagle, and human appeared to blend into one being, as though transmogrified into some winged six-legged creature from the old myths" (102). Pemberton has heard the rumors that "Serena fed the eagle the hearts of animals as well, to make the bird fiercer, but Pemberton had never seen her do such a thing and believed it just one more bit of the camp's lore about Serena" (175). Like *Macbeth*'s witches, Serena is believed to control the natural elements, and when Galloway loses his hand, one of the men claims it was not a tourniquet that saves his life but Serena's power: "She just commanded it to stop and not a drip flowed out after that" (186). Finally, when she is pregnant, another man describes a ritual he believes Serena practices: "I heard she's just eating bloody beef for her breakfast and supper. . . . To make that young one of hers all the fiercer. And that ain't the half of it. Come the night she bares her belly to the moon, soaking in all its power" (201).

Serena is not the only female to be assigned supernatural abilities in Rash's novel. The mother of Galloway, Serena's right-hand man, is a sort of seer—blind from cataracts but able to "see things other folks can't" (56). Like Shakespeare's witches she often prophesies characters' futures. She can even find people who do not want to be found, such as those whom her son has been tasked to murder. She tells her son, for example, that Rachel and her baby have gone to a place that "was a crown set amongst the mountains," a mountain community the reader learns is called Kingsport (284).

As part of the disruption of the natural world, Serena and Pemberton's destruction of the landscape is complete and unprecedented in this book, a feat that both are proud of. Rash wrote that as "the crews moved forward, they left behind an ever-widening wasteland of stumps and slash, brown clogged creeks awash with dead trout" (115). In their conversations the loggers express regret: "Used to be this creek held some of the sweetest water in these parts," Ross says. "The chestnut trees that was up at the spring head give it a taste near sweet as honey" (333). Another logger responds, "Used to be thick with trout too, this here stream. There was many a day you and me took our supper from it. Now you'd not catch a knottyhead" (334). Another says, "Looks like that land over in France once them in charge let us quit fighting. Got the same feeling about it too. . . . Like there's been so much killed and destroyed it can't ever be alive again. Even for them that wasn't around when it happened, it'd lay heavy on them too. It'd be like trying to live in a graveyard" (334–35). Finally the men "contemplated the wasteland strewn out before him where not a single live thing rose" (336). Twice in the novel, as Joshua Lee pointed out in "The Pembertons and Corporate Greed: An Ecocritical Look at Ron Rash's *Serena*," Rash offered a beautiful scene only to pollute it with human action; one time Galloway tells

Pemberton that they will "not find better water" than the spring up ahead, only to spit "a brown stream of tobacco juice into" it when they reach it (Rash 358). In another scene Pemberton jokes sarcastically about the beauty of Kephart's waterfall, only to hear Harris remark he "may piss in it" (167).

The Pembertons' belief that nature exists only for their use is evident in other actions as well. When the couple goes hunting, for example, they have Galloway bait the meadow for a month to draw in the deer and give the hunters an unfair advantage. Then they kill a dozen deer but do not use the meat; they leave the carcasses in a pile to rot. Rachel, in contrast, sees the mountains as sacred, a "sheltering, . . . as if the mountains were huge hands, hard but gentle hands that cupped around you, protecting and comforting, the way she imagined God's hands would be" (197–98).

Serena's disruption of the natural world is also evident in her use of the eagle to hunt and kill snakes, and the loggers sense that something is not right with her actions. Once the eagle reduces the snake population, rats overbreed and cause headaches at the camp. Snipe explains to the other men that Serena's "eagle has done upset what the Orientals call the yen and the yang. . . . The way things is balanced. Everything in the world has its natural place, and if you take something out or put something in that ought not be out or in, everything gets lopsided and out of sorts" (158–59). As in all aspects of life, though, Serena believes laws—both societal and natural—do not apply to her and to Pemberton; she tells her husband, "We're beyond them" (152). Lee believed this basic "disregard for the general sanctity of life" eventually leads to their downfall: "It is this lack of care regarding the sanctity of life that pervades these two characters throughout the entire book which leads to the demise of both the forest, their relationship, and ultimately, the characters themselves" (44–45).

The witches in *Macbeth* read signs and omens in nature, and this has a counterpart in *Serena* with the group of loggers who serve as a sort of Greek chorus in the novel. Once Serena marries Pemberton and moves to the camp, McIntyre sees in the future "unnatural weather," "famines and pestilence," and "snakes and scorpions and all such terrible things falling out of the sky" (63). His predictions prove true, especially the third one, when the eagle flies overhead with a rattlesnake in its grasp, and the snake slips and falls: "The men hadn't seen the eagle overhead, and the serpent fell among them like some last remnant of Satan's rebellion cast from heaven," causing panic and at least one man to faint (104). After this happens the men become superstitious of Serena and her creatures, and Ross claims, "I'd no more strut up and tangle with that eagle than I'd tangle with the one what can tame such a critter" (107).

The unnaturalness of Serena, her behavior, and her creatures creates awe and fear among the men. She is perceived as almost godlike. When Serena arrives back at the camp for a meeting, Wilkie is struck by her appearance and notes to the preacher: "There's a true manifestation of the godly. . . . Such an image gave the Greeks and Romans their deities. Gaze upon her, Reverend. She'll never be crucified by the rabble" (134). And like a god, Serena tells Pemberton, "The world lies all before us" (168). Once, as Serena, Pemberton, and Galloway move away from sight, Rash noted they "appeared to wobble and haze, miragelike. Then they were gone as if consumed by the air itself" (229). Eventually their murders become so numerous and brazen that the men replace their worship of her with fear. When they see her on her horse with her eagle, one man says, "You want a portent of something bad a-coming there it is" (227).

Serena is linked to the moon throughout the novel, probably not as a symbol of the female as much as an allusion to Diana, the goddess of the hunt. Rachel calls the moon "a hunter's moon" once, remembering her father "claimed blood on the moon meant blood on the land" (311) The vision of the moon seems to follow Rachel wherever she goes as she tries to escape Serena, not a soothing light in the darkness, but rather one that "exposed" her. She feels that "Mrs. Pemberton and Galloway held sway over even the moon and stars and clouds. That they'd waited for this night and this night alone to find her and Jacob" (311). Female supernatural power again is illustrated in Galloway's mother when she attends Pemberton's birthday party. Like Macbeth, who is given reassuring words from the witches that he cannot be killed—"for none of woman born / Shall harm Macbeth" (4.1.80–81)—Galloway's mother tells Pemberton, "They ain't one thing can kill a man like you" (344). Both men are deceived, though—Macbeth being killed by Macduff, who "was from his mother's womb / Untimely ripped" (5.8.15–16), and Pemberton, who is killed not by one thing but by many: poison, snakebites, and ultimately a panther.

The disorder first of gender and then of nature is finally played out in its fullest form in society. Macbeth's kingdom is in disarray, and the doctor sums up the atmosphere: "Foul whisp-rings are abroad. Unnatural deeds / Do breed unnatural troubles" (5.1 75–76). Carole S. Vance linked the personal with community in gender and sexuality when she wrote, "The study of sexual behavior, valuable in its own right, is a powerful tool for raising innovative questions about social relations and social structure" (372). Understanding the breakdown in gender, then, helps in the analysis of the breakdown in society.

Serena's subversion of the female affects the community negatively, creating confusion and chaos among the men and in the town, and, as in *Macbeth,* life cannot be normal again until order is restored. For Macbeth and Lady Macbeth, this means their deaths so that the rightful heir can receive the crown. At the end of the play, when Macduff enters with Macbeth's head, he hails the new king, Malcolm, and announces, "The time is free," meaning the kingdom is liberated from the "dead butcher and his fiendlike queen" (5.8.55; 5.8.69). In *Serena* death is also required to put things right. First, Pemberton is killed by Serena with the help of Galloway, but Serena's death takes much longer. Rash was, perhaps, suggesting that the devastation the couple has perpetrated on the land and the community is so severe that it takes a generation for it to be put right. Earlier in the novel, Kephart tells Pemberton that "it pleased him to know [Pemberton would] die and eventually [his] coffin would rot, and how then [he would] be nourishing the earth instead of destroying it" (117). This kind of atonement does not happen overnight, though; the land will not be "fed" by Pemberton until so much damage is done that it cannot be put right for a long time.

The same is true for the death of Serena. Pemberton's illegitimate son, Jacob, must grow up, become a man, and track down Serena in Brazil. There, still with the aid of Galloway, she has continued her assault on the land. Most likely because she does not want Kephart's prophecy to come true—that she might nourish the land rather than destroy it—she orders a coffin for herself that "*won't rot or rust*" (369). Jacob, by the light of the moon that has defined Serena, dispatches both Galloway and Serena. Galloway dies quickly, but Serena, godlike to the end, staggers outside where the guard believes he sees "*a garland of white fire flamed around her head*" (371). She dies, literally, standing up, onlookers claim, naked and vulnerable for perhaps the first time.

This comparison and contrast of *Serena* and *Macbeth* leads to an interesting and rather perplexing question. Was Rash somehow suggesting that Serena must be a traditional female in order for the world to work well? Is the "natural" state for women that of submission and extreme femininity? It is hard to believe in the second decade of the twenty-first century that a fiction writer could be making such a traditional and obviously oppressive point. While Shakespeare might have been intimating that women should remain true to their feminine traditions and that subverting those roles causes chaos, death, and destruction, Rash's purposes are probably much different and might have something to do with the idea of nature that pervades the novel. Femaleness has long been linked to nature, as opposed to masculinity that has often been connected to culture. Nature is frequently referred to by the pronouns "she" and "her," for example, and often people speak of Mother Nature. Charlene Spretnak believed that man's estrangement from nature (while women remained linked to it) began as early as 4500 B.C. when "the nature-based and female-honoring religion of the Goddess in Europe, the Near East, Persia, and India" was replaced with "an omnipotent, male Sky-God," thereby "removing that which is held sacred and revered from the life processes of the Earth" (11). In the seventeenth century, scientists and philosophers took it further by "reinforcing aggressive attitudes toward nature" by speaking "out in favor of 'mastering' and 'managing' the earth." These scientists reinforced the connection that has long been made between women and nature, and "the new image of nature as a female to be controlled and dissected through experiment legitimized the exploitation of natural resources" (Merchant 188, 189). Even Emerson, in "The Young Americans," believed "this great savage country" must meet its "master" (223).

Serena's offense, then, that leads to chaos and destruction may not be her denial of the feminine so much as it is her denial of the female "Nature." Her subversion of gender is a subversion of the gender associated with nature. As a woman she has lost touch with her connection to the "life processes of the Earth," as Spretnak called them, choosing instead to embrace the culture of the masculine. When Serena denies her feminine side, she aligns instead with the destruction of nature, thereby choosing culture and the masculine, throwing the environment—and everything else—out of balance. Dominance and destruction—not balance and harmony—become important to her, and therefore nature and the community suffer. This could also explain why Serena is unable to bear a child. While masculine forces certainly take their toll on nature, nature "is not completely incapable of defending itself against the forces that seek its destruction" (Lee 55). Lee compiled a list of ways nature fights back in the novel, including an extended winter and loggers being killed by falling branches, rattlesnake bites, bears, and cougars. He also pointed out that as Pemberton dies, he hears a "cry like that of an infant" (Rash 367), perhaps a reminder of the child nature did not allow them to have: "To prevent the further spread of malfeasance from any child that might have been spawned between these two, nature seems to retaliate against them" (Lee 55). Rachel, then, can be seen as a survivor—and even a hero—not because she is more feminine, but because she embraces nature, protects it, and honors it.

Earlier in the novel, Pemberton muses that Serena is "beyond gender" (180), perhaps neither male or female, or perhaps both. As in Shakespeare's witches who announce, "Fair is foul, and foul is fair" (1.1.10), Serena offers us contradictions and chaos, brought about by the disruption of a woman who refuses to connect with the nature that is within her and around her. Perhaps both Serena and Lady Macbeth could have been both female and powerful if they had looked to the natural world to sustain them.

Works Cited

Butler, Judith. *Gender Trouble: Feminism and the Subversion of Identity.* 2nd ed. 1990. New York: Routledge, 2007.

de Beauvoir, Simone. *The Second Sex.* New York: Bantam, 1952.

Emerson, Ralph Waldo. "The Young American." *Ralph Waldo Emerson: Essays and Lectures.* New York: Library of America, 1983. 213–30.

Ick, Judy Celine A. *Unsex Me Here: Female Power and Shakespearean Tragedy.* Office of the Vice Chancellor for Research and Development, University of the Philippines, 1999.

Kimmel, Michael. "Masculinity as Homophobia: Fear, Shame, and Silence in the Construction of Gender Identity." *Theorizing Masculinities.* Ed. Harry Bord and Michael Kaufman. Thousand Oaks: Sage, 1994. 119–41.

Lee, Joshua. "The Pembertons and Corporate Greed: An Ecocritical Look at Ron Rash's *Serena.*" *James Dickey Review* 29.2 (Spring/Summer 2013): 44–60.

Maslin, Janet. "Couple Creates an Empire by Felling Trees and Anyone in Their Way." *New York Times* October 6, 2008. Web.

Merchant, Carolyn. *The Death of Nature: Women, Ecology, and the Scientific Revolution.* New York: Harper and Row, 1980.

Rash, Ron. *Serena.* New York: HarperCollins, 2008.

Shakespeare, William. *Macbeth.* New York: Signet Classic, 1995.

Spretnak, Charlene. "Ecofeminism: Our Roots and Flowering." *Reweaving the World: The Emergence of Ecofeminism.* Ed. Irene Diamond and Gloria Feman Orenstein. San Francisco: Sierra Club, 1990. 3–14.

Vance, Carole S. "Gender Systems, Ideology, and Sex Research." *Powers of Desire: The Politics of Sexuality.* Ed. Ann Snitow, Christine Stansell, and Sharon Thompson. New York: Monthly Review, 1983. 371–84.

Willis, Rachel. "Masculinities and Murder: George Pemberton in Ron Rash's *Serena.*" *James Dickey Review* 29.2 (Spring/Summer 2013): 13–34.

RASH'S SHAKESPEAREAN ECOLOGIES

Autopoietic and Allopoietic Remediations of *Macbeth* in *Serena*

Tripthi Pillai and Daniel Cross Turner

Our essay offers an object-oriented exploration of contemporary Appalachian writer Ron Rash's novel *Serena* (2008) and focuses on undead reverberations of objects and ecologies that haunt Rash's narrative vis-à-vis William Shakespeare's *Macbeth* (c. 1606).[1] Setting forth a multitude of allusive reverberations with *Macbeth,* the novel keys on the machinations of a 1930s timber baroness who lays waste to the landscape and inhabitants of the western North Carolina mountains just before the establishment of the Great Smoky Mountains National Park in the region. Connections between the two texts are rife, yet the novel's elusive allusiveness occludes one-to-one correspondences and instead responds to a swarm of calls, a mass of past voices that reemerge as unruly shades driving and disrupting the present as well as anthropocentric constructions of time and place.[2]

Undead Ecologies

There are specific parallels between characters, although these are by no means exact or exclusionary but shift readily: Pemberton as Macbeth (before becoming king); Serena as Lady Macbeth (in exhorting her husband to murder); Serena as Macbeth (as Machiavellian maneuverer and prime mover of the bloodletting); Pemberton as Lady Macbeth (after fading into a conscience-darkened shell of the former self); McDowell as Macduff (in offering meaningful resistance to tyranny or monopoly); and Ross as, well, Ross (in his studied slipperiness, equivocating on the edges of the main fray). *Serena* also plays on, and against, "the Scots Tragedy" with a slew of local Appalachians whose surnames bear their Scots genealogical and, it is suggested, psychic inheritance: from the logging crew members (Ross, Stewart, Henryson, McIntyre), to the camp overseer (Campbell) as well as doctor (Cheney), to the local sheriff (McDowell), to Serena's handpicked henchman (Galloway) and his prophetic mother, who bears witchlike properties. The stereotypical brooding moodiness of the Scots or Scots Irish, their "shared dourness" of spirit and "darksomeness" of mind (185), balances their reputed stoicism and stalwart penchant for honorable resistance to the last full measure. The Appalachian workers are described as "highlanders," again rhyming the landscapes and psyches of the North Carolina mountains with the Scottish highlands of Shakespeare's play. Rash also alluded to the theory, now discredited, that the new world highlanders hold tight linguistic ties to the old world, their dialect reflecting closely "Shakespearean" habits, for "their speech harks back to Elizabethan times" (13). Furthermore *Serena* and *Macbeth* both teem with overleaping ambition, endless equivocation, and heads of corpses; bloody daggers; blood; uncanny prophesies; spectral yet all too real forms; unnatural, if not supernatural, figures; anxieties over reproduction and inheritance; and, paradoxically, intensities of absolute presentness. Hollow crowns, poisoned chalices, and cursed or blighted plant life also reverberate across and through the texts.

As these image patterns imply, an aura of undeadness sequences through and between both texts. In addition to these obvious instances of death and deathliness, undeadness also emerges in equally powerful, if more figurative ways. The most potent link between *Serena* and *Macbeth* for our purposes arises through each text's representation of massive upheavals in the ecological order. In both cases the things of nature refuse to be confined to the humans' perception of them as inert, inanimate, dead matter. On the contrary the nonhuman surround expresses agency across the human domain, resisting the conceit of a "human domain" as intact, separate. In both Rash's and Shakespeare's works, we see a posthuman emphasis on the shaping power of nonhuman actants that condition, sometimes control, human experience and sociopolitical structures.

Undead ecologies in *Macbeth* and *Serena* materialize through shared tropes that we will discuss in full below, including atmospheric pressures (fair or foul weather and other phenological anomalies), the recalcitrance of nonhuman animals, and the woods moving or being removed. Such animate and animating environmental forces are undead in their material vibrancy and capacity to outstrip anthropocentric ideologies: ecological objects in *Macbeth* and *Serena* outlast humanly inflicted damages, undermining the human to the point of death, and beyond. Ecocritical discourses have pointed to the slippery hierarchy of subject (human/cultural) and object (nonhuman/natural). Our essay extends the ecological scope of Rash's Shakespearean remediation by placing it within an object-oriented ontology. The philosophically, ethically, and politically charged inquiry of this object-oriented ontology, or speculative realism, dispenses with traditionally held distinctions of subject and object, claiming instead the multivalence of only one type of being—object-being.[3] Per Graham Harman, objects "have genuine reality at many different scales, not just the smallest," and they "withdraw from all types of relation, whether those of human knowledge or of inanimate causal impact" (106).

In this context undeadness illuminates subtle interchanges between the animate and inanimate, worrying the lines between the two and challenging an anthropocentric ecology that is fastened to hard-line separations and hierarchies between what Levi Bryant defines as "autopoietic" and "allopoietic" objects. While such objects often function smoothly together within given environments, they can also "operate in tension and in conflict" ("Knots" 9). Autopoietic objects, which include living objects and social systems, possess the ability to multiply themselves, chiefly through modes of reproduction. Conversely, allopoietic objects are objects that "do not reproduce themselves through their own operations" but are able nonetheless to "constitute the way in which they are open to other entities in the world" (Bryant, *Democracy of Objects* 141). Autopoiesis characterizes "machines or objects that produce their own elements and 'strive' to maintain their organization across time"; their key feature is "that they produce *themselves*" (163). By contrast allopoiesis describes "machines produced by something else. Generally the domain of allopoietic machines refers to inanimate objects" (163). In short, speculative realism maintains all matter comprises objects, albeit various types of objects that do not necessarily open up to one another or forge meaningful and systematic connections with the environment.[4]

Our essay adapts emergent taxonomies of object-oriented ontology to probe the undeadness of particular autopoietic and allopoietic objects that constitute the environments of *Macbeth* and *Serena.* As beings that hop across textualities and centuries from Shakespeare to Rash, autopoietic and allopoietic objects often blur lines of separation that the anthropocentric imagination enforces, refusing both narrative demise and transparency. As transmogrified beings they become rogue agents that are also monstrous reverberations of other objects and narratives. Ultimately the redoubled power of undeadness as allusiveness and as ecology in Rash's remediation of the Renaissance text amplifies fractures in the progressive logics (linear, temporal, systematic) of narrative that repeatedly attempt but ultimately fail to delineate the living from the dead, the past from the future, and the nonhuman object from its echo in the human.

Atmospheric Pressures

"'Nature' is a difficult word," Jeffrey Cohen reminded us in *Stone: An Ecology of the Inhuman.* Indeed nature is a baffling if constant presence in *Serena* and in *Macbeth.* Like the "lithic" that Cohen stated "is tangled in narrative" and simultaneously is "prod as well as hindrance, ally as well as foe, a provocative and complicit agency," nature in these texts mobilizes a paradoxical energy that pushes the temporal and spatial limits of humans' engagements with it (12). In fact nature penetrates both the physiological and psychic autonomy of the human subject and renders it a leaky object, as vulnerable to the consumption and domination of rivaling substances as it is capable of colonizing other beings and spaces. Both Macbeth and Serena come close to recognizing the influence of other agents or machines in their flows of production—the production of temporal power (Macbeth) and the production of capital (Serena). Yet they each fall short of realizing the full force of the influence nonhuman flows have on their own beings and productions. In *Serena* characters' intentionality is dismantled by the Appalachian surround, by trees that turn rogue and by nature, more generally, that operates against the linear progress designed by the human, entrepreneurial machines at work in the world of the novel. In *Macbeth,* too, human ambition is dismantled by a fiercely unstoppable and—more dangerous—indecipherable nature. In the play's ecology, the transmogrification or becoming rogue of autopoietic machines (humans, animals, trees) is brought about by the actions of allopoietic machines—of spells, for example. In becoming actants the objects eliminate the hierarchy of animate and inanimate being and starkly reveal what anthropocentric ambition strives to conceal: that "the distinction between autopoietic objects and allopoietic objects is not a hard and fast or absolute distinction, but is probably a distinction that involves a variety of gradations and intermediaries" (Bryant, *Democracy of Objects* 163).

If, to the human eye seeking natural order, the reformed and deformed environment of *Serena* is a picture of nature gone awry, in *Macbeth* it stares at the world turned upside down, its movements and upheavals manifested in paradox. The most famous incidents of a paradoxical nature come early in the play, when the witches draw attention to an environment at once "fair" and "foul," smothered in "fog and filthy air" (1.1.12–13). "The multiplying villainies of nature" and human rebellion quelled by Macbeth's "brandished steel" manage only to reveal greater contradictions, for "from that spring whence comfort seemed to come / Discomfort swells" (1.2.27–28). Crucially Macbeth's prowess at diffusing the intentionality of radical human rebellion is lauded as *natural* but not human action. In fact his actions are described in terms of animality. The wounded captain's simile at the beginning of the play likens Macbeth, the soon-to-be Thane of Cawdor, to an eagle or a lion that overpowers its prey instinctually and without struggle. But to his king, who collates natural and monarchic order as one entity, Macbeth epitomizes filial connections: the captain praises the Thane as his "valiant cousin" and a "worthy gentleman" who serves his own kind (1.2.24).

In an obvious sense, Macbeth and Banquo serve King Duncan as loyal subjects; they admit that their violent production is meant entirely for their monarch's reception and the propagation of his power. In response to his king's articulation of the impossibility of giving proper thanks to Macbeth for a job well done, the Thane claims, "Your highness' part / Is to receive our duties, and our duties / Are to your throne and state children and servants, / Which do but what they should by doing everything / Safe toward your love and honor" (1.4.23–27). Macbeth (and Banquo) point to dutiful action as a reward in itself, one that needs no further recompense than the continued security of the system it serves. Macbeth behaves like a predictable autopoietic machine when he assures Duncan that his heroic actions are intended at propagating the present monarchic system. (Autopoietic machines, we may recall, are not simply those that are capable of reproducing their own kind biologically but also those that enable the reproduction and expansion of social systems.)

But the violent productivity of autopoietic machines is always already a threat to the stability of the system they serve. Macbeth and Banquo are manifestations of this paradoxical energy, and their labor must continually be harnessed by the exercise of conventional authority. Duncan's welcome to his prized soldiers is an exercise in harnessing the men's agential potential. On the one hand, he recognizes the need to sustain the culture of loyalty by offering systematic material rewards for proper service. So not only does he fit Macbeth and Banquo with new titles, the material benefits of which they can reap in the present, but he also promises his loyal soldiers future rewards of greater worth than the ones they now receive. Notably he uses an agrarian metaphor to make his point about planned growth within his realm—"I have begun to plant thee and will labor / To make thee full of growing" (1.4.28–29). By comparison Serena offers her eagle the same reward repeatedly: a chunk of steak in return for each service it performs. Duncan's promise of autopoietic economic futurity stems from his tacit recognition of the anthropocentric desire for both difference and increase in reward, whereas Serena's reliance on the simple repetition of a finite reward stems from her anthropocentric reduction of the animal's desire. Put differently, Duncan understands Macbeth as a complex machine that must continually be appeased because it can never be fully trained, while Serena sees the eagle as a simple one, trained by her exclusively to meet her requirements.

On the other hand, the king acts on his need to confine the soldiers' power by rendering it a function that is virtuous only as long as it propagates a normative monarchic ideology founded on lineage, in other words, on the basic reproductive function of the autopoietic machine that is the king. Thus, almost in the same breath that he announces to Macbeth and Banquo the present and future prosperity they have earned, Duncan declares his biological son Malcolm as the sole inheritor of his royal "estate" (1.4.37). With his declaration the king resituates his heroic warriors, particularly Macbeth, within the paradoxical realm of leadership in servitude, of exceptional heroism as normative action.

But Duncan's actions come a scene too late for them to solidify the Thane of Cawdor's autopoietic framework. Allopoietic seepage has already begun to erode Macbeth's being, for the witches he encounters in act 1, scene 3 have initiated the dismantlement of his previously coded humanity, their agency mobilizing in him the blurring of autopoietic and allopoietic lines that would characterize his actions throughout the remainder of the play. Mostly Banquo speaks for both men in the scene that unfolds between the human and hybrid machines. The "weird sisters" are almost unrecognizable as humans, much less as women: "they look not like th' inhabitants o' th' earth / And yet are on't," he notes (1.3.32, 41–42). The men's puzzlement over the witches' being continues: "You should be women, / And yet your beards forbid me to interpret / That you are so" (1.3.45–47). Like the "transmogrified" object in *Serena* that is the "horse, eagle and human" assemblage (102), the witches also dissolve the boundaries of corporality; as Macbeth observes once they have disappeared, "what seemed corporal" to him, and autopoietic, has "melted / As breath into the wind" (1.3.81–82)—as matter that merges the force of human exhalation with the nonhuman energy of wind.

The witches are hypernatural objects insofar as they possess a peculiar ability to form a cohort with the nonhuman elements in nature to alienate the human from his imagination of his being "as the metaphysical core of the universe" (Harman 107). For example their partnership with the nonhuman agents of nature enables them to "sail" the seas in "a sieve" fueled by the force of oceanic currents and "winds," the help of which enables them not only to "drain" shipmen "dry" on "tempest-tossed" "barks," but also dislodge sleep from the human eye: "sleep shall neither night nor day / Hang upon his penthouse lid. / He shall live a man forbid," they predict of the sea captain whose wife refused to share the treat of "chestnuts" with one of them (1.3.8–21). Indeed, in the play, sleep, a defining characteristic of the animate world inhabited by humans, is a thing lost by the human as a result of his strife with the hypernatural surround produced by the terrifying amalgam of autopoietic and allopoietic agency. Preparing to murder his king and guest, Macbeth observes that, while "o' er the one half-world / Nature seems dead, and wicked dreams abuse / The curtained sleep," he combines his inhuman energy of ambition with the nocturnal powers of "pale Hecate," "the wolf" and the "ghost" to commit regicide (2.1.50–57). With Duncan's murder "Macbeth does murder sleep," as well. He moves steadily from losing night's peaceful rest, which now is filled with "the affliction of . . . terrible dreams / That shake [him] nightly" to forgoing it entirely despite his wife's warning to him that he "lack[s] the season of all natures, sleep" (3.2.19–29, 3.4.142).

In giving up sleep, Macbeth distances himself from the limits of autopoietic being while forging a connection with the hypernatural world. His wife, by comparison, is never able fully to abandon the property of sleep: her sleep walking may well be induced by the human guilt she experiences for her part in the murders of Duncan, Banquo, Lady Macduff, and her children, but she still clings, however marginally, to the exercise of a function that situates her within autopoietic being. While critics have often emphasized the connection between Lady Macbeth and the witches, it is Macbeth who becomes witch by removing himself from the core of anthropocentric and normative being. Transformed by the hybrid conjunction of autopoiesis and allopoiesis, he "conjure[s]" with the witches in act 4, scene 1 to "untie the winds and let them fight / Against the churches" and against "navigation." He demands a conference with the witches' "masters," even at the expense of paradoxical natural movement unleashed as chaos: "though bladed corn be lodged and trees blown down, / Though castles topple on their warders' heads, Though palaces and pyramids do slope / Their heads to their foundations, though the treasure / Of nature's germens tumble all together / Even till destruction sicken, answer me / To what I ask you" (4.1.72–85). The upheaval he desires is the stuff that feeds others' nightmares—not simply of others in the play who deem Macbeth a "hellhound" and monster (5.8.3), but also of our own nightmare vision of the natural world turning against us.

In *Serena,* too, sleep is disrupted as a simple signifier of autopoietic being. While nightmares disrupt Serena's rest early in the novel, as the transmogrified machine that blurs the distinctions between human and nonhuman natural objects and propels the accumulation of capital, she transcends the limits of both memory and guilt by regaining peacefulness in sleep: "she slept well now, in a deepness beyond dreams," she confesses to Pemberton, who notes her nightmares vanished immediately after she trains her eagle, like "ghosts might who find a house they've haunted suddenly vacated" (118). But what she gains in slumber the highlanders lose in their hierarchical footing within the natural environment. Underestimating nature's capacity for resistance, Galloway loses his left hand to an accidental axe blow by a young man whose "knee buckled" as the drenched ground beneath him slipped. Other workers also fall prey to the onslaught of the attacking surround—so much so that Dr. Cheney remarks, "It seems the men are getting killed at a rather prodigious rate these last few weeks" (187). As apocalyptic visions of the havoc caused by their work litter the men's imaginations, nature turns increasingly bellicose, an unkillable machine that makes humans wield axes against themselves, turning to naught men's power over their own and others' movements.

The Recalcitrance of Nonhuman Animals

The image of woods that are removed while *re-moving* the human recurs through Rash's novel and works in conjunction with figures of nonnative animality in the narrative. Serena's importation of a Berkute eagle from Kazakhstan to kill rattlesnakes so work can continue unabated by the threat of rattlers among the understory and slash provides a vivid instance of allopoiesis in the narrative. As a nonnative species introduced to effect "unnatural" changes in a given ecosystem, the Mongolian eagle is a rouge machine and reflects what Craig Dworkin defined as ambient fauna. The imported, retrained animal is in southern Appalachia to produce nothing of its own—it is nonautopoietic in its incapacity to multiply its own material being—and therefore epitomizes Serena's efforts to breed a self-consuming ecology. It represents an "abnormal" or allopoietic species introduced to "renormalize" the human work environment; as ambient fauna, the eagle's presence vacillates in a dubious category of belonging only as a chief foreign or alien species introduced to kill "normal" species, to disassemble the autopoiesis of "normal" species and alienate the native. Set against the irruptive force of the eagle are instances of the crumbling autopoietic being of indigenous animal life. By the end of its first month of work, the eagle has exterminated seven rattlesnakes, "including a huge satinback that panicked Snipes' crew when it slipped from the bird's grasp mid-flight and fell earthward. The men hadn't seen the eagle overhead, and the serpent fell among them like some last remnant of Satan's rebellion cast from heaven" (104). The lay preacher McIntyre falls into a dead faint and subsequently loses the power of speech for several months. Offering another grim echo of *Macbeth* ("Light thickens; and the crow / Makes wing to the rooky wood" as "black agents to their preys do rouse" [3.2.51–52]), a raven then signals an uncanny warning: it "flew overhead, wing shadow passing over the men like a dark thought. Dunbar flinched when he saw the bird's shadow, looked upward" (107). Ross wishes for restabilized autopoietic order: "If I had my rathers I'd take them rattlesnakes where the Good Lord put them. . . . At least then you'd not have the worry of them dripping out of the sky onto you" (104). Instead something wicked every which way comes, for "it's trouble coming from every direction now" (107).

Because the eagle is highly efficient in sighting, snatching, and killing rattlers (it destroys forty-two rattlesnakes total [326]), its forced allopoietic presence produces a hazardous series of natural disorders. It enables the human workers to be more productive, thereby speeding the decimation of the forest ecosystem, and also exposes Serena as a nonregenerative being whose productivity is based entirely on the Appalachian workers' ability to reproduce their own labor within a compulsory system that makes money for the Pembertons. The men worked faster now "in part because there hadn't been a single rattlesnake bite since the eagle's arrival" (115), but as the crews move forward, the woods move back. The workers leave behind an undead ecology, "an ever-widening wasteland of stumps and slash, brown clogged creeks awash with dead trout" (115). The land, stripped of its natural "green" producers of oxygen, transforms into a graveyard for aquatic creatures: "Even the more resilient knottyheads and shiners eventually succumbed, some flopping onto banks as if even the ungillable air offered greater hope of survival" (115).

The Berkute eagle's prowess leads to mass overpopulation of rats infesting workers' stringhouses. Dunbar notes that, come winter, "the rats has pretty much laid claim to my stringhouse," while Ross complains he used the toxic compound Paris Green in his stringhouse and "them rats ate it like it was no more than salt on popcorn" (158). Snipes responds that "the thing to kill them is snakes, . . . but that eagle has done upset what the Orientals call the yen and the yang" (158), for "everything in the world has its natural place, and if you take something out or put something in that ought not be out or in, everything gets lopsided and out of sorts" (158–59). Snipes makes analogy to the phenological imbalance of having spring all year round, in which case there would be "too much aliveness" in the nonhuman environs (159). The reality is, however, that winter has come early to the mountains this year (61) and stays late (173). Ross ponders the hazardous ecologies created by the eagle's allopoietic impact, raising "his gaze to take in the gray and brown valley floor, the scalped ridges of Noland Mountain" (159), countering Snipes's example of eternal spring and excess aliveness with the bleak matter confronting them—too much deadness. "So what happens when there ain't nothing left alive at all?" (159), Ross questions, and the answer that surrounds the men like fog and filthy air lies in the partnership between the nonreproductive duo of eagle and Serena, which bares the monstrous consequence of autopoietic-allopoietic merger: a world where there is, paradoxically, "too much aliveness" and "nothing left alive at all."

The Woods Moving/Being Re-moved

Bryant cited the example of trees to illustrate how "the spatial proximity and overlap of natural (autopoietic) objects, human and nonhuman" mobilizes a complex network of flows of production that "influence the movement and capacities of other machines" (Bryant, "Knots" 8). "A tree," he stated, "is a machine that draws on flows of sunlight, water, carbon dioxide, and soil nutrients to produce things such as oxygen," a substance consumed by other autopoietic machines that enables their smooth operation ("Knots" 8). While animality gauges the friction between allopoietic and autopoietic systems in *Serena,* in each text it is the trees that matter most vibrantly. The most trenchant illustration of undead ecology—that is, of the animate, if ahuman, environs impacting the human realm in forceful, unmanageable ways—is the shared image of a disembodied forest moving while being removed. Both Serena and Macbeth present the ostensibly "unnatural" formation of forests without trees, and trees without forests, with collateral impacts on indigenous animal species.

Famously the three witches prophesy that "Macbeth shall never vanquish'd be until / Great Birnam wood to high Dunsinane hill / Shall come against him" (4.1.114–16). Their equivocation about the disruption of human ambition by hypernaturality is lost on Macbeth, who is cognizant of the potency of nature's upheaval: "Stones have been known to move and trees to speak; / Augurs and understood relations have / By maggotpies and choughs and rooks brought forth / The secret'st man of blood, he claims" (3.4.123–26). Yet, once convinced by his wife of his supremacy as architect of his own and others' fates, he interprets the witches' statement as a declaration of his invincibility as hybrid autopoietic-allopoietic being. Ironically Macbeth falls prey to the stock anthropocentric delusion that he controls the movements of both the human and nonhuman worlds. In doing so he also falls prey to Malcolm's rival scheme of human and ahuman symbiosis, by means of which he erodes the tyrant's power. Malcolm commands each man in his army to become a transmogrified being that encompasses woodsman, tree, and surreptitious warrior: "Let every soldier hew him down a bough / And bear't before him. Thereby shall we shadow / The numbers of our host and make discovery / Ere in report of us" (5.4.4–7). In the end the witches' prediction holds truth, and as Malcolm's troops uproot the foliage of Birnam Wood, removing it "unnaturally" to high Dunsinane hill, Macbeth is vanquished on Macduff's blade by the violence of a hypernatural environment that is capable of dislocating the human.

Macbeth's bloody stabbing death in the play forecasts Serena's eventual fate in the novel. Serena is linked throughout with the supernatural—especially in a literal sense of holding sway *over* or *above nature*. Like Macbeth, Serena proves not unkillable. But her ability to wield a power of undeadness over the natural surround is expressed not only through her apparent timelessness (her utter, intact presentness that elides all traces of past facticity), but also through her seeming mastery over woodland ecosystems spanning into the hemispheric and global South as she transitions her timber corporation from the southern Appalachians to South America. Through much of the narrative, it seems her supernatural control will repeat itself "until the woods were gone" (15).

And yet "then more woods" (15): for the woods are never fully removed. Despite Serena's intensive timber harvesting, the woods reterritorialize. After near annihilation they recompile, a resurrected force. They resist the stratification imposed on the mountain terrain by the Pembertons' clear-cutting operations. The woods take on elements of the Deleuzean body without organs, exceeding and dissolving the strata constructed by the workings of market capital. Such strata "consist of giving form to matters, of imprisoning intensities or locking singularities into systems of resonance and redundancy" (Deleuze and Guattari 45). Stratification thus represents "acts of capture . . . like 'black holes' or occlusions striving to seize whatever comes within their reach. They operate by coding and territorialization upon the earth; they proceed simultaneously by code and by territoriality" (45). But if these codings appear as "judgments of God" à la Serena's supernatural, that is, above-nature power, "the earth . . . constantly eludes that judgment, flees and becomes destratified, decoded, deterritorialized"

(45). Even as the woods are cleared from nearly every parcel of the Pembertons' land holdings, the ineradicable trace of vitality still haunts the place: "It was Snipes' crew who cut the last tree. When a thirty-foot hickory succumbed to Ross and Henryson's cross-cut saw, the valley and ridges resembled the skinned hide of some huge animal" (Rash 333).

In spite of this gashing, the forest carries the animus of an imposing animal, inspiring a moment of sublime reflection on the part of the men, even if, to borrow Žižek's terms, it is a glimpse not into "sublime spiritual immortality," but into "the obscene immortality of the 'living dead' which, after every annihilation, recompose themselves and clumsily carry on their activities" (53). The woods are marked with animation, if not sentience. The trees take on a grotesque life of their own. A cross-cut blade's sawing of a tulip poplar sounds like "inhalations and exhalations" as if "the tree itself were panting" (Rash 111). The woods are often cloaked in posttraumatic imagery, trees turning "bleak and skeletal" (184), like "layers of gauze" veiling the underlying wound (48). Pemberton himself admits the trauma he and Serena have imprinted on the nonhuman surround: "He looked down at the vast dark gash they'd made on the land. Pemberton stared at the razed landscape a long time, wanting it to be enough" (261). If by way of Serena's overvaulting ambition and her endless if hollow will to power, too much is never enough; the trees nevertheless recant, recoil. After McDowell sets fire to the original camp, Pemberton experiences a fleeting hope that the damage done to the woods can be as easily undone when he watches workers remove the rails and crossties to move camp further into the mountains: "Pemberton looked past the men to where only wooden crossties remained, some blackened by the fire, others not. They blended so well into the landscape as to be barely discernible. Pemberton remembered helping lay the rails across these same crossties, and he head a sudden sensation he was watching time reverse itself. The world blurred, and it seemed possible that the crossties would leap onto stumps and become trees again, the slash whirl upward to become branches. Even a dark blizzard of ash paling back in time to become green leaves, gray and brow twigs" (339). The fantasy is like time reversing itself through space. The landscape reanimates, reverts, as the woods are remade, while the rail lines as built environs are unbuilt into forestland again. Pemberton's vision invokes the inverse of Birnam wood to Dunsinane encroaching, and the illusion is no less affecting for being just that—illusionary.

Deforestation and its collateral damages are impressed through mergings of human-nonhuman nature that inscribe a dark reciprocity. "There's men falling dead near about fast as the trees" (301), reckons Ross, and "before long they'll be fittin' us for [wooden] coffins ahead of time" when loggers will "be planted in the ground," treelike, "before you've got a chance to stiffen up good" (246). A memorable instance of the human merging with the tree comes when Snipes's crew finds itself beneath a heavy, spear-sharp sycamore limb, "one end quilled with smaller branches, the other sheared to a narrowing sharpness," hanging thinly among high popular branches "as if deciding" whether to fall and strike the men below (187). Agency is ascribed explicitly here, and the trees as vibrant matter turn deadly. The limb crashes down, impaling Dunbar (187): "The limb fell toward Dunbar, whose back arched as his axe struck wood the same instant the sycamore limb entered between his collar bone and spine. Dunbar's face smashed against the ground as his knees hit, the rest of his body buckling inward. The white limb had not snapped or slipped free from the flesh. It remained embedded in Dunbar's back like a stalled lightning bolt, and as the limb's angled weight succumbed to gravity, Dunbar's body slowly, almost reverently, lifted to a kneeling position, as if to be given a last look at the world" (187).

Reciprocity between human and nonhuman elements is expressed in the immediate response between Dunbar's axe striking live wood and the coincidental impact of the dead limb that human effort has unloosed from its autopoietic system as part of the sycamore and rerouted as an allopoietic intrusion into the human organization of the work crew. The vitality of the wood proves fatal, a grim endgame of give and take with nature. Rash infused the scene with religious discourse. The sycamore limb enacts a jump-cut crucifixion and descends rapid-fire *ex alto,* as if a judgment of God or gods, "like a stalled lightning bolt." Dunbar's body moves with the eerie momentum of the undead and assumes, beyond his outstripped will, the attitude of prayer: his near-dead corpse is filled with a life not its own as his form, darkly transfigured into a human-nonhuman hybrid, is "slowly, almost reverently, lifted to a kneeling position, as if to be given a last look at the world" (Rash 187). His eyes, notably, are not bent toward heaven, but to the ecological surround, to "the world" in all its obstinate materiality—a shocking *tableau mourant,* fashioned with and by the vibrant material of the forest. He is one with nature. The workers conceive, in a sense unavailed to Serena, the strident power of the woods, of the undead will of the ecology they work to destroy: "Snipes knelt and laid his hand on the dying man's shoulder. Dunbar's eyes shifted in awareness of Snipes' presence, but as he left the world he offered no last words or even a final sigh, only one tear that welled in the corner of his right eye before slowly rolling down his check. Then he was dead" (187). The dread silence of the man's passing signals how *natura naturans* gets the final say insofar as its inarticulate materiality is beyond words, beyond cultural strata of meaning making and consequence. The intended instrumentality of the trees as timber has broken down, and the trees bounce back with dire recoil. The woods assert themselves, resisting their designated equipmentality as dead objects to be inputted in the allopoietic machinations of the marketplace, their status as goods not good. If, in *Serena,* we lose our drive to undermine objects by perceiving them as static substances that serve us within *our* environment, paradoxically we also lose the desire to "overmine" them reductively as materials connected intimately with our own substantiality. So, while "humans lose their place as the metaphysical core of the universe," it is only "because *no* object is allowed to occupy that core, including the inanimate sort" (Harman 107). Nothing works, holds, centers—not us or not not-us.

As we have proposed through our readings of atmospheric pressures, unruly animality, and moving/removed forests, various animate and inanimate objects in *Serena,* relocated and remediated from *Macbeth,* compete with one another for centrality in an environment that refuses to absorb their agency passively but instead posits itself as an active and mobile resistor of both animate and inanimate forces and wills. The arrhythmic movement of these objects between selective exposure or "presence" and operational closure or "withdrawal" generates an undead energy that circulates across the ecologies of these texts, at once spreading the power of nonhuman matter and diminishing the ability of the humans to control the environment. Like the fair-foul atmospherics and the obstinate nonhuman creatures, the trees move and therefore speak volumes about the recrudescence of the dead. *Macbeth* and *Serena* map the violent movements in and of hypernaturality, of nature up in arms against the human.

While the majority of recent dystopic writings about nature focus on the horror that ensues from human abuse of the environment, what distinguishes Rash's narrative of a vengeful nature is his refusal to assign to the forests operational passivity. The trees are not static recipients of the axe's blow; conversely they make their stand. This apprehension of the limits of anthropocentrism, this sounding the depths of ecological autonomy, gains direct expression in Widow Jenkins's testament to Rachel about the staying power of the mountains in conditioning identity: "if you're born here they're a part of you" (197). Her statement is not a backsliding into place-based essentialism but signifies how intently and extensively nonhuman things acclimatize human behaviors, even on an epigenetic level. The sensibility is akin to Rash's account of his eighteenth-century Scots forebears who settled in the western North Carolina Appalachians. During a personal conversation in 2010, Rash mused that he believed his ancestors who farmed these mountains "felt an ominous presence when working these fields under the rock-cast shadows: the immensity of the hills summoning something of human fate and mortality, as if the rolling Appalachians were so many tombstones, an ever-expanding *mise-en-abîme* of *memento mori*" (Turner 18). Rash proposed an experiential connection with the nonhuman habitat, one that dovetails with Casey Clabough's espousal of somatic memory created by a transferrable, if deeply imprinted "sense of place," one infused in our physiological being in the world: "After all, our bodies have digested and continue to carry the trace elements of the soil, flora, air, animals—as well as the often-unconscious psychological impacts of sound, weather, topography, and human interaction—long after we have departed. A connection remains, some of the dimensions of which tend to make our places almost indistinguishable from ourselves" (156). Indeed vestigial elements of past places constitute us physically and psychologically, also troubling strict divisions between the individual human body and nonhuman environs. For better and worse, we are not above or apart from nature, from the past, present, or future.

Nor are our texts discrete units that operate as isolated experiences and insular narratives of human forces of will set to the passive backdrop of a natural surrounding. As a complex remediation of time, place, and narrative, *Serena* eschews notions of "faithfulness" to the donor text to reconsider allusions as part of larger linguistic and cultural networks, to remediate word systems *as* ecologies. Such undead ecologies of intertextuality take on agency, as much as the purportedly sovereign figure of the author. Responding to a post-Barthesian dissemination of authorship and authority in the wake of the Death of the Author, Linda Hutcheon argued that adaptations represent "mosaics of citations that are visible and invisible, heard and silent; they are always already written and read" (210), offering "the comfort of ritual combined with the piquancy of surprise" (4). Remediation continuously presents breakneck switchbacks between ritual comfort and the element of surprise, a swarming call-and-response so intense that surprises are really no surprise. Spectral voices and undead speech are uncontained, not ruled. Rash(ness) does not house Shakespeare(ness), except as a haunted house, except for the ways in which ghosts rarely speak plainly, if at all, but equivocate: they repeat verbatim scenes from the inapproachable past, hovering betwixt some other sphere and our own time and place. Likewise Shakespeare(ness) does not house Rash(ness). In Gaston Bachelard's terms, the poetic image "is not an echo of the past. On the contrary: through the brilliance of an image, the distant past resounds with echoes, and it is hard to know at what depth these echoes will reverberate and die away" (xvi). Rash recalled Shakespeare, made remediated images resonate with new meanings, and the distant past resound with endless echoes. The remediated text is itself a transmogrified being: like the characters within it that morph unpredictably and unsystematically into messy amalgams of autopoietic and allopoietic being, the novel blurs lines of and from the play just as much as it disrupts lines that divide human experiences of temporality and location, amalgamating through allusions the natural, unnatural, and hypernatural environments within which *all* machines are capable of operational closure and aggressive resistance.

Notes

1. The understanding of undeadness here coincides with the concept as expressed in Anderson, Hagood, and Turner, eds., *Undead Souths.* Describing a continuum of posthumous phenomena, undeadness exposes the physical underpinnings of human

subjectivity as transformations in and of the body spark and shadow mutations in and of consciousness.

2. Rash contended that *Serena* is more than a simple "retelling" of *Macbeth:* "I wanted to create an Elizabethan novel. When I say this I sound so pretentious but . . . I wanted it to feel that way. So you evoke Shakespeare certainly but also very consciously evoke Marlowe" (Morrow 152). Rivlin noted that reading *Serena* as a sort of updated backwoods *Macbeth* is a reductive approach, which may have more to do with using "Shakespeareaness" as a branding mechanism to push books and target an audience. Morrow used a range of textual and paratextual materials, including the initial novel cover, blurbs, and reviews, to demonstrate that "Shakespeare is used as a component of the marketing strategy to guide reviews of the novel as well as to attract consumers to purchase the book" (138).

3. For recent approaches in object-oriented ontology, see Bennett; Barad; and Morton. Cohen's *Prismatic Ecology* specifically addresses the ecological implications of understanding the material vibrancy of the nonhuman environs, as does the concept of the "parahuman" in Allewaert's *Ariel's Ecology.*

4. Bryant further elucidates the nature of "machinic ecologies": "Never imagine an environment is an inert container, transcendent to the entities that inhabit them. . . . Insofar as beings are always moving and becoming, environments are therefore ever shifting machinic ecologies. Objects are defined not by their qualities, but their forces, their power, what they can do. Because entities or substances are defined by their doings and interactions, they deserve to be called machines. . . . The merit of the term "machine" is that it leads us to attend to how things operate, to what they do. It leads us to think of powers and activities, not properties. Do not first list a set of properties nor a use, but ask what things (objects), living and nonliving, human and nonhuman, do" ("Knots" 6).

Works Cited

Allewaert, Monique. *Ariel's Ecology: Personhood and Colonialism in the American Tropics, 1760–1820.* Minneapolis: University of Minnesota Press, 2013.

Anderson, Eric Gary, Taylor Hagood, and Daniel Cross Turner, eds. *Undead Souths: The Gothic and Beyond in Southern Literature and Culture.* Baton Rouge: Louisiana State University Press, 2015.

Bachelard, Gaston. *The Poetics of Space.* 1954. Foreword by John R. StilGoe. Boston: Beacon, 1994.

Barad, Karen. *Meeting the Universe Halfway: Quantum Physics and the Entanglement of Matter and Meaning.* Durham: Duke University Press, 2007.

Bennett, Jane. *Vibrant Matter: A Political Ecology of Things.* Durham: Duke University Press, 2010.

Bryant, Levi R. *The Democracy of Objects.* Ann Arbor: Open Humanities Press, 2011.

———. "Knots: For an Interactivist Ontology." Umeå universitet. Umeå, Sweden. May 27, 2015. Keynote address.

Clabough, Casey. *Inhabiting Contemporary Southern and Appalachian Literature: Region and Place in the Twenty-First Century.* Gainesville: University Press of Florida, 2012.

Cohen, Jeffrey Jerome. *Prismatic Ecology: Ecotheory beyond Green.* Minneapolis: University of Minnesota Press, 2014.

———. *Stone: An Ecology of the Inhuman.* Minneapolis: University of Minnesota Press, 2015.

Deleuze, Gilles, and Felix Guattari. "10,000 B.C.: The Geology of Morals (Who Does the Earth Think It Is?)." *A Thousand Plateaus.* New York: Continuum, 1987. 44–82.

Dworkin, Craig. "Normal Flora and Ambient Fauna." *Qui Parle: Critical Humanities and Social Sciences* 19.2 (2011): 2–4.

Harman, Graham. "Gold." In *Prismatic Ecology: Ecotheory beyond Green.* Ed. Jeffrey Jerome Cohen. Minneapolis: University of Minnesota Press, 2013. 106–23.

Hutcheon, Linda. *A Theory of Adaptation.* New York: Routledge, 2006.

Morrow, Christopher L. "Acknowledgement, Adaptation and Shakespeare in Ron Rash's *Serena.*" *South Central Review* 30.2 (2013): 136–61.

Morton, Timothy. *Hyperobjects: Philosophy and Ecology after the End of the World.* Minneapolis: University of Minnesota Press, 2013.

Rash, Ron. *Serena.* New York: HarperCollins, 2008.

Rivlin, Elizabeth. "The Ghost of Shakespeare in Ron Rash's *Serena.*" Conference presentation. Southern American Studies Association. January 31, 2013. Charleston, South Carolina.

Shakespeare, William. *Macbeth.* Ed. Stephen Orgel. *The Complete Pelican Shakespeare.* Stephen Orgel and A. R. Braunmuller, gen. eds. Middlesex: Penguin, 2002. 1616–50.

Turner, Daniel Cross. "From Blue Ridge to Blue Sea: On Teaching a Southern Literature and History Travel Course." *James Dickey Review* 28.2 (2012): 8–19.

Žižek, Slavoj. *In Defense of Lost Causes.* New York: Verso, 2008.

Part III

WAR, MEMORY, VIOLENCE

THE CIVIL WAR AND BEYOND IN APPALACHIA

A Historiographical Essay

Adam J. Pratt

On January 18, 1863, in the Shelton Laurel Valley of Madison County, North Carolina, Confederate troops rounded up and executed thirteen noncombatants, among them young boys and old men, who were rumored to be Union sympathizers. The thirteen murdered men, as well as at least some of their killers, were from Madison County. That these men, who presumably knew one another prior to the conflict, could fight and even kill their acquaintances and neighbors is one of the darkest chapters of the American Civil War, and it demonstrates how and why this particular county became known as "Bloody Madison." For decades Ron Rash has been obsessed with the Shelton Laurel Massacre, and he has used it in a range of poems, essays, and short stories, and it provides the overarching themes and drama for his 2006 novel *The World Made Straight.* On multiple occasions Rash has gone so far as to say that the massacre has and continues to "haunt" his personal imagination, and thus it likely should come as no surprise that the massacre has bubbled up in his literary imagination repeatedly and in some of his most poignant and probing explorations of southern Appalachia.[1]

The seventeen-year-old protagonist of *The World Made Straight,* Travis Shelton, finds himself caught in the crosshairs of historical forces beyond his understanding, as he contends with drug dealers, rural poverty, elusive trout, and the almost unfathomably dark event that transpired not only in his native Madison County but also to members of his own family. In the novel Travis drops out of high school and ends up living in a trailer with Leonard Shuler, a former high school history teacher who now illegally sells drugs and alcohol. With Leonard's help Travis makes a series of discoveries about his family's history. Travis's most surprising realization, perhaps, comes when he learns that his kinfolk were Unionists, and that some of them were murdered at the Shelton Laurel Massacre. This event, and the rest of the war, echoed throughout Appalachia, and Rash's novel hints at the lingering effects of a violent civil war on a region, its communities, and the individuals still struggling with the consequences of historical violence. Throughout the novel Travis struggles "to make sense of the notion that time didn't so much pass as *layer over things,* as if under the world's surface the past was still occurring" (86, emphasis in original). For many the reckoning needed to make sense of their past never materialized; for many the war had ceased to end.[2]

Historians, too, have struggled with dealing with the Civil War in Appalachia. In his 2001 historiographical essay, "Feelin' Mighty Southern," Noel Fisher made a case that scholarly output on the Civil War in southern Appalachia since the 1960s has tended to overemphasize socioeconomic data at the expense of qualitative sources that accentuate "the fears, resentments, and rage that fracture these regions" (345–46). Moreover, he argued, historians have sanitized their portrayals of the ferocity of "irregular violence" that categorized much of Appalachia's wartime experience. Perhaps most egregious, historical scholarship has collapsed the differences between Appalachia and the rest of the South. For Fisher it was the spirit of dissent "that emerged so quickly after war began and became so intense" that naturally speaks to the inherent differences in the South's various geographic (sub)regions. Violence and dissent, then, are two themes that make the Civil War particularly Appalachian. Such a distinction is crucially important for examining Rash, because he is a writer who identifies first and foremost as an Appalachian, rather than a southern, writer.

This essay will highlight the significant research published on the Appalachian South since the publication of Fisher's article in 2001. Although much of the work being done on the region still explores the phenomenon of Unionism, it has also embraced more complicated explanations for the occurrence of divided communities. Political divisions and economic rivalries all played a part in how communities split and how individuals decided loyalties. More recent scholarship also brings the story of Civil War memory in those divided communities into the twentieth and twenty-first centuries. The meaning of the war after the fact was often just as contentious as the actual bloodshed itself. This gets to the second point of this essay: explaining the historical context behind Rash's *The World Made Straight,* in particular the events of the Shelton Laurel Massacre. The violence and bloodshed that rocked western North Carolina were not isolated phenomena. Numerous Appalachian communities suffered a lack of unity for a variety of reasons. By the twentieth century, many of those divisions had been papered over, and the façade of a Confederate heritage reigned supreme. While this chapter does not provide an extended analysis of Rash's primary texts, which John Lang has done in the subsequent chapter, my aim is to survey the historiography relevant to Rash's fiction and poetry. Understanding the Civil War and its aftermath in southern Appalachia can help us better explicate the characters captured in Rash's many works who are obsessed with and haunted by the Shelton Laurel Massacre.

If any single historical development unites Appalachia's history, it is the presence of violence. Although Noel Fisher charged historians with downplaying the severity of violent activity during the war, more recent works have highlighted the phenomenon. Indeed the prevailing trend is the discussion of the violence that did not end with the war, but continued unabated. Although the public imagination holds the Hatfields and McCoys as the sole evidence of postwar violence, scholars have begun to flesh out the Civil War's impact on community life as the impetus for mountain feuds. Even works of popular culture buy into the idea of a violent Appalachia. Beyond *The World Made Straight* and its more recent film adaptation (2015), FX's show *Justified* also explores manifestations of violence and community relationships as it follows U.S. Marshal Raylan Givens around Kentucky.

As American culture moves toward more realistic portrayals of violence, its causes and aftermath, Civil War scholars, especially those who focus on Appalachia, have been following suit. Upward of seven hundred thousand soldiers gave their lives for their causes during the Civil War, an unprecedented total in the history of American warfare.[3] Fighting between armies devastated the landscape wherever they came into contact, and, by the war's end, cities that upheld the Confederate war effort faced the destructive fury or at least occupation of Union armies. Most of the fighting did occur between uniformed men on both sides, though frequently guerrilla warfare upset the home front, especially in the border states. In Appalachia the war took on a different tone. More ambivalent about secession and the Confederacy, communities in the mountain South, as we see in *The World Made Straight,* were divided from the outset. The region's past, one also marred by violence, seemed to dictate the course that the fighting in Appalachia would take. New historical research on the violence that has plagued the region contextualizes the war but does not explain completely the internecine violence many experienced.

Blood in the Hills (2012), a collection of essays edited by Bruce Stewart, explores various facets of historical violence that colored the region's past. What is unique about the volume is that it consigns the problem of historical violence to the entire region, not exclusively the southern portion of Appalachia. In Stewart's collection Kevin Barksdale argued that Americans in Appalachia turned to violence as a means of establishing locally oriented governments. Unsatisfied with previous scholarship that condemned early settlers to violent behavior because of their ethnic heritage (in this case Scots Irish), Barksdale instead sought alternative motivations for their engagement in brutality. He wrote, "More compelling explanations grounded in specific historical circumstances and a complex collision of political and economic forces" better describe backcountry violence (25).[4] Discontentment in the area was fueled by inept state leaders, state indebtedness, and Cherokee resistance. Settlers in what is now east Tennessee saw the state as either unresponsive to its claims, at best, or downright uncaring, at worst. In 1784, when the state ceded its western lands to the federal government to help alleviate its debt crisis, western leaders "manufactured outrage" at the legislation (even though they supported it) and turned the anger into an independence movement that culminated with the creation of a new state, Franklin. Two competing camps, one supporting the state of Franklin and another supporting the governor, arose in the backcountry. The lack of unanimity in the community's opinion presaged much of the region's experience during the Civil War and demonstrates the diverse set of opinions that could divide neighbors, especially when those opinions were rooted in politics. Rather than a unique example of violent expression, frontier violence plagued eastern North America as it transitioned from a site of imperial contest and collaboration to a hegemonic republic. Republican politics gave way to fracture; politically motivated violence accompanied those political changes. By the nineteenth century, Appalachia's violent legacy permitted bloodshed when local political control was threatened by a larger, more powerful entity.

Such contested power structures at both the local level and beyond are illustrated in Bloody Madison and Rash's novelization of the massacre that occurred there. When the Civil War erupted, the seeming lack of control over local participation in a national war pointed to the possibility of employing violence to compel obedience. Parts of southern Appalachia, in particular, which had been divided on the issue of secession, soon became hotbeds of dissent.[5] Though other southern communities, most notably the "Free State of Jones," also expressed resentment toward the Confederacy and Jefferson Davis's administration, the bulk of southern dissent toward the Confederacy came from mountainous communities. In Rash's novel Leonard states, "That caused Jeff Davis a lot of headaches. Bad enough for the South to fight the rest of the United States, then add to that a bunch of homemade Lincolnites. Of course, men like Colonel [who was partially responsible for the massacre] used the term bushwhackers, which made it easier for something like Shelton Laurel to happen" (*World Made Straight* 94). The division over secession in those mountainous regions moved past that debate and into the war. Community studies abound that demonstrate the flux undergone by Appalachian residents before and during the war. More recently scholarship has brought much of that conflict, like Rash's confused protagonist, into the twentieth century as a means of highlighting historical memory and continued community divisiveness.

John Inscoe and Gordon McKinney examined the effects of the Civil War in the highlands of western North Carolina in *The Heart of Confederate Appalachia* (2000). The coauthors noted that slaveholders, as in other areas of the South, held hegemonic sway over local society and economics. Slaves themselves were less numerous than in other parts of the Confederacy, and they were more frequently hired out or worked side by side with white tenant laborers; because of the limitations to agriculture imposed by topography, the largest slaveholders in the area were merchants rather than planters (16–20). The Whig Party controlled the area, at least until the 1850s, when the Democrats became ascendant and promised to protect the institution. Secession brought about discordant political ideas, or at least concentrated them, as the authors maintain that the two-party system had remained viable throughout the antebellum period. Ten of the seventeen counties in the region opposed immediate secession in February 1861 but lined up behind the movement after Confederates fired on Fort Sumter in Charleston harbor. When President Lincoln called up troops to suppress the rebellion after the incident, many cautious southerners became convinced that only by seceding from the United States could they protect their rights. As young men flooded out of the area to fight, upholding the loyalties of those who remained proved a struggle. Inscoe and McKinney maintained that Unionism was not nearly as rampant in western North Carolina as it was in other parts of the southern highlands. When it did surface, though, it was the product of "the exigencies of war" and not "deeply held love of the Union or opposition to slavery or slaveholders" (86). Desertion proved particularly distressing, because large numbers of troops could leave their units and seek solace with locals. As wartime tensions mounted, guerilla violence, especially Unionist raids and pro-Confederate reprisals, became a serious problem in the region, for it "blurred the lines between combatants and noncombatants and obscured the rules of war that defined both" (120). The Shelton Laurel Massacre that so haunts Rash's personal and literary imagination was an extreme, but not isolated, example of that problem. Desertion from the Sixty-Fourth North Carolina coupled with a Unionist raid on the town of Marshall provided Confederate general Henry Heth with enough provocation to order the regiment to clear out guerillas in the area, which ultimately led to the execution, under the command of Lieutenant Colonel James A. Keith, of thirteen boys and men not far from their homes (160–70).[6] Military incursion by the Union army in 1864 brought military occupation to the region, and a sense of resignation on the part of Confederates.

Working in tandem with the main thrust of Inscoe and McKinney's argument is an exploration of economic expansion in the region. The authors went to great lengths to examine the diverse operations of antebellum residents, and rather than a static region, they saw dynamism. During the buildup to secession, residents tried first to declare economic independence from the Yankees (36–38).[7] As the war progressed, economic hardship followed. For example the Asheville Armory, continually vexed by labor shortages and transportation problems, had difficulty fulfilling contracts and procuring raw materials. Once the war concluded, towns in western North Carolina suffered from a lack of development and opportunity. The railroad became king, and the industries needed to secure its reign were found in Appalachia. The moneyed metropolis soon turned the region into a colonial dependency that supplied the coal and timber needed to expand the railroad's reach. Travis Shelton's Appalachia still felt the reverberations of this economic expansion. Once coal and timber went into decline, many Appalachian residents turned to selling drugs, as we see in *The World Made Straight*, or became reliant on federal aid to make ends meet.

Inscoe and McKinney's *The Heart of Confederate Appalachia* explodes long-held myths surrounding the Appalachian experience in the Civil War: a seemingly harmonious and homogenous region, largely unscathed by economic development, found itself divided, first by secession and then by war. Rather, political competition had remained a hallmark of life in the region. As the war progressed, the demands of the Davis regime and wartime disaffection meant an increased number of deserters and guerillas. Much like Barksdale's exploration of early political violence showed, what western North Carolinians wanted was local self-determination. When that became impossible, raids and bushwhacks made life in isolated areas uncertain, and neighborliness declined. By the end of the war, military occupation ended the immediate cycle of violence, but wartime divisions continued into Reconstruction and allowed for economic exploitation once the rest of the nation "discovered" Appalachia.

Other studies corroborate the findings made by Inscoe and McKinney. Robert Tracy McKenzie's *Lincolnites and Rebels* (2006) explores how east Tennessee, more than anywhere else in the southern Appalachians, was a hotbed of Unionist support. At the heart of Unionism in the "metropolis" of Knoxville was Parson William Brownlow, a Methodist circuit rider and editor of a Whig newspaper. A man of strong antipathies, he spent his twenties in battle against Baptists and Presbyterians, and his later career engaged with Democrats. Though Brownlow was quick to separate himself from President Lincoln (and thus the epithet "Lincolnite"), he blamed secession on the aggressiveness of southern planters (75). Unionist Home Guard units drilled and prepared for eventual confrontations with Rebels and struck in November 1861. Burning important railroad bridges ahead of an imminent federal invasion, Unionists struck first but were left to fend for themselves when William Tecumseh Sherman's planned march fizzled in Kentucky. The Confederates occupied the city; local jails filled with political prisoners, though Brownlow himself was sent north. During Confederate occupation Unionists profited by selling scarce goods to Confederate forces, while awaiting liberation. When federal armies did take the city, Unionist sympathy expanded.

But even Unionist forces in East Tennessee could not remain united. Divided over the direction of Lincoln's war policy regarding slavery, emancipation, and military service, more conservative Unionists broke with Brownlow when he returned to the federally occupied city. Some openly supported General George McClellan, the Democrat opposing Lincoln in the election of 1864 (McKenzie 192). The parson urged "swift and severe retribution" against Confederates once the war ended and began suing a litany of Rebels for damages associated with imprisonment and banishment. Showing the complicated nature of loyalty, many Unionist lawyers defended former Confederates and thwarted Brownlow's plans (198, 202). McKenzie's treatment of Civil War Knoxville concludes with a brief spat of violence between former Rebels and Unionists that culminated with the lynching of a black Union soldier. The message was clear; reunion would occur in Knoxville the way it would in much of the South: along racial lines and at the end of a noose.

Other men were also killed to inspire reconciliation, and such stories can further illuminate the Confederate soldiers' motivation for killing thirteen Union sympathizers in Madison County. Brian McKnight told of Champ Ferguson, a notorious Confederate guerilla warrior who operated around the Cumberland valley on the Kentucky-Tennessee border. McKnight's *Confederate Outlaw* (2011) is the story of how Ferguson came to be known as one of the more vicious Rebel partisans, who reportedly killed over forty men; in addition Ferguson's circumstances provide an interesting parallel to the Confederate vigilantism meted out at Shelton Laurel and depicted in *The World Made Straight*. Coming of age in Clinton County, Kentucky, Ferguson shared the "cracker characteristics" of his time and place. He owned a still and had a reputation as a drinker and gambler, and it was rumored that he passed counterfeit money (19). In 1860 Ferguson found himself living among Unionists. McKnight cited a 1973 study that listed Clinton County as the fourth most loyal county in the state (36). Even the Ferguson family was divided over the issue of loyalty. His brothers sided with the Union army, while he was arrested for disloyalty, which is how his foray into partisan warfare began. Escaping his captors Ferguson then set out for the relative safety of Tennessee to kill for the Confederate cause.

Much of the rest of Champ Ferguson's Civil War was spent in Tennessee, where he aided the Confederate war effort by attacking Unionist guerillas. McKnight skillfully traced Ferguson's trail of bloodshed through the Cumberland region, and although his focus is local in nature, he never lost sight of the wider drama unfolding around the nation. For example he discussed John Hunt Morgan's 1862 raid, which Ferguson joined. By serving under Morgan, Ferguson was one step closer to being a Confederate operative, but he never enlisted. In fact the liminal space Ferguson occupied allowed him "to move fluidly between irregular and regular warfare" (81).[8] Ferguson frequently took prisoners only to kill them with his knife, his favored method of dispatching enemies. He also tortured captives. But "I killed men to get them out of the way, only; I took no pleasure in torturing them," he said to one reporter after he captured and killed two Unionists (99). As his repute grew, Ferguson took on more responsibility as he gained followers enamored with the partisan lifestyle. In 1864, working with more conventional Confederate forces, Ferguson's band participated in the Battle of Saltville in October. It was there that Ferguson and his men deliberately targeted and killed black Union soldiers. On the night of the seventh, he went so far as to sneak into a Union hospital and murder two black soldiers as they convalesced (150).

In the spring of 1865, Ferguson was captured and brought to Nashville to stand trial for his crimes. Charged with fifty-three murders, Ferguson's lengthy trial ended with a guilty sentence that was read in October. In spite of appeals for leniency sent to President Johnson, he was hanged later that month, a process that took over a half-hour to end the life of the notorious Confederate outlaw. Although it is usually reported that the commandant of the Andersonville Prison, Hartman Wirz, was the only Confederate hung for war crimes, Ferguson also fits that bill—even though he never officially enlisted as a Confederate soldier. Though Ferguson's execution violated the spirit of how former Confederates were handled, he received more consideration than the victims of the Shelton Laurel Massacre. The fact that a reputed killer went through the legal process before being executed shows the differences in the ways that backcountry disputes were handled compared to more official proceedings. After his capture Ferguson was brought out of the world of backcountry violence and into a federal courthouse where he pled his case. Those thirteen men and boys at Shelton Laurel had no such chance.

T. R. C. Hutton explored the purpose of community violence in *Bloody Breathitt* (2013). The eponymous county, squarely in the eastern reaches of Kentucky, became bloody during the Civil War, much like "Bloody Madison" did in western North Carolina. The partisan warfare in Breathitt, a pro-Confederate county surrounded by a sea of Unionism in a state that declared neutrality, "blurred the distinction between social relations and military strategy" (38). Hutton also parsed socioeconomic motivation in rather sophisticated ways. He noted that slavery and prewar party affiliation did amount "to something almost approaching class consciousness," for Confederate sympathizers tended to be Democratic slave owners with access to fertile bottomlands. Conversely Unionists tended to be poorer and lack the means of purchasing slaves (48–52). Unionist Home Guard units, which were sponsored by the state and brutally enforced

Unionism, often came into conflict with pro-Confederate State Guard units or partisans. As was the case in Madison County, North Carolina, at the time of the Shelton Laurel Massacre, much of the fighting and dying that occurred in Breathitt happened between men who knew one another. It made the fighting more personal, more vicious, and also more difficult to forget. The memory of the war, and the fact that white Kentuckians were staunchly Democratic in the wake of slavery's abolition, brought the violence into a new era.

That violence in Appalachia persisted beyond the end of the Civil War should not be a surprise. Residents of the southern highlands who decided on secession as the best way to preserve local government saw their faith misplaced in the Davis administration. The centralizing habits of the Confederate government made many mountaineers question their loyalty. Unionism flourished in communities across the region, and the fractious nature of those decisions lingered. In the same way that southerners after the fact convinced themselves and the nation that the war was about the growing power of the federal government, southern highlanders also misplaced the meaning of the war. As the war's racial legacy gave way to reunification and romanticism during the Spanish-American War, white Americans after the war whitewashed its meaning, rather than accept the emancipationist legacy championed by African Americans and their Republican allies.[9] The reality of the Civil War as a complicated, lived experience for millions of Americans, fraught with meaning, gave way to a memory of a war that became a tool for white southerners to deny basic rights to blacks. It should not be a surprise, then, that Travis Shelton was a product of that false memory; in spite of the fact that secessionists massacred his Unionist ancestors, he still wore a shirt with the battle flag of the Army of Northern Virginia. Leonard reminds him, "If you'd wore it up here in the 1860s it could have gotten you killed, and by your own blood kind" (*World Made Straight* 28). Yet cognitive dissonance was not at work in Leonard during this exchange. He had simply succumbed to the narrative of the Civil War endorsed by white southerners. Perhaps South Carolina's recent removal of the Confederate battle flag from the grounds of the statehouse illustrates this point. Americans forgot the divisiveness wrought by the war and chose instead to remember romanticized aspects of the conflict that focused on heroism and gallantry.

In contrast Appalachian scholars have done an astute job of recapturing the dissent, confusion, and violence that marked Appalachia's experience during the Civil War and beyond. Likewise Ron Rash's novel *The World Made Straight* also recaptures the complexities of the Civil War in Appalachia, and how the echoes of that conflict shape the modern world. Never wholly loyal to the Confederacy, fractured mountain communities could never go back to the way they once were. *The World Made Straight* is an excellent example of how those communities are still reeling from the changes wrought by the Civil War. For acknowledging the impact of the Civil War on Appalachian life and the momentous wake it left in the lives of those who experienced it, Rash should be commended for offering a novel so keenly aware of the nuances of southern Appalachian history.

Notes

1. For more information on the Shelton Laurel Massacre, see Phillip Shaw Paludan's *Victims: A True Story of the Civil War.* For an example of Rash's own interpretation of the event, see his essay "The Facts of Historical Fiction."

2. The recent conclusion to the Civil War's sesquicentennial saw many historians weigh in on the war's perpetuity. See, for example, David Blight's "The Civil War Isn't Over."

3. On the reevaluation of Civil War dead, see J. David Hacker's "A Census-Based Count of the Civil War Dead."

4. Some historians have argued that Confederate tactics, and therefore southern violence in general, stemmed from its Scots Irish heritage. Most notably see Grady McWhiney and Perry D. Jameison's *Attack and Die: Civil War Military Tactics and Southern Heritage.* It is not inaccurate to say that much of the eighteenth-century backcountry was populated by "borderers," or migrants from northern England, Scotland, and Northern Ireland who were accustomed to "incessant violence"; see David Hackett Fischer's *Albion's Seed: Four British Folkways in America* (626). Ethnocultural analysis can lend some explanatory weight to the problem of Appalachian violence, but it should not be seen as the sole or even the primary contributing factor.

5. Historians tend to look at class differentiations as markers for support or opposition to secession. Richard Drake argued that "common farmers" were more likely to remain Unionist while slaveholders in Appalachia tended to support the Confederacy. It should be noted that the mountain South's Unionism did not necessarily preclude support for the institution of slavery (93–95).

6. The interpretation offered by Inscoe and McKinney largely follows the more detailed account provided in Paludan's *Victims.*

7. Scholars have long argued that economic dynamism was part and parcel of the Appalachian experience. See, for example, Robert D. Mitchell's collection *Appalachian Frontiers: Settlement, Society, and Development in the Preindustrial Era,* as well as Wilma A. Dunaway's *The First American Frontier: Transition to Capitalism in Southern Appalachia, 1700–1860.* Any discussion of the southern economy is incomplete without an analysis of slavery. Though Inscoe and McKinney figure slavery into their analysis, other historians downplay the significance of slavery in the mountain South. One exception is Dunaway's masterful *Slavery in the Mountain South.*

8. Much of McKnight's strength comes from his understanding of the war's context in the Cumberland region. See his *Contested Borderland: The Civil War in Appalachian Kentucky and Virginia.*

9. On the changing memory of the Civil War, see David W. Blight, *Race and Reunion: The Civil War in American Memory.*

Works Cited

Barksdale, Kevin T. "Violence, Statecraft, and Statehood in the Early Republic: The State of Franklin, 1784–1788." *Blood in the Hills: A History of Violence in Appalachia.* Ed. Bruce E. Stewart. Lexington: University of Kentucky Press, 2012. 3–25.

Blight, David. "The Civil War Isn't Over." *Atlantic* April 9, 2015. https://www.theatlantic.com/politics/archive/2015/04/the-civil-war-isnt-over/389847/.

———. *Race and Reunion: The Civil War in American Memory.* Cambridge: Harvard University Press, 2001.

Drake, Richard. *A History of Appalachia.* Lexington: University of Kentucky Press, 2004.

Dunaway, Wilma A. *The First American Frontier: Transition to Capitalism in Southern Appalachia, 1700–1860.* Chapel Hill: University of North Carolina Press, 1996.

———. *Slavery in the Mountain South.* New York: Cambridge University Press, 2003.

Fisher, David Hackett. *Albion's Seed: Four British Folkways in America.* New York: Oxford University Press, 1999.

Fischer, Noel. "Feelin' Mighty Southern: Recent Scholarship on Southern Appalachia in the Civil War." *Civil War History* 47 (December 2001): 334–46.

Hacker, J. David. "A Census-Based Count of the Civil War Dead." *Civil War History* 57 (December 2011): 307–48.

Hutton, T. R. C. *Bloody Breathitt: Politics and Violence in the Appalachian South.* Lexington: University of Kentucky Press, 2013.

Inscoe, John C., and Gordon B. McKinney. *The Heart of Confederate Appalachia: Western North Carolina in the Civil War.* Chapel Hill: University of North Carolina Press, 2000.

McKenzie, Robert Tracy. *Lincolnites and Rebels: A Divided Town in the American Civil War.* New York: Oxford University Press, 2006.

McKnight, Brian D. *Confederate Outlaw: Champ Ferguson and the Civil War in Appalachia.* Baton Rouge: Louisiana State University Press, 2011.

———. *Contested Borderland: The Civil War in Appalachian Kentucky and Virginia.* Lexington: University of Kentucky Press, 2012.

McWhiney, Grady, and Perry D. Jameison. *Attack and Die: Civil War Military Tactics and Southern Heritage.* Tuscaloosa: University of Alabama Press, 1982.

Miller, Wilbur R. *Revenuers and Moonshiners: Enforcing Federal Liquor Law in the Mountain South, 1865–1900.* Chapel Hill: University of North Carolina Press, 1991.

Mitchell, Robert D., ed. *Appalachian Frontiers: Settlement, Society, and Development in the Preindustrial Era.* Lexington: University Press of Kentucky, 1991.

Paludan, Phillip Shaw. *Victims: A True Story of the Civil War.* Knoxville: University of Tennessee Press, 1981.

Rash, Ron. "The Facts of Historical Fiction." *Publisher's Weekly* April 10, 2006. 78.

———. *The World Made Straight.* New York: Henry Holt, 2006.

Stewart, Bruce E., and Paul H. Rakes, eds. *Blood in the Hills: A History of Violence in Appalachia.* Lexington: University Press of Kentucky, 2011.

"I AM HAUNTED STILL"

The Shelton Laurel Massacre in Ron Rash's Work

John Lang

Anyone familiar with Ron Rash's 2006 novel *The World Made Straight* knows the integral role played in it by the Shelton Laurel Massacre of January 1863, during which Confederate troops in Madison County, North Carolina, murdered thirteen noncombatant Union sympathizers ranging in age from twelve or thirteen to more than sixty. That massacre confirmed the county's Civil War–era reputation as "Bloody Madison." But the atrocity had haunted Rash for more than a quarter century before *The World Made Straight* was published. "In the [late] 1970s and '80s," Rash told interviewer Thomas Ærvold Bjerre, "I started writing some poems about Shelton Laurel and got more and more interested in it," though none of those poems seems to have been published until 1998 (220). Rash also referred to the "decades of research" that contributed to the novel, including research on nineteenth-century medicine, for in writing the book Rash created twelve italicized ledger entries purportedly written by Dr. Joshua Candler, who served with the Confederacy's Sixty-Fourth North Carolina Infantry Regiment, the unit responsible for the massacre ("Facts of Historical Fiction" 78). While the ledgers are Rash's invention, Dr. Candler was an actual person—and Rash's great-great-great-great-grandfather—who might have been present at the killings and might even have been ordered to participate in the slaughter. For Rash that massacre became emblematic of what Melville in *Billy Budd* called "the mystery of iniquity" (128) and emblematic of human beings' rejection of the divine command to love one's neighbor.

As Rash declared in an essay entitled "Shelton Laurel" in the *North Carolina Literary Review*, "One of the most troubling aspects of history is how some of the worst atrocities have occurred among people who have shared a particular place . . . and thus coexisted for generations, as in Nazi Germany, and, more recently, in Rwanda, Cambodia, and Bosnia" (115), and "as in Madison County, N.C., among my own ancestors, during the Civil War," he added in his essay

"The Facts of Historical Fiction" (78). Rash has highlighted this massacre not only by placing it at the center of *The World Made Straight* but also by publishing three brief essays on the event and more than half a dozen poems about it, including one poem each in the issues of *Appalachian Heritage* (fall 2002) and the *Iron Mountain Review* (2004) that featured his work, a clear indication of how central Shelton Laurel is to his artistic vision. His second and third books of poetry, *Among the Believers* (2000) and *Raising the Dead* (2002) both contain two additional poems either about the massacre itself or about its continuing impact on the residents of Madison County, while *Waking* (2011) offers yet another such poem. Although the first of Rash's essays on Shelton Laurel, "The Facts of Historical Fiction," did not appear until after the publication of most of these poems and nearer to the release of *The World Made Straight,* the essay illuminates the poems as well as the novel. All three essays conclude with the single-sentence paragraph, "I am haunted still," a statement that helps explain Rash's ongoing engagement with this event throughout his literary career.

In "The Facts of Historical Fiction," Rash emphasized both his own family's possible role in the massacre and the relevance of that violence to more recent "internecine atrocities." He also pointed out the divided loyalties among people in mountain communities in the South, noting that Madison County, for example, "was evenly split between Unionists and Confederates during the war" and that Shelton Laurel itself was a "Unionist hotbed" (78). It is the image of twelve year-old David Shelton—murdered in cold blood despite his pleas for mercy—that haunts Rash as this essay closes. The other two essays Rash published on the massacre both bear the title "Shelton Laurel," a phrase Rash sometimes has used as a place name, the site of the massacre, while at other times the term designates the massacre itself. The first essay appeared in the twenty-fifth anniversary issue of the *Iron Mountain Review* (2007) as a response to the editor's request for a brief piece on the author's principal "allegiances." The other essay, an expanded version of the one in *Iron Mountain Review,* was published in 2008 in *North Carolina Literary Review.* Both these essays provide much more autobiographical information than does "The Facts of Historical Fiction," including an account of a childhood experience incorporated into *The World Made Straight,* when Leonard Shuler criticizes Travis Shelton for wearing a Confederate flag T-shirt (28–29), just as an uncle had criticized young Ron for sporting a Confederate cap ("Shelton Laurel," *North Carolina Literary Review* 114).

In these later essays Rash mentioned that Dr. Candler's brother Zachary also served in the North Carolina Sixty-Fourth, while the author's great-great-great-grandfather, Martin Rash, served with Union forces from that state. The latter, Rash remarked, "did not join the Union army until after the Shelton Laurel massacre," adding that "several of my older relatives believe his enlistment was a response to the killings" (116). The pathos of Rash's account of David Shelton's murder in these later essays is enhanced by David's telling the soldiers "that he forgives them all for killing his father and brothers" before futilely pleading to be spared (116). The longer essay in *North Carolina Literary Review* also mentions one of Rash's key historical sources: a *New York Times* account of the massacre dated July 1863.[1]

That article, perhaps not surprisingly, contains several factual errors, however, so Rash relied, as he indicated on the acknowledgments page of *The World Made Straight,* on "Phillip Paludan's excellent book *Victims,*" the most extensive historical analysis of the massacre (291). But Rash's novel follows the *New York Times* article in declaring David Shelton to be twelve years old, not thirteen, although Rash's poems "Shelton Laurel" and "Good Friday, 2006: Shelton Laurel" refer to "Shelton's youngest son" as "thirteen years old" (*Raising the Dead,* 23; *Waking,* 60).

The seven poems Rash has devoted to the massacre and its bitter legacy tend to underscore the brutality at Shelton Laurel, what "Madison County: 1864," the first of these poems to be published, calls "an intimate politics / of atrocity" (*Among the Believers* 11).[2] Set in the year following the massacre, the poem focuses on the violence perpetrated by both sides during a time when men "authored new testaments from / Jehovah's old laws," phrasing that suggests the subversion of Jesus's New Testament ethic of love for one's neighbor in favor of the *lex talionis* of the Old Testament's Jehovah. The poem concludes with a reference to Shelton Laurel's Widow Franklin, to whom Leonard Shuler alludes in *The World Made Straight,* using her as an example of atrocities committed by Union forces, for she had been forced to watch them burn down her home and kill three of her sons (*The World Made Straight* 199; Paludan xxii). Paludan recounted her testimony, during a post–Civil War trial, about the way she raised her boys (22), words of advice paraphrased by Rash in the poem's final lines: "If you die, die like a dog, / your teeth in somebody's throat."

The second Shelton Laurel poem in *Among the Believers,* "Allen's Command," immediately follows "Madison County: 1864" and, as its title suggests, deals with the nominal commanding officer of the North Carolina Sixty-Fourth, Colonel Lawrence Allen, although it was actually Lieutenant Colonel James A. Keith, according to Paludan, who ordered the execution of the thirteen prisoners (85), and it is Keith whose name is most often associated with the massacre in *The World Made Straight.* Yet whoever gave the command to kill the prisoners, the consequence of that order were dire: "Those fortunate / died from musket balls, the rest / hoe-hacked like snakes, their one grave / danced on to push them deeper / into hell" (12). Rash's dance imagery here mirrors that used in the *New York Times* article of July 24, 1863. Whereas most of Rash's poems about the massacre use his characteristic seven-syllable line, "Shelton Laurel" in *Raising the Dead* differs by being an epistolary poem in blank verse, a letter penned by one of the soldiers ordered to serve on the firing squad that winter day. That letter, written one week after the massacre, the soldier intends to deliver to his sister. In the letter he explains that although he aimed his rifle away from the prisoners, he is haunted by the bloodshed he witnessed. In fact the cruelty of the massacre impels him to desert his regiment and to take refuge in a cavern, a setting suggestive of the atavistic violence the atrocity manifests. While the unnamed soldier envies the cavern's blind fish "for all they haven't seen" and hopes that "with enough time" he too might "cease to see these things I tell you of" (24), the impulse that underlies these poems is the desire to confront the violence that seems inherent in human nature, not to look away but to make visible the ongoing impact of humanity's persistent recourse to the "politics / of atrocity." In this poem Rash also made it clear that human beings themselves must assume responsibility for renouncing such violence, for the natural world is portrayed as indifferent to the massacre: "when it ended the sun burned in the sky / like any other day. The French Broad still / flowed southward down to Asheville" (23). Admirable for being repelled by the slaughter, this soldier has withdrawn, at least temporarily, into a passivity and longed-for blindness that Rash has rejected.

"The Dowry," the following poem in *Raising the Dead,* though set in the postwar period, centers on a conflict arising from the continuing animosity the war engendered in Madison County, between the poem's principal antagonists, named Candler and Shelton. Having lost a hand in the war, Colonel Candler refuses to allow his daughter to marry the "homemade Yankee" Jake Shelton "until / what he'd lost to a sniper / filled that sleeve again" (25). The resulting stalemate is resolved only when Jake brings the colonel his severed right hand, Jake's wrist "blood-staunched by a lover's knot" (25). This poem inspired Rash's short story of the same title published in *Nothing Gold Can Stay* more than a decade later. Although in that story the antagonists' surnames are changed to Davidson and Burke and the local pastor, not Burke, sacrifices his hand to appease Colonel Davidson, Madison County remains the setting for the events depicted. In both story and poem, Rash underscored the intense antipathy and intransigence that mark the maimed Confederate officer. The dramatic sacrifice required to overcome such antipathy reflects Rash's consciousness of the severe obstacles that hinder forgiveness and reconciliation. As in Dietrich Bonhoeffer's theology, with its rejection of what Bonhoeffer famously calls in *The Cost of Discipleship* "cheap grace," so from Rash's religious perspective mutual accord among adversaries requires compromise and self-sacrifice. Only intense empathy and heart-felt commitment to an ethic of love for one's neighbor have a chance of defusing such entrenched hostility.

The single poem, "Good Friday, 2006: Shelton Laurel," that addresses the massacre in *Waking* concludes the fourth of that book's five sections, one that contains three other poems about the Civil War or veterans of that conflict. In this poem Rash again dealt with the fate of David Shelton: "he had asked / one mercy, not to be shot / like his father—in the face," a mercy the boy appears to have been denied (60). For the poet returning repeatedly to this event, the poem's final sentence is crucial, for if "the land / unscrolls like a palimpsest," so does human history, with its horrible layering of atrocity on atrocity despite the lessons the past might teach. The Good Friday setting of the poem may be meant to link David's innocent suffering with that of Jesus, but it may also be intended to invoke the forgiveness that both the crucified Christ and David offered their executioners. By dating the experience as occurring in 2006, the year *The World Made Straight* was published, Rash once again affirmed the ongoing relevance of the past to the present, one of the major themes throughout his fiction and poetry.

The two uncollected poems on the massacre, "Bloody Madison" and "At Shelton Laurel," differ from those already discussed because both present a speaker identifiable as Rash himself. The former poem focuses on Dr. Candler, the speaker calling him "my ancestor," as Rash did in his essays. In contrast to those essays, however, in which Rash explained that he did not know exactly what Dr. Candler had done at Shelton Laurel or whether the doctor was even present at the massacre, this poem assumes that Candler helped to kill the folks he had previously saved from disease and death. "Each poultice and splint and stitch / enabled that future end," Rash wrote ironically, death becoming the "quick, merciful cure" for the suffering the doomed prisoners anticipate.

In "At Shelton Laurel," Rash recounted a winter visit he made to the site of the massacre like the visit he described having made there during the spring of 2003 in his two essays titled "Shelton Laurel," the visit that prompted him to begin writing *The World Made Straight* ("Shelton Laurel," *North Carolina Literary Review* 116). A less accomplished poem than the others, it nonetheless sheds light on the novel because in the poem Rash attributed to his father sentiments that the novel places in the mouth of Leonard Shuler's grandfather, who gives to Leonard Dr. Candler's ledgers. According to the poem, it is Rash's father who told him, "haunted places make us feel / less real than they are" (5; cf. *The World Made Straight* 86, 202). Whereas in this poem, set nearly a century and a half after the massacre, the visiting speaker's "white steps / vanish in white," in "Allen's Command" "red / blossomed the snow," and in "Shelton Laurel" "the snow had turned from white to red." Part of the impulse that led to Rash's novel on the massacre was his desire to inscribe on the white or blank page of his reader's consciousness a bloody event that speaks to so much of human history, including that of the twentieth and twenty-first centuries. As he remarked in the longer of his "Shelton Laurel" essays, "We live in an era that, much to its own peril, seems incapable of even acknowledging there is a past, much less that some resonance of that past might linger in a particular place" ("Shelton Laurel," *North Carolina Literary Review* 116). For Rash the aim of historical fiction, "the best that any work of historical fiction has to offer," is "a chance to grapple with the mysteries and complexities of the past, in hopes of seeing the present a little clearer" ("Facts of Historical Fiction" 78).

In *The World Made Straight,* those historical mysteries and complexities are developed primarily through the fictional ledger entries ascribed to Dr. Candler. (As I have noted in *Understanding Ron Rash,* those ledgers are a literary creation reminiscent of the ones Isaac McCaslin reads by his grandfather in Faulkner's *Go Down, Moses* [73].) Dr. Candler's, dating from 1848 to 1863, are in the possession of Leonard Shuler, the doctor's great-great-grandson. Rash presented twelve italicized entries from the ledgers and had Leonard refer to two others. It is, in fact, with a ledger entry that the novel opens, so readers of the book need to pay careful attention to those entries, which detail the care Dr. Candler provides to some of the very people who later become victims of the massacre, including David Shelton and his family. Such background knowledge enhances the irony of the doctor's presence at Shelton Laurel, whatever role he may have played in the violence there.

The first ledger entry, dated August 5, 1850, records the doctor's visits to three patients, among them Maggie Shelton, seven months pregnant and suffering from uterine bleeding (3), while the second, dated August 12, 1852, lists the names of three additional patients, including Nance Franklin and Dewey Morton, the latter later reported to have died of fever in an entry dated January 17, 1863 (185). Adding to the irony of the doctor's visit to Nance Franklin is the fact that the doctor's fee is paid in part by work done to repair the doctor's roof by her two oldest sons, whom she is later forced to watch murdered by Union soldiers (199).

The third ledger entry, dated September 12, 1856, lists among the doctor's patients both Joe Woods, already fifty-eight years old in that year, whom Paludan considered the oldest person murdered at Shelton Laurel (97), and Billy Revis, who ironically survives the threshing machine that mangles his arm in 1856 to serve in the North Carolina Sixty-Fourth, losing two toes to frostbite in January 1863 and later becoming the person who delivers the dead doctor's final ledger to Candler's widow in May 1865 (260–61). Both the fourth and fifth ledger entries document additional contacts with the Shelton family: a James Shelton (Paludan named two James Sheltons as among the massacre's victims [5]) and David Shelton himself, whom the doctor saves from scarlet fever when David is eight years old according to a ledger entry dated December 21, 1859 (79–80). It is this entry that Leonard "had turned to most often over the years," wrote Rash (115), as Leonard presumably ponders how Dr. Candler could both save the child's life and stand by while that life was snuffed out some four years later.

Rash used these entries not only to portray the doctor's relationships with his patients but also to trace the country's drift toward war and the war's impact on the doctor. An entry dated May 13, 1861, for instance, describes the doctor's treatment of various patients who have been arguing and brawling over the issue of North Carolina's secession from the Union, this entry having been written almost exactly a month after the attack on Fort Sumter that initiated the Civil War. Dr. Candler treats Lawrence Allen, later the Colonel Allen who commands the North Carolina Sixty-Fourth, for aphonia, Allen having lost his voice championing secession. Seemingly out of place in the ledgers' focus on healing and medicine, Dr. Chandler, for the first time, comments on the politics of the day: "Would it be that not just Allen but Zeb Vance and his Raleigh firebrands would get aphonia to quiet their braying about states rights" (101). This entry mentions several other patients, including Julius Candler (presumably a relative of the doctor, perhaps the "first cousin" who joined "the Union forces" [206]) and Abney Shelton, both bleeding from "fisticuffs" sparked by the debate over secession, which the doctor calls "this folly," hoping it "may yet be prevented" (102). A week later, however, North Carolina did, in fact, secede, and Dr. Candler found himself serving among Confederate troops. The final ledger entry in the first of the novel's two parts, an entry dated January 2, 1863, reveals that the doctor is on the last day of a furlough in Marshall, the county seat, where he treats four female patients, the men apparently absent on military duty.

While each of the seven chapters in part 1 is preceded by a ledger entry, part 2 begins immediately with chapter 8, perhaps to emphasize how hectic the doctor's life has become. All the entries in part 2 are less detailed than those in part 1, as if hastily composed. Like the last entry in part 1, two deal with events in January 1863, the crucial one dated January 17, the day before the massacre, and identified by the doctor's location, Shelton Laurel (185).[3] After identifying various patients treated, that entry concludes with the word "Others," a term that Leonard assumes refers to the women of Shelton Laurel who were whipped—and brutalized in others ways, Paludan says (96)—to force them to reveal the whereabouts of their fathers, husbands, and sons (181). Leonard also speculates that "Others" might refer to some of the prisoners, whose fate Dr. Candler could not have foreseen.

Even more significant from Leonard's viewpoint is the absence from the ledgers of any entry for January 18, an omission that suggests Dr. Candler finds the massacre literally unspeakable. "No January entry had been torn or cut out," Leonard observes, though he does find an entry for January 19, one readers of the novel never see, being told only that the entry contains "no mention of the prisoners or of Shelton Laurel" (204). Rash mirrored the doctor's silence by omitting any ledger entry before chapter 11, even though entries do precede chapters 9, 10, 12, 13, and 14, the brief final entry written by a friend of the doctor to report Candler's death and burial and to request that the ledger be delivered to the doctor's widow (255). In the massacre's aftermath, Candler appears to come to believe that his silence at Shelton Laurel was a species of complicity, for one ledger entry recounts his being "waked by a vexing dream" (209), while another, his last, dated June 17, 1863, describes his having received a mortal wound. "Much pain as God is just," he writes. "Refuse anodynes. Want mind clear to pray for my soul, ask forgiveness for what cannot be hidden from my Maker" (223).

The reconciliation with God that Dr. Candler seeks is paralleled in the novel's time-present action by Leonard's unfolding relationship with seventeen-year-old Travis Shelton, a high school dropout for whom Leonard becomes a surrogate father after the teenager comes to live in Leonard's trailer following a conflict with his biological father. A former history teacher who has lost his job—as well as his wife and daughter—after being falsely accused of drug possession, Leonard recognizes Travis's natural intelligence and intellectual curiosity, encouraging the boy's interest in his ancestors and their fate at Shelton Laurel—and also persuading Travis to obtain a G.E.D. Yet, ironically, Leonard now supports himself by selling drugs and alcohol out of his trailer, an occupation he decides to terminate as his friendship with Travis deepens. The contrapuntal structure that Rash employed in this novel, alternating Dr. Candler's ledger entries with events in the late 1970s, indicates the past's continuing impact on the present. As Travis acquires more knowledge of the massacre, his empathy and commitment to others' well-being also intensify. And as Leonard's relationship with Travis strengthens, Leonard ultimately escapes the passivity that has marred his life, though he does so only at the cost of that life, further evidence that Rash has rejected easy resolutions to deep-seated conflicts. Through his relationship with Travis, Leonard hopes to make partial amends for his Candler ancestor's involvement in the massacre, a stance that reflects one of Rash's major aims in writing this book, which he characterized as a novel "that posits the possibility of past wrongs set straight" ("Shelton Laurel," *North Carolina Literary Review* 116).

It is Leonard who first corrects Travis's misconception that it was Yankees who murdered his kinfolk at Shelton Laurel (29), thus sparking the teenager's desire to learn more about the massacre. Leonard gives Travis a book with a chapter on the killings, and after reading that material, Travis proposes that the two visit the site the same morning, an excursion Rash detailed in chapter 5, during which, using Leonard's metal detector, Travis locates a pair of glasses, one frame missing its lens, that are later proven to be David Shelton's, as Travis initially suspects (90, 117). It is during this visit that Leonard first tells Travis, "You know a place is haunted when it feels more real than you are," and that Travis ponders "the notion that time didn't so much pass as layer over things, as if under the world's surface the past was still occurring," an idea that corresponds to Rash's use of the term "*palimpsest*" in his poem "Good Friday, 2006: Shelton Laurel" (*Waking* 86; Rash's italics). Chapter 5 enables Rash to provide background information about the massacre—David Shelton's last words, for instance, and a description of the mass grave in which the victims were buried—and about the nearly equal division of loyalties between the Union and the Confederacy in Madison County. Nevertheless, says Travis, "You'd think they [Colonel Allen's forces] wouldn't have done such a thing to their own neighbors" (93), to which Leonard responds, "History argues otherwise" (94). Significantly Paludan likewise stated that he was drawn to the Shelton Laurel Massacre because of his interest in what Robert J. Lifton called "the atrocity-producing situation," especially as that concept relates to the Holocaust and the My Lai massacre by American troops in Vietnam (Paludan ix, xx).

Rash kept David Shelton and the massacre in the reader's consciousness by having Leonard repeatedly reflect on the ledgers or read a passage from them (as he does in chapters 4, 6, and 9); although Dr. Candler's name does not appear in the novel until page 116, the physician's first name, Joshua, appears on the following page. To this point an earlier reference to Leonard's "Grandfather Candler" is the only link between Leonard and the doctor (77). Chapter 8, the first chapter in part 2, extends this emphasis on the massacre because Travis has been reading *The Civil War in North Carolina,* which mentions the whipping of women in Shelton Laurel, including one eighty-five-year-old (160). In chapter 8 Leonard also recalls reading the *New York Times* article of July 24, 1863, entitled "Barbarous Outrages Perpetrated upon Union Men by the Rebels" (164). Gradually revealing the details of the massacre, Rash complicated the reader's response to it in chapter 9 by having Leonard "imagine" what the doctor's actions might have been on the eve of the massacre as Candler interacted with those Others (181–83). Such imaginative reconstruction of the past is precisely what Rash himself undertakes in this novel, envisioning the dilemma confronting his own ancestor. At the same time, Rash implicitly recommended to his readers that they humanize the other through the power of empathy, a key term introduced in the novel during Travis's first encounter with Leonard (23).

Leonard and Travis make a second visit to Shelton Laurel in chapter 11 on the anniversary of the massacre, January's chill and snow reinforcing the coldhearted action of the perpetrators of those murders. During this visit Leonard evades Travis's question about Leonard's ancestry, commenting only that "the Shulers came from Swain County in the 1890s," and thus concealing his connection to Dr. Candler, uncertain how Travis might react to such a revelation. It is during this visit, too, that Travis dons David Shelton's spectacles in an effort to see the scene from David's perspective, something Leonard declines to do when Travis hands him the glasses, an action that underscores Leonard's customary tendency toward passivity and disengagement, a stance that he finally overcomes in the novel's penultimate chapter because of his growing commitment to Travis. Chapter 11 adds further details about the massacre and its principals, among those details the death of Lieutenant Colonel Keith's fourteen-year-old nephew shortly after the boy joined the Sixty-Fourth and Leonard's assumption that "Lieutenant Keith and Colonel Allen had chosen this open area [where the massacre occurred] deliberately, for they knew eyes watched from nearby cliffs and ridges," the killings being "a performance for the men who hadn't been captured" (206).[4]

The climactic chapters of *The World Made Straight* revolve not around the massacre but around the conflict between Travis and the Toomeys over Dena, the thirty-four-year-old drug addict who has also been living with Leonard. Heavily in debt to the Toomeys for the drugs she has used, Dena has become ensnared in debasing sexual abuse by the Toomeys, a situation from which Travis rescues her, prompting the Toomeys' search for both. Because Travis's father had recently told Travis of Leonard's Candler lineage ("His momma's great-granddaddy helped kill off near every member of your family" [231]), Travis distrusts Leonard but has no other potential allies in his confrontation with the Toomeys, who are killed, along with Leonard, when he grabs the steering wheel of the pick-up truck in which he has been compelled to ride with them, forcing the vehicle over the side of a mountain road.

Although Rash strains credibility as the novel reaches this resolution, it seems clear that both Travis and Leonard have learned one of the key lessons of Dr. Candler's experience at Shelton Laurel: not to remain a bystander, for the bystander's passivity makes him or her complicit in evil. This lesson is one Rash reinforced in part by having some of the action of the novel's lengthy penultimate chapter set at Shelton Laurel, where the Toomeys catch up with Travis and Dena, though Leonard enables Travis and Dena to escape. Later, following the truck accident, as the injured Leonard approaches death, he considers how "Joshua Candler had made the choice to side with the shooters that January morning" (282), a choice Candler's ledgers reveal the doctor later regretted and a choice Leonard rejects in his final struggle with the Toomeys. To an even greater degree, Travis embraces empathy and compassion in his rescue of Dena, qualities absent from the perpetrators of the massacre and absent from those responsible for the other atrocity-producing situations that Rash's fiction frequently invokes. The novel's closing sentence places Travis on a route of "ascent," the road's "straighten[ing]" echoing the book's title, which itself alludes to Isaiah 40:3 by way of Handel's *Messiah* (289, 159). Moreover, in saving Travis and Dena, Leonard has partially redressed the violence enacted at Shelton Laurel.

Some of Rash's more recent fiction continues to address Shelton Laurel or analogous atrocities, such as *Saints at the River,* which prefigures his concern with such subject matter through journalist Allen Hemphill's book on the genocide in Rwanda and Allen's experiences as a reporter in Kosovo, as well as through environmentalist Luke Miller's Peace Corps service in Biafra. In the short story "Dead Confederates," Rash alluded to Shelton Laurel without naming that event when the caretaker at the cemetery—somewhat surprisingly, perhaps, to the uninformed reader—allows the grave robbing to proceed because the second Confederate officer being disinterred served in the North Carolina Sixty-Fourth and the caretaker's great-grandmother, who "sided Union," had been whipped by soldiers seeking information about her men folks' location (*Burning Bright* 62–63). In Rash's 2012 novel *The Cove,* likewise set in Madison County, the author has kept the memory of Shelton Laurel alive by naming his female protagonist Laurel Shelton and by having Laurel's elderly neighbor Slidell recall the murders of his father and sixteen-year-old brother by outliers who considered them Union sympathizers (81). One reviewer of this novel suggested that Laurel's ancestors may have fled to Tennessee after the massacre because her parents are described as moving from that state to purchase land in the cove in the late nineteenth century (Martin). Similarly the extreme sacrifice required to effect reconciliation in the short story "The Dowry" in *Nothing Gold Can Stay* becomes more comprehensible if examined in relation to Rash's poem of the same title, whose principal characters, as mentioned earlier, are named Candler and Shelton. *Nothing Gold Can Stay* also includes a story entitled "A Servant of History," its denouement centering on the consequences for the protagonist of his failure to recall the parties involved in the Glencoe Massacre of 1692. And Rash's short story "Outlaws," the final selection in *Something Rich and Strange* (2014), includes a character named Jason who participated in the My Lai massacre and who takes strange comfort from the first-person narrator's published story (a fiction) about Jason's having lost both hands in a train accident. According to Jason that story brings comfort because in his recurrent dreams about My Lai, he can no longer reenact his part in the killing (433).

As such recent stories as "A Servant of History" and "Outlaws" demonstrate, Rash has remained haunted by what Lifton (again, as quoted in Paludan ix, xx) called "atrocity-producing" situations. For Rash the Shelton Laurel Massacre typifies on a smaller scale this larger historical phenomenon and represents the profound flaw in human nature that leaves Tracy of his first book convinced "we live in a fallen world," a world desperately in need of redemption (*The Night the New Jesus Fell to Earth and Other Stories of Cliffside, North Carolina* 43). In *The World Made Straight,* Rash's allusion to Handel's *Messiah* indicates one source of such redemption. But Rash's fiction and poetry also underscore the need for heightened awareness of humanity's capacity for evil and conscious cultivation of such virtues as empathy, compassion, and love for one's neighbor. While this didactic dimension of his work might strike some readers as platitudinous, his fiction and poetry record the myriad ways people betray this ethic of love, and his writing thus acknowledges the intense challenge these precepts continue to pose—not as abstract ideas to be contemplated but as a way of life to be enacted.

Notes

1. A typo in the *North Carolina Literary Review* printing of Rash's essay cites the date of this *New York Times* article as July 14, 1863, but the article was actually published on July 24.

2. "Madison County: 1864" was originally published in *Carolina Quarterly* 50.2 (1998): 47.

3. Phillip Shaw Paludan's *Victims* contains an appendix that discusses the "two conflicting dates for the massacre" (137), but Paludan believed that "it is highly likely that the proper date is January 18" (139). In *The World Made Straight,* Rash followed Paludan in this regard, but in his essays "Shelton Laurel" and "The Facts of Historical Fiction" Rash used January 23 as the date of the massacre.

4. Although Keith held the rank of lieutenant colonel, in *The World Made Straight* Rash usually referred to him as Lieutenant Keith (161, 182, 206). On one occasion, however, the officer is referred to as Colonel Keith (282).

Works Cited

"Barbarous Outrages Perpetrated upon Union Men by the Rebels." *New York Times* July 24, 1863: 3.

Bjerre, Thomas Ærvold. "'The Natural World Is the Most Universal of Languages': An Interview with Ron Rash." *Appalachian Journal* 34 (2007): 216–27.

Bonhoeffer, Dietrich. *The Cost of Discipleship.* New York: Macmillan, 1959.

Lang, John. *Understanding Ron Rash.* Columbia: University of South Carolina Press, 2014.

Martin, D. G. "Ron Rash's 'The Cove'—Laurel Shelton or Shelton Laurel." Chapelboro.com, April 8, 2012. http://chapelboro.com/pages/10065369php?archive=l&pid=231614. Accessed July, 25 2015.

Melville, Herman. *Billy Budd, Sailor. Melville's Short Novels.* Ed. Dan McCall. New York: Norton, 2002. 103–70.

Paludan, Phillip Shaw. *Victims: A True Story of the Civil War.* Knoxville: University of Tennessee Press, 1981.

Rash, Ron. *Among the Believers.* Oak Ridge, Tenn.: Iris, 2000.

———. "At Shelton Laurel." *Iron Mountain Review* 20 (2004): 5.

———. "Bloody Madison." *Appalachian Heritage* 30.4 (2002): 28.

———. *Burning Bright.* New York: HarperCollins, 2010.

———. *The Cove.* New York: HarperCollins, 2012.

———. "The Facts of Historical Fiction." *Publishers Weekly* April 10, 2006: 78.

———. *The Night the New Jesus Fell to Earth and Other Stories from Cliffside, North Carolina.* 1994. Columbia: University of South Carolina Press, 2014.

———. *Nothing Gold Can Stay.* New York: HarperCollins, 2013.

———. *Raising the Dead.* Oak Ridge, Tenn.: Iris, 2002.

———. *Saints at the River.* New York: Holt, 2004.
———. "Shelton Laurel." *Iron Mountain Review* 23 (2007): 71.
———. "Shelton Laurel." *North Carolina Literary Review* 17 (2008): 114–16.
———. *Something Rich and Strange: Selected Stories.* New York: HarperCollins, 2014.
———. *Waking.* Spartanburg, S.C.: Hub City, 2011.
———. *The World Made Straight.* New York: Henry Holt, 2006.

THE DEVIL AT THE BOTTOM

Southern Honor Culture in the Novels of Ron Rash

Edward J. Whitelock

"Still waters run deep . . . and the devil lays at the bottom" (212). These are the recollected words of Deputy Bobby Murphree's grandmother as Ron Rash's debut novel, *One Foot in Eden,* nears its end. In a literal sense, still waters can be indeed deceptive in their nonthreatening appearance but deadly when taken for granted. Such is the situation that opens Rash's second novel, *Saints at the River,* when Ruth Kowalsky steps into the middle of the seemingly calm Tamassee River only to be swept away over the falls and drowned in a hydraulic. But Grandmother Murphree's statement is figurative, and intended as a different kind of warning: The appearance of calm and order in daily life can be just as deceptive, and just as deadly. The southern culture of honor, that ambiguous set of deeply held principles and practices traceable back to the Anglo-Saxon honor code and seeded into the landscape by the Scots Irish and Welsh immigrants who populated the Appalachian and southern regions of the United States in the eighteenth and nineteenth centuries, has long served to create an appearance of calm and order, and it has proven as deadly as any seemingly placid river gorge. It is the devil at the bottom of southern gentility and social propriety.

Southern honor culture is commonly known but little understood, easy to satirize in our popular culture but difficult to analyze. Stereotypes abound: think of Yosemite Sam as the old southern plantation master chasing the impudent Yankee, Bugs Bunny, back across the Mason-Dixon Line in the controversial 1953 Warner Brothers cartoon "Southern Fried Rabbit." Such a caricature, and so many others like it,[1] connects with an audience because of widespread familiarity with the stereotype of thin-skinned southern bellicosity. But as with all stereotypes, the seemingly simple proves highly complicated. Clarifying honor's place in general culture has been acknowledged as difficult. Elizabeth

Fox-Genovese noted that the "elusiveness of the concept of honor has bedeviled scholars and played havoc with those whose behavior scholars try to understand" (Fox-Genovese and Genovese 106), while Whitley Kaufman reminded us that "[honor] is not a simple idea but a complex ethos" (558). Specifying honor's deep hold on and within southern culture has proven exceptionally challenging, but scholars have identified a number of defining characteristics.

Edward Ayers called southern honor culture "simultaneously potent and elusive," noting that since its proponents failed to record its workings from the inside, historians have been forced to "reconstruct it out of fragments, glimpsed encounters, passing comments" (19). Bertram Wyatt-Brown, the first to comprehensively examine the subject, did exactly that in his classic study *Southern Honor: Ethics and Behavior in the Old South,* turning to literary texts along with memoirs, letters, and the standard stuff of the historian to construct a deeper understanding of the topic. Wyatt-Brown, in constructing his working definition of the term, argued that fiction serves as a valuable historical resource because "storytelling, fictional or historical, satisfies a basic human curiosity to learn how it all came out" (xiv). Wyatt-Brown's then-controversial approach has, over time, proven prescient in clarifying the breadth of influence that southern honor culture exerted in the broader culture. "Above all else," he contended, "white southerners adhered to a moral code that may be summarized as the rule of honor," and he connected that characteristic to the south's historical violent streak (3). "Honor," Wyatt-Brown summarized, "is reputation" (14), and the maintenance of that reputation comprises most of the unwritten but commonly understood rules of the code.

Richard E. Nisbett and Dov Cohen built on Wyatt-Brown's work in their *Culture of Honor: The Psychology of Violence in the South,* contending that the Scots Irish and Welsh descendants of precolonial herding cultures who populated Appalachia and the American South brought their code of honor with them. In this society "the individual is prepared to protect his reputation . . . by resort to violence" (xv). Further Nisbett and Cohen emphasized that, in matters of personal honor, "there are high costs for backing down from a challenge, *and everyone knows it* [Nisbett and Cohen's emphasis]. . . . Insults cannot be ignored, because a man's reputation for strength and toughness is compromised until he proves himself through violence, or at least through dominant or aggressive behavior signaling a capacity for violence" (38–41). This honor code was exclusive to white males, and in the highly class-stratified South, questioning one's manhood or his ability to provide for his family or to protect his property was experienced as an insult. And as Ayers noted, "All knew that the failure to respond to insult marked them as less than real men, branded them, in the most telling epithets of the time, as 'cowards' and 'liars'" (13). Kenneth Noe called this affront "the central insult in Southern honor culture" (1095), while Kenneth

Greenberg noted that a southern gentleman "would rather kill or be killed than accept the affront" (32).

While seeking to define southern honor culture, these scholars have agreed, as well, on another significant feature, its amorphousness. Personal reputation rests at the center of the honor culture, around which a collection of widely understood and accepted behaviors and beliefs revolve. Wyatt-Brown identified family allegiance, prescriptive revenge, and reliance on oath taking among this collection, referring to them as holdovers from Indo-European "primal honor" (34). Orit Kamir noted that "an honor culture glorifies as honorable conformity to its honor code, while debasing deviant conduct and constructing it as shameful" (196), while Ayers emphasized the importance of reputation first noted by Wyatt-Brown, declaring honor "a system of values within which you have exactly as much worth as others confer upon you" (13). These defining elements coalesce into an observable working definition of southern honor culture. Here is where Wyatt-Brown's inclusion of fiction as a tool for the historian proves so valuable. Ron Rash, a writer who contended, "Southerners among Americans . . . have the deepest sense of history" (Bjerre 218), can be considered, through his fictional representation of the Appalachian South, an active participant in the exercise of exploring and clarifying the southern honor culture for a broader audience. Zackary Vernon called Rash a "firm believer in W. J. Cash's idea that 'many Souths' exist simultaneously" (104), which reflects on Rash's ability to portray the many distinct elements of the honor code at work through the storyteller's tools.

Major characters and key plot points in Rash's novels are directly guided by allegiance to or challenges of the southern honor culture and its code. I will examine how the treatments of southern honor culture in Rash's first five novels construct a comprehensive representation and critique of the honor code. Defining those characteristics as conformity to the code, family allegiance, prescriptive revenge, reliance on oath taking, and the maintenance of one's reputation, we can see that these novels emphasize one of these elements above all others. Each novel is not, of course, exclusive in its treatment of any one aspect of the honor code, but one can identify a singular, dominant element of the code in each of Rash's novels. But the devil is always in the details of how the honor code guides his narratives. The major plot points of *One Foot in Eden* are shaped by conformity to the code, while bonds of family allegiance guide the characters' decisions in *Saints at the River.* Prescriptive vengeance bookends the action of *The World Made Straight,* and, while *Serena,* too, is a novel filled with vengeance, the code's bond of oaths dominates the shaping of that narrative. Finally, *The Cove* offers a blistering critique of the code's emphasis on reputation.

The honor code served first as a means of maintaining order, its strictures designed to uphold a sort of frontier law. "Fighting, shooting, stabbing, feuding, and shotgun weddings," Ayers told us, "were considered legitimate and inevitable results of honor confronting honor" (79). Further, as Grady McWhiney noted in *Cracker Culture,* "It was customary of Southerners and other Celts to settle their personal disputes, especially those related to their honor, outside the courtroom" (169). The deadly confrontation between Billy Holcombe and Holland Winchester in *One Foot in Eden* can be seen as just such a scenario. This novel, more than Rash's others, is most shaped by its characters' obedience to the code, their acquiescence to its ability to provide order outside of the parameters of prescribed law. Billy and Amy Holcombe are immersed in the honor culture, deeper so when Billy becomes a landowner, purchasing his farm from Holland Winchester's father, who taunts him as he signs the deed, "A Holcombe owning land. . . . You're getting above your raising, boy" (121). That comment would sting, deeper so for Billy's inability to do anything other than accept it as he signs his name. But, having done so, he and Amy can focus on the next step in gaining communal respectability—raising a family. They discover, however, that Billy's bout of childhood polio has left him sterile. As the community questions their childlessness, Amy reveals Billy's limitation, effectively unmanning him in the eyes of their community, and Billy responds angrily, "Damn you to hell for talking of it with others" (66). Already sensitive to his reputation owing to his parents' poverty, Billy sees this breaking of a confidence as more damning, even, than Amy's eventual breaking of their marriage vows.

Holland Winchester's manhood, on the other hand, is never doubted. He is almost a model for Nisbett and Cohen's southern male proponent of the honor culture, projecting "a stance of willingness to commit mayhem and to risk wounds or death for himself" rather than tolerate an insult (xv). His violent character is revealed in the novel's opening, when Sheriff Alexander finds him in the bar following a fight. Holland meets the sheriff's challenge by calmly displaying the dried, severed ears he carries in a pouch, souvenirs from his Korean War service (6). Holland is a man who has lived by the code and whose family embraces it. Even his mother never questions the justification of Billy's having killed Holland when the time comes; she only demands its verification so that satisfaction in kind can be later demanded and met. Holland further unmans Billy when he lays with Amy, cuckolding him. Because of his own allegiance to the code, he understands that Billy has no recourse but to respond with violence, pointing the gun barrel to his own chest during their confrontation and admitting "I'd have killed a man who done to me what I done to you" (127). That Holland's war experience and sincere love for Amy and the baby she carries has softened him is not, in this context, a sign of personal growth but is rather perverted by the code into a weakness.

Both Holland and Billy understand the frontier justice that is due, and neither questions it. Billy chooses to conform to the honor code, not just in shooting Holland as revenge for his cuckolding, but even more so when he agrees to keep Amy's secret and raise the child, Isaac, as his own son. This latter act is a bold and bald act of manipulation of the code, engineered by Amy, and one for which they could both be damned if their secret were ever revealed. And it is revealed, though Isaac as quickly buries it again, dropping Holland's just-recovered bones into the rising waters that will also consume both Amy and Billy. Isaac ultimately chooses loyalty to the family that raised him and, like his parents, ironically maintains conformity to the code through his deception. Rash's treatment of this element of the honor code is to problematize it, something he has done with each novel. If conformity to the code is supposed to be a socially accepted stance, Rash has gone out of his way to demonstrate a situation wherein such conformity creates a deeply moral dilemma.

The next element of the honor code, familial loyalty and, by extension, loyalty to place and home, plays a role in all of Rash's novels. Sheriff Alexander's tenuous relationship with his brother and estrangement from his father in *One Foot in Eden* stems solely from his decision to move from the family farm to town. Such "getting above one's raisin'" creates the gulf between Travis Shelton and his father in *The World Made Straight.* Family bonds will complicate Hank Shelton's ability to marry and start his own farm in *The Cove,* and it is Pemberton's choice to remain loyal to his bastard son that brings about his undoing in *Serena.* The theme of family allegiance runs most strongly, though, in Rash's second novel, *Saints at the River,* where the theme of family allegiance, like that of obedience to the code, is problematized and complicated by the messiness of being human.

Maggie Glenn, like Sheriff Alexander, has chosen to leave her family and community for a life in the city. She returns to Oconee County, "the Dark Corner" as outsiders call it, as a photo-journalist assigned to a regional story quickly growing into a national cause. Ruth Kowalsky's drowning in the Tamassee River and the subsequent entrapment of her body within a hydraulic below the falls set off a conflict between her wealthy northern family, who want to retrieve her body, a local environmental group led by Maggie's ex-lover, Luke, who wish to protect the river from any exception of law that could lead to its further destruction, and the members of the valley's impoverished logging community, whose meager livelihoods lay threatened equally between the forces of environmental protection and commercial development. Maggie describes herself as "a woman who [has] spent much of her life focusing on surfaces to reveal deeper meanings" (13), yet she ultimately fails to live up to this self-assessment, mostly because of her conflicted resistance to the codes into which she was born. Her estrangement from her father is tangled in the complex vortex of the code, as she simultaneously refuses to forgive him his failure to live up to his responsibility of paternal protection while defending her own youthful choice to take Luke, the rash environmentalist, as a lover. Maggie's brother, Ben, remains permanently scarred from the scalding he had received when their father left them alone to buy cigarettes, forgetting the pot of hot soup boiling on the stove. She refuses to accept her father's admission of guilt just as she refuses to acknowledge that her relationship with Luke was, under the strictures of the code, rationally viewed by many as an act of defiance not just to her father but to the community as a whole, who depended on the logging industry to survive.

Although she is welcomed upon her return, Maggie is held at arm's length because her loyalties are forever in question. Her inability to see truly below the surface of things is reflected in the photograph she takes of Herb Kowalsky, standing above the falls and wiping away what appears to viewers as a tear but is actually a gnat. The photograph and its false interpretation elicit widespread sympathy for the Kowalskys and their temporary dam project, effectively winning the battle for that side. Maggie, who by her own account views the past as a black-and-white photograph (178), simplified and static, is a counterexample of familial allegiance, a lesson in the complexities of breaking away from such strictures. If there is a sense of calm at the surface of any family dynamic, it is hiding a devil of a treacherous undercurrent.

Conversely we see the principle of familial allegiance emphasized among the townspeople of the river valley, particularly via Maggie's twin cousins, Randy and Ronnie. The locals consistently demonstrate connection and an understanding of familial bond, forming a united front that accepts the outsiders but maintains a boundary beyond which only family may pass. It is family obligation that guides their daily lives and choices. When Randy makes his decision to dive into the dangerously swelling river in an attempt to retrieve Ruth's body while the temporary dam above him buckles under the strain, he does so not because of the content of Ellen Kowalsky's plea for her daughter's proper burial, but because he understands the bond of family and the power of one's pledge. Despite Herb Kowalsky's bluster and the hubris of the dam engineers, despite, even, Ronnie's warning, Randy dives into the river because it is the honorable thing to do. It does not matter that Kowalsky has called them all "hillbillies" (56); Randy risks, and ultimately sacrifices, his life in an act of courage that demonstrates his commitment to the code of family. As in *One Foot in Eden,* Rash took this principle of the honor code and gave it life in complicated, contradictory circumstances that force the reader to question the very values represented as virtuous.

Family, too, provides much of the conflict in Rash's third novel, *The World Made Straight.* Travis Shelton's discontent with the life of a tobacco farmer creates an unbridgeable gulf between himself and his father. Furthermore his relationship with Leonard Shuler, his mentor and protector, is complicated and sorely tested by the revelation, gleefully dispensed by his father, that Leonard is a descendant of the Candler clan, who massacred members of the Shelton family in a harrowing and bloody Civil War event still remembered among the hill folk. What complicates their relationship one hundred years after the horrible event are the trappings of Anglo-Saxon blood vengeance that remain still woven into the southern honor code. When Travis asks why he had not told him of his own lineage, Leonard responds, "Because it would have changed things between us. It shouldn't. . . . But it would have" (269).

The novel opens with a reworking of Rash's story "Speckled Trout." Character names are changed,[2] but the main story remains the same. Travis discovers a plot of marijuana plants while hiking deeper into "the back of beyond" in search of better fishing holes. He steals a few plants and drags them back to a friend who introduces him to local drug dealer and former high school teacher Leonard Shuler, who buys the plants and offers to buy more. Travis returns to the pot plot twice more, but on that second return steps into a bear trap, falling into the hands of the notorious Carlton Toomey and his son, Hubert. As Nisbett and Cohen noted, the honor code is specific in what must be done to protect one's possessions against thievery: "Potential predators will go elsewhere rather than risk dealing with a man who knows how to defend himself and his possessions and who appears to not be afraid to die" (xv). Carlton must uphold that rule of the code but plays with Travis when he acknowledges, "Coming back up here the second time took some guts. Even if I'd figured out you was the one I'd have let it go, just for the feistiness of you're doing it" (36). This is most likely a hollow promise, because Toomey has Travis gasping at his feet like a hooked trout pulled from the stream. Travis must pay for his greed and stupidity, of this there is no doubt under the code. Hubert would rather just kill him, and Carlton suggests that they have done as much to others when he says, "I think we done used up our allotment of accidental drowning around here" (36). This line of dialogue, absent from the original story, offers some hope for Travis's life but does not absolve him from punishment. Where in his original story Rash left readers to expect the worse, here Travis will get to live, albeit it with a distinct limp that everyone can see in order to understand its origin. Carlton is sincere when he says, "I'm sorry I have to do this, son," but it is not a statement of regret. Rather it is an acknowledgment that both he and Travis have a role to play within the code, and Carlton, hawkbill in hand, carefully carving into Travis's heel until the tendon snaps, is doing what is made necessary by Travis's foolish actions (38).

Carlton Toomey is perhaps Rash's most fearful villain. Serena may compile a higher visible body count, but Toomey's every snakelike gesture promises violence. He has woven the honor code so tightly around his being, it is twisted into justification for all manner of criminal activity; there is honor among these thieves, albeit a warped version, but one to which Carlton ascribes all value. When he appears at Leonard's trailer, rattling the bag of pills out of his car window like a rattlesnake, Carlton is upholding a vengeance code. Leonard is obligated to purchase the extra pills because he has participated in the theft against Carlton by buying the weed from Travis. He must now make good on this honor debt (49). Carlton, further, has no qualms in prostituting Dena because, in his logic, she brought that debt on herself when she made the choice to swallow the pills she was supposed to be selling (245). That he can sing gospel in a voice sweet enough to bring tears to a convict's eyes and do so with sincerity only adds to the complexity and ominousness of the character.

The World Made Straight is a novel of prescribed vengeance enacted under the honor code though ultimately thwarted through an act of self sacrifice. The Toomeys' vengeance can be escaped only through death, which is why Leonard grabs the steering wheel that sends their truck off the road and into the gorge. After the crash Carlton offers an oath to Leonard, promising if he gets them both out of the chasm alive, he will forgive all debts, both those to be paid in cash and those owed in blood. He offers, even, to "swear it on my own son's blood," pointing to the body of Hubert protruding from the wrecked truck's windshield (281). Leonard will not accept that oath, watching as Carlton breathes his last breath before himself succumbing to his injuries, knowing that Travis and Dena are now safe, made so by his own self-sacrifice, the only means of ending the process. In Rash's treatment of prescriptive revenge, readers see, again, a complication of what is supposed to be the simple rule of a straightforward code. No party is fully innocent, for while Carlton Toomey is certainly the villain of the novel, it is Travis's initial theft that sets events in motion.

Much has been written about Rash's most acclaimed novel, *Serena,* and there is much to cover in the complex, masterful tale, including its Shakespearean references, its examination of gender roles, and its embedded environmentalism. For all the novel's violence, it might seem surprising that this is not the primary element that ties the novel to the honor code. Rather *Serena* is a novel of oath making and oath breaking, and it is this element of the honor code that dominates the novel's plot.

Serena begins with the clash of two of Pemberton's oaths, his sincerely given oath of betrothal to Serena and the outcome of his insincere seduction of Rachel Harmon. Whatever false promises he made the illiterate girl, her father meets the Pembertons' train to exact his vengeance for that oath's betrayal. Pemberton quickly dispatches the elder Harmon in an impromptu knife duel, disemboweling him in front of a crowd of lumbermen, the sheriff, and the Pembertons' business partners. Pemberton is acutely aware of the honor culture into which he has inserted himself and is happy that "the highlanders," as he repeatedly refers to the loggers, have witnessed this act, as he believes they will hold him in higher esteem for it: "Now they knew he could kill a man . . . they'd respect him" (10). What's more, the duel with Harmon amplifies Pemberton's pledge to Serena, for he has now successfully fought for and defended her. Serena immediately responds with what Jack K. Williams identified as the "pride in being fought over" (19), condescendingly advising Rachel to sell her dead father's knife because, while rightfully Pemberton's prize, "it's all you'll ever get from my husband and me" (10).

For all the novel's violence, it is the many oaths that the Pembertons make or break and their perspective on oaths of service or honor that moves the narrative forward. Serena's first act when introduced to the camp is to enter into a bet with the impudent logger Bilded, who spits when hearing Pemberton's decree that the men are to consider Serena his equal in command. When she wins the wager, correctly calculating closest to the total board feet generated by a massive tree cut down at her command, she demands that the declared oath be met, docking Bilded two weeks' pay, even after Campbell expresses concern for the lumberman's wife and young children. "All the better," she declares. "It will make a more effective lesson for the other workers" (36).

Pemberton and Serena hold all around them accountable to their oaths as a means of maintaining their place atop the mountain hierarchy, and it does not take them long to demonstrate that, in keeping with the honor code, they will resort to violence when they see an oath broken. When Buchanan begins to waver in his promise to stand firm with the Pembertons against selling to the national park interests, Pemberton murders him in a staged hunting accident, which serves to convince Wilkie that his best interests lie in selling his share of the lumber country to the Pembertons. Now in charge of the entire tract, Pemberton and Serena systematically remove through violence anyone whose actions strike them as disloyalty, from business partners, to workers and anyone in their service. When Serena saves Galloway from bleeding to death, he pledges his troth to her and becomes a weapon as deadly to any who would cross her as is the eagle she trains to rid the lumber camp of rattlesnakes. When Harris manipulates his promises to his own advantage, succeeding in actually getting the better in a business deal over the Pembertons, Serena sends her assassin after him to avenge the insincerely given oath. When the foreman, Campbell, quits without permission, he is not trusted to keep the Pembertons' secrets and is tracked down and murdered in bed (283). When Dr. Cheney, who cannot from the beginning hide his disdain for Serena, fails in his doctor's oath to "first do no harm," his insufficient treatment leading directly to the death of their newborn child, he is dispatched (217).

Even Pemberton himself will become Serena's victim when he breaks his pledge of exclusive devotion to her, acting to save Rachel and his bastard son from Galloway's clutches. In trying to save them, Pemberton miscalculates that the former sheriff, McDowell, will keep his secret, but McDowell reveals

Pemberton's payment to Galloway before the assassin kills him, knowing Serena will not accept so close a betrayal and ensuring that Galloway will ultimately do what McDowell himself could not: kill Pemberton. But it must be emphasized that Pemberton dies not as justice for any of his crimes against his business partners, the highlanders, or nature itself, but because he has broken his oath to Serena. The novel may end with a final act of blood vengeance in accordance to the honor code, when Jacob Harmon kills the elderly Galloway and Serena as they sleep in their Brazilian mansion, but it is the blood of oaths, not vengeance, that flows most deeply in this novel. And again, in presenting his theme, Rash complicated it, placing in the "keeper of oaths" role a couple undeserving of trust or honor. Once again we see a supposedly order-inducing code utilized for its opposite intended effect.

Like all of Rash's novels, *The Cove* is set amid real history though it does not set out to tell a historical tale. As *One Foot in Eden* references the Lake Jocassee Dam project and *The World Made Straight* is shaped by the Shelton Laurel Massacre, this novel references the *Vaterland* incident of World War I, with the allegedly mute flute player, Walter, being an escapee from that ill-fated ship's band. History echoes so strongly here that Rash named his heroine Laurel Shelton, a direct allusion to *The World Made Straight* and an indication that her body, like that innocent meadow, will be defined and defiled by the foolish and stubborn adherents to an honor code. In this novel that foolishness is embodied in the character of Chauncey Feith, a person so reprehensible that Rash himself cut two chapters featuring him from the paperback edition of the novel, correctly figuring that readers do not need to spend any extended time with this character to understand his ugliness.[3] Through Feith *The Cove* is a novel that examines, and mocks, personal reputation within the southern honor culture.

Chauncey Feith is identified from the start as a hollow poseur, hypersensitive to others' opinions and possessed of a delusionally heightened sense of self-worth. The pampered son of the owner of the town's savings and loan, who taught him that "refusing to drink anything other than brown liquor was the sign of good breeding" (64), Chauncey has managed to avoid active service in the war by serving as the local recruitment officer. Readers first encounter him in his spit-shined uniform buying a round of drinks in Meachum's bar and worrying that "they were watching to see if he'd sip like a nancy-pants or drink like a man" (65). He spends most of his time filling himself with false pride, trying to convince himself that his recruiter's job requires the same kind of courage as serving in the field, even quietly cursing those who "act brave one time, maybe for just a few seconds" and then find themselves honored as heroes (69). He understands only the glory of war and is unable to see its brutality, even when faced with Hank Shelton's lost hand or Paul Clayton's gas-ravaged lungs. Chauncey believes he can charm and cajole his lasting reputation through government service, daydreaming of the future statue to be built in his honor and the proud, dutiful wife who will stand by his side at the ceremony, placing in that role the secretary of the senator who condescendingly indulges Chauncey's delusions and harnesses his self-importance for his own purpose (146).

But Chauncey is not honorable, and his manipulations of his reputation reveal him as a holdover of the antebellum gentry, an elitist and obsolete class with no place or bearing in the current time. His weakness is exposed with the revelation of Walter as the escaped German, just as Chauncey's long-planned parade and presentation are about to start. Chauncey wants to wait and call authorities in the face of the forming lynch mob. "It's called proper protocol," he stammers. But when Linville Wray, one among the mob, calls out, "I've got another name to call it," Chauncey, rather than standing up to the challenge and doing what is right, gives in to avoid the implication of cowardice, leading the mob forward in their murderous folly (227).

When Chauncey accidentally discharges his pistol, striking and killing Laurel, he is unwilling to take the blame for his actions, accusing Boyce of having ridden too close and jostled him. "You tell that to Hank. . . . He'll kill you for this," Boyce replies (242). Knowing the truth of it, and of Hank's justification for revenge under the code, Chauncey sneaks back alone to where Hank has been tied to his porch and murders him, still too cowardly to look directly at the man while he shoots him (246). He is still concocting the fanciful tale of his heroism for the townspeople when he falls into the uncovered well, never to be heard from again. Here again Rash's fiction problematizes a defining element of the honor code. "Honor is reputation," Wyatt-Brown definitively stated (14), yet, in Chauncey, Rash created a despicable character whose blinkered pursuit of personal reputation lacks all honor, exposing a great flaw within the system itself. Those who would so strive for such a hallowed reputation are often among the hollowest of souls, and those who assist them in the name of honor often serve its opposite.

One element of the southern honor culture remains unexplored, that of women's roles within the code. In Rash's novels this element might just be the most surprising, informative, and important among his many treatments of the code. Rash's female characters are nearly unanimous in their challenges to the honor code, either bucking against its strictures or working to manipulate it to their own advantage. Only the strung-out, prostituted Dena of *The World Made Straight* seems to settle for her role. That novel, which has been criticized among Rash's works as the weakest in its portrayals of women, still presents the strong if not fully formed character of Laurie, Travis's girlfriend, who possesses a single-minded commitment to avoiding the many pitfalls of her poverty. In general and as a collection, Rash's female characters offer an additional critique of the southern honor culture.

Numerous scholars have commented on women's place within the southern honor culture. Ayers contended that honor "offered women nothing except prestige by association with a male relative. Women played the crucial roles of audience and reward for conflict between honorable men, but nothing more" (29). Wyatt-Brown echoed this passive expectation, stating, "Southern women were to embody the virtues of subservience" (50). Robert Elder noted that "while honor was undoubtedly a male-dominated ethical system, women were vital participants in their own as well as their . . . family's honor" and clarifies those expectations as "a reputation for sexual purity, sustained by restraint, prudence, and modesty in every area of life" (583–84). Rash's major female characters, as we have seen, defy these passive, subservient expectations and often in surprising ways.

As previously noted Amy Holcombe uses her affair with Holland not to escape from the maternal responsibilities of marriage but to create and uphold them for herself and Billy. She is noteworthy in taking matters into her own hands, but she ultimately does so in order to fit into the code, as a nurturer, the mother of a child and wife to a virile man capable of giving her that child (or at least agreeing to play that role in the public eye). Laurel Shelton, an outsider who cannot, like Amy, change her status by manipulating herself into the code, quietly but persistently pushes against it, whether embracing her reputation as a witch to scare the local gossips or choosing to be seduced by Jubel Parton so that she may experience what she has convinced herself no man will want to give her through commitment. When Walter shows her otherwise, she embraces him passionately and makes her plans to escape with him to the North. Maggie Glenn struggles, as we have seen, with the outcomes of her choices, but she never questions having made them. Her desires are too broad for the strictures of the code. Serena does not manipulate the code but rather embraces it, subverting it by inserting herself into the male role. This constitutes, of course, the greatest challenge to the code, since she is not, by its own definition and through her gender, allowed to brandish it the way she does. It does not take her long, though, to find its formalities restrictive, so she throws the thing off, like the costume it was, in favor of outright rule by terror. If it is not already apparent, surely through his application of the honor code to his female characters, it is obvious that Rash holds the whole of the tradition in question.

Discussing Rash's importance, Vernon said, "The strength of much of Rash's work is its depiction of southern Appalachian history as it was and is, flinching away from neither the good nor the bad," and he contended that Rash's work "reconcile[s] the many contradictory roles Appalachia has played in the American imagination" (121). The same can be said for Rash's treatment of the southern honor code in his first five novels. Rash carefully characterizes its multiple elements and then problematizes them to reveal the system's contradictions and flaws. Blind conformity to the code often creates the opposite of order. Family bonds do not protect us from all harm and sometimes mislead us. Vengeance is rarely clear-cut. Oaths are only as good as their makers. And reputation is the abode of the scoundrel. All these elements of the southern honor culture, intended to serve order and maintain a surface of calm, hide a devil at the bottom. As Wyatt-Brown contended, "The ethic of honor was designed to prevent unjustified violence, unpredictability, and anarchy. Occasionally it led to that very nightmare" (61). Ron Rash's first five novels demonstrate this truth through masterful storytelling. The southern honor culture might be the subject of pleasant nostalgia in some corners or of mild mockery in others, but as a historical instrument of social order and justice, it represents a deeply flawed, indeed dangerous system. Grandma Murphree's warning should be heeded.

Notes

1. For more on violent stereotypes of southern Appalachia, particularly feuds involving the honor of "blood kin" and the media sensationalism of the Hatfield-McCoy tragedies, see Blee and Billings.

2. In the O. Henry Award–winning story, the main character is named Lonny. Rash changed the teenager's name to "Travis" to indicate themes of movement, or "traveling" between past and present, transgression, and the continuous crossing of social, personal, historical, psychological, and spatial borders, and as a clue that Travis, unlike Leonard, will be able to escape "landscape as destiny" and traverse the mountains to a new future.

3. As John Lang noted, Rash's trimming of Chauncey Feith's role in the paperback version, along with Rash's piercing headnote to the softcover edition, establishes "that the paperback version must be considered definitive as the author's preferred vision" (96).

Works Cited

Ayers, Edward L. *Vengeance and Justice: Crime and Punishment in the Nineteenth-Century American South.* New York: Oxford University Press, 1986.

Bjerre, Thomas Ærvold. "'The Natural World Is the Most Universal of Languages': An Interview with Ron Rash." *Appalachian Journal* 34.2 (2007): 216–27.

Blee, Kathleen M., and Dwight B. Billings. "Where 'Bloodshed Is a Pastime": Mountain Feuds and Appalachian Stereotyping." *Back Talk from Appalachia: Confronting Stereotypes.* Ed. Dwight Billings, Gurney Norman, and Katherine Ledford. Lexington: University Press of Kentucky, 1999. 119–37.

Elder, Robert. "A Twice Sacred Circle: Women, Evangelicalism, and Honor in the Deep South, 1784–1860." *Journal of Southern History* 78.3 (2012): 579–614.

Fox-Genovese, Elizabeth, and Eugene D. Genovese. *The Mind of the Master Class: History and Faith in the Southern Slaveholder's Worldview.* Cambridge: Cambridge University Press, 2005.

Greenberg, Kenneth. *Honor and Slavery.* Princeton, N.J.: Princeton University Press, 1996.

Kamir, Orit. "Honor and Dignity in the Film *Unforgiven:* Implications for Social Theory." *Law and Society Review* 40.1 (2006): 193–233.

Kaufman, Whitley. "Understanding Honor: Beyond the Shame/Guilt Dichotomy." *Social Theory and Practice* 37.4 (2011): 557–73.

Lang, John. *Understanding Ron Rash.* Columbia: University of South Carolina Press, 2014.

McWhiney, Grady. *Cracker Culture: Celtic Ways in the Old South.* Tuscaloosa: University of Alabama Press, 1988.

Nisbett, Richard E., and Dov Cohen. *Culture of Honor: The Psychology of Violence in the South.* Boulder, Colo.: Westview, 1996.

Noe, Kenneth. "'Damned North Carolinians' and the 'Brave Virginians': The Lane-Mahone Controversy, Honor, and Civil War Memory." *Journal of Military History* 72.4 (2008): 1089–115.

Rash, Ron. *Chemistry and Other Stories.* New York: Henry Holt, 2007.

———. *The Cove.* New York: HarperCollins, 2012.

———. *One Foot in Eden.* New York: Henry Holt, 2002.

———. *Saints at the River.* New York: Henry Holt, 2004.

———. *Serena.* New York: HarperCollins, 2008.

———. *The World Made Straight.* New York: Henry Holt, 2006.

Vernon, Zackary. "Commemorating vs. Commodifying: Ron Rash and the Search for an Appalachian Literary Identity." *Appalachian Journal* 41.1/2 (Fall 2013/Winter 2014): 104–24.

Williams, Jack K. *Dueling in the Old South: Vignettes of Social History.* College Station: Texas A&M University Press, 1980.

Wyatt-Brown, Bertram. *Southern Honor: Ethics and Behavior in the Old South.* New York: Oxford University Press 1982.

A HUN ON THE LOOSE

World War I and *The Cove*

Thomas Ærvold Bjerre

Judging from the critical consensus surrounding *The Cove* (2012), Rash's fifth novel is considered a somewhat disappointing novel, especially coming after the widely lauded *Serena* (2008). But many reviewers and critics have barely touched on one of the novel's essential themes: war. Instead the focus has been on already established themes and tropes in Rash's work: the natural world (specifically southern Appalachia) and its people, the recovering of the region's lost voices, and education as escape, as well as the novel's love story, its "thriller" plot, or its "fairy tale" aspects (Wilhelm 23). Granted, *The Cove* is certainly much more than a war story, and in some ways Rash's handling of World War I serves as a way of fleshing out existing themes. To readers familiar with Rash's work, the name of the novel's protagonist, Laurel Shelton, brings associations to Shelton Laurel, the site of the Civil War massacre at the heart of *The World Made Straight* (2006). As Rash elaborated in an interview, one of the ironies is that the "dehumanization" that occurs in *The Cove* is in some ways an echo of the region's previous massacre (Vernon 38). However, *The Cove*[1] invites a closer reading with a focus on the extent to which the novel fits into the well-established tradition of war literature. A few critics have placed the novel in the context of war, calling it an "anti-war novel" (Martin) or drawing parallels to today's harassment and suspicion of American Muslims (Le Guin). And while John Lang correctly noted that war is among Rash's "most obsessive subjects" (98), *The Cove* has yet to be viewed as a war novel, or perhaps more accurately, a novel of war literature.

Unlike the Civil War, the traces of which are physically and psychologically present to this day in Rash's Appalachia, World War I was somewhat of an anomaly in that the fighting took place outside of the United States. But World War I also brought about unique changes to the region. Discussing William Faulkner's debut novel *Soldier's Pay* (1926), John T. Matthews pointed out how the "drastic, even violent onset of modernity" brought on by World War I was felt "all the more acutely" in the South, "the most distinctive and conservative region in the country" (238). This point was also discussed in Zackary Vernon's interview with Rash and fellow North Carolina writer Terry Roberts.[2] Roberts noted how southern isolationism was even more profound in the mountains: "World War I and World War II were the first significant instances of international exposure between the mountains and Europe, as well as Europe and the mountains" (Vernon 41).

So how does Rash approach World War I in *The Cove*? A place to start is Randall Stevenson's observation that the "Great War . . . refuses to remain buried in the past." It has been kept "firmly present in the mind and memory of later decades. Yet it has been remembered variously. Its lengthening shadow has been repeatedly reshaped . . . by the changing cultural landscapes across which it has fallen" (vii). The cultural landscape of *The Cove* can be said to be the United States as seen from Appalachia in 1918. The action is set in the final months of World War I, but the setting is familiar Rash territory: the Appalachian Mountains. While the front line is literally thousands of miles away, the novel features war-related characters such as returned veterans, a German citizen, and a manic army recruiter, as well as the home-front population: women and old or crippled men. So while we can clearly argue that it is a World War I novel, another way of reading *The Cove*—and extending Rash's use of indirection even further—is as a commentary on contemporary America during the War on Terror. At least that seems to be what Rash intended, as he told Vernon: "Sometimes the most effective way to talk about the present is to talk about the past. I would argue that *The Cove* is as much about what is happening in the United States right now as it is about the past" (38). World War I might just be the ideal mirror in which to reflect our current time. As Stevenson argued, "if the Great War refuses to remain buried in the past, it is because the shock, disillusion, and fractured faiths of that first, fundamental modern crisis have so long continued to shape the world in the present, from 1914 all the way to the postmodern age" (viii). In some ways the events of 9/11 as well as the Bush administration's handling of them also amounted to "shock, disillusion, and fractured faiths," certainly for Ron Rash, who declared *The Cove* to be "about The Other" and "about those scoundrels who advocate intolerance and advocate war, although they never go themselves, people just like Chauncey [Feith]," the manic army recruiter (Vernon 38). In the revised paperback version of *The Cove,* Rash again pointed to the link between the past and present, urging readers who wish for more of Chauncey to "close the book and look around" (n.p.).

As with any other subject, notions of war are influenced by earlier representations, or, as Paul Fussell asserted in his seminal work on World War I, *The Great War and Modern Memory* (1975), it seems "impossible to write an account of anything without some literature leaking in" (173). My specific focus in exploring *The Cove* as war literature will be on language or representation as well as its handling of characters, more specifically the deconstruction of certain binary categories of people often associated with war. But let us begin with the issue of how to begin: In his introduction to the 2013 edition of Fussell's book, Jay Winter argued that war is "too frightful, too chaotic, too arbitrary, too bizarre, too uncanny a set of events and images to grasp directly. We need blinkers, spectacles, shades to glimpse war even indirectly. Without filters, we are blinded by its searing light" (x). This dilemma has been a driving force in much of Rash's fiction. But Rash has always (re)presented war through indirection, by means of "blinkers, spectacles, shades." This applies to Rash's treatment of the past in general, but in terms of representations of war, we find the indirect approach in the veterans haunted by their war experience in *One Foot in Eden;* in stories like "Nothing Gold Can Stay" and "Three A.M. and the Stars Were Out"; in the bitter Civil War strife that haunts the contemporary community in *The World Made Straight* (where a pair of eyeglasses from the Civil War plays an important part for the contemporary protagonist); and in the parents worrying about their daughter who is deployed to Afghanistan in "Twenty-Six Days."[3] Rash has yet to write a story or novel set in an actual war zone at the time of war. It has remained distant in one way or another, and regarding *The Cove,* its American setting adds an additional layer of indirectness to World War I. John T. Mathews asserted that the very remoteness of World War I characterizes "America's distinctive relation to the Great War" (217).

Much like Jay Winter argued about the difficulty of grasping war directly, Kate McLoughlin summed up the "generic difficulty" facing "all those who seek to convey the complex, massive phenomenon that is war. How indeed to begin, to end, to find appropriate words?" (*Authoring War* 4). Likewise Didra DeKoven Ezrahi pointed to the "basic tension" between the "instinctive revulsion against allowing the monstrous to be heard" and the equally powerful "instinct against repressing reality, against the amnesia that comes with concealment" (2). The inadequacy of words to convey war is one of war literature's main tropes (Fussell 185), and McLoughlin referred to the dilemma using the rhetorical trope "adynation" ("War and Words" 15), meaning "the impossibility of addressing oneself adequately to the topic" (Vickers 491, qtd. in McLoughlin, "War and Words" 15).

While *The Cove* is not self-reflexive in the same way as much of the war literature that McLoughlin discussed in *Authoring War,* it still reflects and explores the troubled relationship between language and conflict. In *The Language of War,* James Dawes distinguished between what he called "disciplinary" and "emancipatory" models of the relationship between language and violence. The former posits language and violence as "mutually constitutive," while the latter sees language as an alternative to violence, making the two "mutually exclusive"

(1). As Dawes explained it, language and violence exist on a spectrum: "on one end unconstrained violence, on the other unconstrained language, and in between an ambient blending" (3). In *The Cove* we find examples from both ends of the spectrum and of course also the "ambient blending" between the two poles (Dawes 3). Chauncey Feith, the jingoistic recruiter caught up in a paranoid fervor, sees language as a threat, or to use Dawes's models, as disciplinary, as "a method of disciplining and controlling violence in order to concentrate its effects" (1). When Feith goes to the college library at Mars Hill to remove books written in German, he sees books "lined up row after row as if poised for an attack" (139). Even the German language itself "looked sinister, especially the two dots that resembled a rattlesnake bite. The words could mean anything," Feith surmises (141).

The censorship that Feith is exercising corresponds with the anti-German sentiment in the United States during World War I, where the Committee on Public Information (CPI) was in charge of informing the public about the war effort. Even though the CPI provided factual information to the press, its literature and propaganda was fused with a "distinct emotional edge" and a theme of "wartime unity" (Keene 35). David Trask pointed to how the mobilization of hearts and minds led propagandists to produce "a spate of heated articles to stimulate the hatred of the enemy and support for the war effort" (7). The increasing patriotic fervor created an atmosphere of paranoia in which German Americans went from being "one of the most assimilable and reputable of immigrant groups" to one suspected of treason and disloyalty, the latter being "the gravest sin in the morality of nationalism" (Higham 196). Chauncey Feith feeds these fears when he tells the crowd at a war bonds drive: "We must remain ever vigilant, because the Hun will become even more desperate and devious, not just overseas but here in Madison County, where we of late have all but been overrun with likely imperial agents" (117). Rash also showed how the anti-German sentiment has festered in the community at large through other characters as well as conversations and by including propagandistic and anti-German posters, writings, and other forms of propaganda, such as the crude "Kaiser Bill" puppet doll, drawn with "daggered teeth beneath a mustache and monocle," sprawled at the entrance to a farm dance, a "pitchfork jabbed through the chest" (112).

One of the results of the anti-German atmosphere was that the teaching of German was banned in almost half of U.S. states because the German language was believed to disseminate "the ideals of autocracy, brutality and hatred" (Keene 35–36). Concurrently, in his speech, Feith demands "the immediate removal of Doctor Horatio Mayer from his position as Professor of Languages at Mars Hill College" (117). Feith adds, "Let us not hear any more cries about free speech, that colleges should embrace any and all sorts of thinking" (118). Clearly

Feith is an example of what Keene deemed "perhaps the greatest threat that total war posed to the future of American democracy," namely the demand that "the American people think as one" (38). This type of censorship, including Feith's removal of German books, demonstrates how "the effect of violence upon language is amplified and clarified" during war, as Dawes put it (2). He expanded: "Wars are born and sustained in rivers of language about what it means to serve the cause, to kill the enemy, and to die with dignity" (15). The simple act of naming, Dawes argued, "is also the most basic and simple act of coercion" (17). While Feith is the most obvious purveyor of this tendency, Rash made sure that the reader sees how the propaganda spreads and becomes naturalized in the community. As Dawes asserted, propaganda, or "dialogue unsutured . . . represents not the violence of language but rather the victory of violence over language" (17).

On the other end of the language/violence spectrum is "unconstrained language" (Dawes 3). This is the emancipatory model "predicated on the idea that social structures built around democratic language practices emancipate us from the reign of force" (Dawes 1). Rash made several allusions to art, including literature, as something that engenders "empathy and a sense of human interconnection" (Lang 98). While this is true of the music Walter plays on his flute, Dawes's emancipatory relation between language and violence can be found in Walter's detailed story of the *Vaterland* ship, a story that Laurel memorizes and repeats, word by word. As Lang argued, the merging of Walter's and Laurel's stories reflects "the power of art to liberate, to enable people to transcend, through the literary or artistic imagination, their time and place and circumstance" (99). However, as often in Rash's fiction, darkness wins out in the end, or, to put it in the context of Dawes's discussion, violence trumps language. Laurel's oral repetition of Walter's experience on the *Vaterland* is an imaginary escape from the cove, a daydream that only hints at coming true. So the language is never truly given form before violence takes over. That is one of the harsh lessons in a novel that explores "some of the human costs" of war (Lang 97).

Apart from the issue of language and representation, the question of what war does to people has been central to war writing since the *Iliad,* as Sarah Cole noted (25). To consider this question, Cole argued, "is, almost inevitably, to think in categorical and binary terms—combatant and civilian, men and women, young and old, injured and healthy, prewar and postwar, enemy and friend." She then argued that war writing follows a "deconstructive pattern," a trope of which is the disintegration of these categories: "war creates distinct types only to miscegenate them" (26). This is certainly the case in *The Cove,* in which Rash complicated the binary categories related to war. In this way he was also writing within an established tradition of war literature. Cole explored four categories: enemy and friend, civilian and combatant, men and women, and injured and healthy (26). Since all four binary categories are at play in *The Cove*, it makes sense to take a closer look at how Rash employed them.

According to Cole, "in each of the four categories," it is "the body that most palpably and irrevocably disrupts the sense of distinctiveness or boundary" (26). Again and again, Cole argued, war literature provides us with the provocative notion that "the dead and wounded body, perhaps counter-intuitively, pushes back against the organizing oppositions of war" (26, 27). While *The Cove* does not feature scenes of death on the battlefield, it does feature several wounded veterans, a severely wounded Walter, as well as killings that are justified as war related. Furthermore some of the veterans who serve as Rash's minor characters fit into commonly accepted notions of veterans scarred either physically or psychologically (Matthews 234–39). For example Tillman Estep, who spends his days drinking at the Turkey Trot, has "lost an eye and had his face scarred rough as a washboard," and his bitterness comes through in his "telling anyone who'd listen that the war was nothing more than a bunch of men killing each other for a few acres of mud" (63). One of Estep's veteran drinking buddies "had come back from Europe convinced, though he'd had no wound, that his guts were torn up," apparently because he had gutted a German (65). The most horrific depiction of a wounded veteran is that of Michael Davenport, who has been gassed: "Black patches covered his eyes. . . . Burn scars welted his face and neck and phlegm clotted each breath" (114). And Paul Clayton, once an idealistic young man who had been "one of the first to join Chauncey's chapter of the Boys Working Reserve" (71) and who volunteered when he turned eighteen, is in a hospital in Washington with scorched lungs and damaged eyes (89). Two of the characters voice indictments of the "new level of horror," as Rash called gas warfare (Vernon 39). Boyce Clayton, uncle of the maimed Paul Clayton, expresses his incredulity: "Even in war, you'd think some things wouldn't be allowed" (89). And after seeing the blinded Michael, Hank angrily tells Laurel: "There's things people ought not to do to each other, even in a war" (115).

The wounded veteran featured most prominently in the novel is Hank. He lost his lower left arm in the trenches of France, but Rash's depiction of him resonates with established stereotypes of the maimed veteran suffering from shell shock and unable to adapt back home (Matthews 234–39): "he had dug in his boot heels and gotten on with his life, whether it was farm work or sparking [his fiancé] Carolyn Weatherbee" (42). Furthermore, despite his obvious handicap, the loss of his arm has not made him less physically able; quite the contrary, in the first of several scenes of Hank performing hard, physical labor, Rash described Laurel watching her brother: "Hank's right bicep was twice as big as the left, the forearm thick and ropy with blue veins that bulged with each pull. He was so much stronger than when he'd first returned from Europe. Strong enough that even one armed, no one, including Jubel Parton, would want to cross him" (13). Laurel's view of Hank echoes a description of the crippled Billy Holcombe in *One Foot in Eden,* whose hard, manual labor also turned him into an almost hypermasculine figure, at least in the eyes of his wife.

According to Sarah Cole, the "soldiers versus civilians" binary is a "primary distinction that strenuously and inevitably organizes the terrain of 'people in war'" (31). But, as she asserted, during the twentieth century, this "core distinction" had been severely challenged, mainly for two reasons. First, because of conscription, the "citizen soldier," whom Cole saw as "a temporary and often non-voluntary combatant" in contrast to the regular career army officer, has become the "primary icon of war" (31). The second reason is the vast increase in attacks on civilians. Both of these reasons for the breakdown of the soldier-civilian binary can be found in *The Cove.* Apart from Paul Clayton, who volunteered the day he turned eighteen, the veterans in the novel, including Tilman and Hank, were conscripted. As Laurel explains, "Hank didn't want no part of that fight but they made him go anyway" (53). Even though Hank fits the category of conscripted soldiers who, according to Cole, "do not view themselves as belonging, in fundamental ways, to the codes and realities of the military" (31), he still performed an act of bravery and was awarded the Purple Heart.

In contrast to the conscripted and hesitant soldiers who have come back disillusioned, the character of Chauncey Feith serves to blur categories further. As the town's army recruiting officer, he is clearly a part of the military, and he certainly sees himself as fundamentally belonging "to the codes and realities of the military" (Cole 31). Feith is an example of the tendency noted by Leo Braudy of enlistment rates being high "among the middle and professional classes, intent on defending their personal honor and their vision of their nation, headpieces stuffed with images of medieval knights" (374). But Feith's idealistic fantasies of war have never been checked by the gory realities of the battlefield. This leaves him in a predicament. Since World War I propaganda "linked personal honor to national interest" (Braudy 376), Feith remains caught up in the myths that are fueled by the propaganda he espouses, but not all civilians in town are enthralled by his strutting and parading in uniform with his loyal Boys Working Reserve. Rumors have it that he became a recruiter because of his father's connection with the local senator. Also the returned veterans view him with utter disgust and treat him as if he were a pariah (an interesting parallel to the way Laurel is treated by most of the community). When Feith enters the Turkey Trot, "no one looked especially glad to see" him (64), and when he pours a veteran a drink and salutes "all men like you what have worn the uniform," Feith hears "a scoff . . . from the back of the room" (68). Perhaps the harshest comment, and one that shows the disintegration of the soldier-civilian category, comes from Miss Yount, the librarian at the college library where Feith is performing his act of censorship previously described. Feith tries to showcase his authority over her—with two of his troop members watching—by looking her square in the eye and saying, "I am not a student . . . I am a soldier." But Miss Yount's tart reply once again leaves Feith humiliated: "'A soldier,' she said. 'Then why aren't you in Europe?'" (142).

The disrespect from the veterans and parts of the community jars Feith, who tries to diminish the accomplishments of the veterans while convincing himself that he is an "unsung hero" whose job requires a "day-to-day courage as you stood up for what you believed no matter what" (69). Even the big welcome home parade that Feith is organizing for Paul Clayton, complete with music and marches, is dismissed by the veterans as a sorry attempt to boost Feith's standing in the eyes of others. Rash made it clear that the lack of respect leveled at Feith and his reaction to it are grounded in notions of masculinity. Drawing on journals, memoirs, and letters from soldiers in the two world wars and Vietnam, Samuel Hynes concluded about the authority of war narratives that "war cannot be comprehended at second-hand" and pointed to the "authority of ordinary men's witness" (1). In this sense, it can be argued, as Hynes did, that "war does make men." But, he went on, "it also isolates them from other men—cuts off the men who fought from older and younger men who did not share that shaping experience." This experience creates what amounts to "a secret society in a world of others" (5). It is exactly this "secret society" that Feith feels left out of, and no matter how fresh-pressed his uniform, how polished his bronze buttons, or how obedient his boys troop (205–9), nothing can bridge the gap between having been over there and having stayed at home.

Feith's predicament is also tied in with issues of homosociality. As Michael Kimmel explained in his *Manhood in America,* "the evaluative eyes of other men are always upon us, watching, judging" (7). Feith is painfully aware of the evaluative eyes, not just of the civilians, but especially of the veterans. Kimmel quoted an army general, saying "every soldier fears 'losing the one thing he is likely to value more highly than his life—his reputation as *a man among other men*'" (5–6, italics in original). Feith's fear of being called a coward, a non-man, is, in fact, what prompts the tragic escalation at the novel's end. On the day of Paul Clayton's homecoming, which Feith has arranged as an indirect celebration of himself, Boyce and Ansel recognize Walter from a wanted poster. Immediately the flame of anti-German sentiment that Feith has been instrumental in fanning flares up among the men: "Let's go get the damn Hun," urges one while others run for "rifles and ammunition . . . plenty of rope," and dogs (210). The men seek out Feith, who for once has a chance to live up to the role of manly leader he has designated for himself: "'You going to lead them, Sergeant Feith?' Wilber asked. 'Of course he is,' Jack said, 'and we'll be with him'" (211). But Feith is more concerned about missing out on the big ceremony, which he hopes will be the first step on his path to a career in politics. So he suggests turning the case over to the sheriff. The men protest, to which Feith stammers: "'It's called proper protocol.' . . . Jubel stared at him. 'I got another name to call it, Feith,' Linville Wray said" (227). The "evaluative eyes" and the threat of emasculation force Feith to set the hunt in motion.

The gender-based complications discussed above also feed into the "men and women" binary that Cole analyzed. Besides the complex issue of masculinity found in Rash's portrayal of Hank and Feith, Laurel and Walter also deserve attention. First of all having Laurel as the novel's protagonist is in itself a way of deconstructing traditional war narratives. The traditional logic of acknowledging war only through direct experience served to strengthen division into male and female spheres. This also meant that because direct war experience was coded as masculine, the home-front experience was coded as feminine, a coding that "tainted" the men who were not at war. But Rash complicated this tradition in his exploration of Laurel. Because of her local superstition, Laurel's status in the community is that of a witch and pariah. Secluded in the cove—"a cursed place . . . most people in the county believed" (17)—Laurel feels "she herself might be a ghost" (19).

Rash destabilized the power relationship inherent in this exclusion by placing much of the narration close to Laurel's point of view. Furthermore her relationship with Walter becomes an alternative to the official community. The first part of Laurel and Hank's relationship is a nurse-patient relationship. In a war-related context, this is significant territory. Discussing the cultural understanding of nurses based on war literature by men, Cole argued that one of the central premises in the cultural understanding of nurses and soldiers is that "(hetero)sexual activity is good for recovery." To the male soldier, desiring the nurse and having sex with her is "to exit the war domain and reenter a productively civilian one" (33). In contrast, Cole argued, women nurses' writings display "an extremely sensitive, compelling, and at times disruptive account of the gender dynamics created in and by the nursing environment" (33). It is to this latter account that Rash's depiction of Laurel can be said to fit. Because even though Laurel can be cast in the nurse role—with Hank complaining that she is "fussing over [Walter] like he's the king of England" (40)—it is not Walter's recuperation that is the primary focus. Rather it is Laurel's blossoming that we witness. As she nurses him back to health, and as their relationship deepens and becomes sexual, Laurel finds new meaning and a sense of purpose with her life to an extent where it frees her from the apparent curse of the cove. When she memorizes Walter's experience of the *Vaterland,* she can finally claim: "it's part of me, and this place can't lay claim on me any more, not really, even if the war never ended" (170). Through words and imagination and through the relationship with an apparent enemy, Laurel's secluded world opens up and frees her.

The "enemy and friend" binary in the novel is not underwritten by any German soldiers. However, the hysterical atmosphere creates enemies out of German Americans and those associated with them. As we saw above, the previously respected Professor Mayer becomes a scapegoat because he teaches German. But the most interesting conflation of the "enemy-friend" binary is found in the character of Walter, or rather, Jurgin Walter Koch, which is his real name (167). While the reader learns early on that Walter has escaped from some kind of prison, Rash deliberately has kept the reader unaware of Walter's exact background. It is revealed to us concurrently with Laurel's revelation. As it turns out, he was a musician on the German ship *Vaterland,* "the world's largest ship in 1914 and for years afterward" (Painter 28). Rash is drawing on actual historical material here: the internment in Hot Springs, North Carolina, of hundreds of German prisoners, termed "enemy aliens" by the Department of Immigration (Painter 27). Most of the prisoners were civilians working on German and Austrian ships. They had been holed up in American ports since Great Britain declared war three years earlier, but when America declared war, the "interned ships became legitimate prizes of war and were immediately overhauled for conversion to troopships" (Painter 27, 28). So Walter is officially an "enemy alien," which explains his decision to pass as a mute. While his initial goal is to catch a train to New York, his relationship with Laurel makes him change his mind. And when Laurel guesses his real identity, Walter has already proven his commitment to a life in the cove.

Rash did not depict Walter as an enemy figure; that role goes to Chauncey Feith, who comes across, especially in the first edition, as almost too one-dimensional in his villainy. But even in the revised version, Feith is clearly the closest the novel comes to an enemy; someone who creates discord in the community, who entices hatred and bloodlust to such an extent that three innocent people are killed. Walter, on the other hand, is an "alien" but one who brings something of value to the small community. He proves his worth through hard physical labor, in that way staking a kind of claim on the cove. But he also adds new positive elements, as symbolized by his flute playing. Laurel describes it as "the prettiest thing I've ever heard" and reflects that music in general "lets you know you're not all of every way alone, that someone else has known the likesomeness of what you have" (52, 53). Hearing the flute in the cabin, Laurel experiences how the "cabin somehow became less gloamy, as though the music pulled in more light through the windows and chink gaps" (54). The connection between Walter the "alien" and Laurel the cursed witch should be obvious. If not, Miss Calicut points it out when she compares the anti-German sentiment with the way the community shuns Laurel: "'To be treated so badly because of a few foolish people,' Miss Calicut sighed, 'but you've had plenty of experience with that, haven't you'" (151). By showing how Laurel and Walter are both cast as others, outsiders, and threats, Rash wove an additional layer to his criticism of paranoid, prejudiced American culture into the story, while at the same time writing into war literature's tradition of creating a "sense of commonality with the enemy" (Cole 28). Walter's contribution to and influence on the local community is also prominent in a central scene that depicts a merging between German and American. Walter and Slidell play the mountain tune "Shady Grove" on their flute and guitar to the amazement of Laurel, Boyce, and Ansel: the "guitar and flute tightly wove their sounds and then untangled them" (92). Ironically, later in the novel, Boyce and Ansel are the ones who initiate the hunt on Walter when they recognize him from the wanted poster.

Rash's employment of the "enemy and friend" dichotomy, so common in war writing, is but one of many examples of the ways in which *The Cove* works as war literature. In his complex exploration of how war is represented and the role language plays, and in his constant renegotiation and dismantling of the binary terms often associated with war, Rash wrote a novel that belongs firmly in the tradition of war literature. *The Cove* builds on historical material to which Rash added his trademark poetic language and his ear for local dialect to weave a story about specific people caught up in a particular conflict. Because Rash's view on World War I is refracted through our contemporary time, one of the somber points the novel makes is that the ramifications of war, be they on the soldiers fighting or on the civilian population on the home front, are timeless. And the novel's tragic vision, common in Rash's writing, serves to condemn the practice of blind patriotism, then and now.

Notes

1. Unless otherwise noted I will be referring to the 2012 paperback edition of *The Cove.* As John Lang noted, most likely because of the criticism of Chauncey Feith as too one-dimensional, Rash took "the unusual step of revising the book substantially before its publication in paperback" (96). In a note prefacing the prologue in the paperback edition, Rash wrote that "two chapters and a number of additional paragraphs" had been removed, thereby "returning Chauncey Feith to minor character status" (n.p.). More specifically chapters 14 and 19 of the first edition have been removed, and chapter 9 has been moved to chapter 13 in the paperback edition. Furthermore, as Lang noted, Rash also made minor revisions, correcting errors and omitting repetitious words or sentences. For these reasons Lang concluded that the paperback edition "must be considered definitive as the author's preferred version" (96).

2. Roberts's novel *A Short Time to Stay Here* (2012) is also set in Appalachia during World War I.

3. All three short stories are from *Nothing Gold Can Stay.*

Works Cited

Braudy, Leo. *From Chivalry to Terrorism: War and the Changing Nature of Masculinity.* New York: Alfred A. Knopf, 2004.

Cole, Sarah. "People in War." *The Cambridge Companion to War Writing.* Ed. Kate McLoughlin. Cambridge: Cambridge University Press, 2009. 25–37.

Dawes, James. *The Language of War: Literature and Culture in the US from the Civil War through World War II.* Cambridge, Mass.: Harvard University Press, 2002.

Ezrahi, Sidra DeKoven. *By Words Alone: The Holocaust in Literature.* Chicago: University of Chicago Press, 1980.

Fussell, Paul. *The Great War and Modern Memory.* 1975. Oxford: Oxford University Press, 2013.

Higham, John. *Strangers in the Land: Patterns of American Nativism, 1860–1925.* New Brunswick, N.J.: Rutgers University Press, 1988.

Hynes, Samuel. *The Soldier's Tale: Bearing Witness to Modern War.* New York: Viking Penguin, 1997.

Keene, Jennifer D. *The United States and the First World War.* Essex: Pearson Education, 2000.

Kimmel, Michael. *Manhood in America: A Cultural History.* New York: Free Press, 1996.

Lang, John. *Understanding Ron Rash.* Columbia: University of South Carolina Press, 2014.

Le Guin, Ursula K. "The Cove." *Guardian* March 16, 2012. http://www.theguardian.com/books/2012/mar/16/the-cove-ron-rash-review. July 25, 2015.

Longley, Edna. "The Great War, History, and the English Lyric." *The Cambridge Companion to War Writing.* Ed. Kate McLoughlin. Cambridge: Cambridge University Press 2009. 57–84.

Martin, D. G. "Ron Rash's 'The Cove'—Laurel Shelton or Shelton Laurel." Chapelboro.com, April 9, 2012. http://chapelboro.com/columns/one-on-one/ron-rashs-the-cove-laurel-shelton-or-shelton-laurel/. Accessed July 25, 2015.

Matthews, John T. "American Writing of the Great War." *The Cambridge Companion to the Literature of the First World War.* Ed. Vincent Sherry. Cambridge: Cambridge University Press, 2005. 217–42.

McLoughlin, Kate. *Authoring War: The Literary Representation of War from the* Iliad *to Iraq.* Cambridge: Cambridge University Press, 2014.

———. "War and Words." *The Cambridge Companion to War Writing.* Ed. Kate McLoughlin. Cambridge: Cambridge University Press, 2009. 15–24.

Painter, Jacqueline Burgin. *The German Invasion of Western North Carolina: A Pictorial History.* Johnson City, Tenn.: Overmountain, 1997.

Quinn, Patrick. "The First World War: American Writing." *The Cambridge Companion to War Writing.* Ed. Kate McLoughlin. Cambridge: Cambridge University Press, 2009. 175–84.

Rash, Ron. *The Cove.* New York: Ecco, 2012.

———. *Nothing Gold Can Stay.* New York: HarperCollins, 2013.

———. *One Foot in Eden.* New York: Henry Holt, 2002.

———. *The World Made Straight.* New York: Henry Holt, 2006.

Stevenson, Randall. *Literature and the Great War.* Oxford: Oxford University Press, 2013.

Trask, David F., ed. *World War I at Home: Readings on American Life, 1914–1920.* New York: John Wiley and Sons, 1970.

Vernon, Zackary. "Writing the Great War: Ron Rash and Terry Roberts." *North Carolina Literary Review* 23 (2014): 30–47.

Vickers, Brian. *In Defence of Rhetoric.* Oxford: Oxford University Press, 1988.

Wilhelm, Randall. "Introduction: Blood Memory." *The Ron Rash Reader.* Ed. Randall Wilhelm. Columbia: University of South Carolina Press, 2014. 1–32.

SUBALTERNS IN THE HOLLERS

Postcolonial Appalachia in Ron Rash's *Serena* and *The World Made Straight*

James Eric Ensley

In an essay on her website, Appalachian author Lee Smith recounted a story in which she took her New England–born mother-in-law on a drive to her hometown in the mountains of western Virginia. Smith's mother-in-law, surprised by the town's visible poverty and the lack of those trappings typically associated with the Moonlight and Magnolias mythos of the South, asked, "Where are all the big houses?" to which Smith replied, "That was someplace else." Indeed Smith has suggested that southern Appalachia exists in geographic limbo, defined by its negative space; after all much of Appalachia is latitudinally part of the South and frequently labeled as part of that region both on maps and in the popular imagination, though many of the South's best known cultural touchstones—Faulkner, plantations, and genteel social interactions to name but a few—fail to reflect the past or present habitus of most of Appalachia's people. That the culture of Appalachia is alien to both southerners and northerners alike has been, as I will elaborate further, a locus for the creation of Appalachian identity.

Smith's assertion that Appalachia is "someplace else, a world away" is one that permeates both insider and outsider imagination of the region, though only infrequently has this imagination led to the cultural products created by its inhabitants or those writing about it to be approached through a postcolonial lens. I offer that the works of many authors who focus primarily on southern Appalachia, in this case specifically the works of Ron Rash, address the complex epistemic and ontological nature of Appalachians' identity and the ways in which Appalachians are both speaking subjects and cultural objects acted on by regional insiders and outsiders alike. It is, of course, unproductive to speculate as to whether Rash or any other Appalachian author has purposefully written postcolonial literature or if they take as their literary subject a region that is already well established as postcolonial. Yet I suggest when viewed through the lens of critical frameworks by postcolonial theorists and deconstructionists like Edward Said, Gayatri Spivak, and Homi K. Bhabha, Rash can be seen attempting the difficult procedure of giving voice to his Appalachian literary entities, voices that speak neither in panegyric or declamation of mountain life and culture that has exemplified writing about the region since the local color movement of the late nineteenth century.

Nevertheless the application of postcolonial literary theory to a region of what is by many measures the world's wealthiest country opens itself up to critique, as post–World War II America is frequently imagined as both prosperous and free of colonial holdings, as seen in the relationships between the United Kingdom and India or France and Algeria, among many others. Prior to examining Rash's novels *Serena* (2008) and *The World Made Straight* (2006) through the lens of postcolonial theory it is necessary to establish Appalachia as an internal postcolonial region of the United States whose culture has been codified as so alien as to be an Other to both the South and an imagined and homogenized American culture. Furthermore it is necessary to establish that much of its population past and even present could be considered subaltern, in that it has been and remains outside the hegemonic social, cultural, and monetary structures of southern and American metropoles.

Postcolonialism and Appalachia: Codifying a Region

Bill Ashcroft, Gareth Griffiths, and Helen Tiffin asserted that the term "postcolonial" entails all the cultures that have been impacted by "the imperial process" from their original interaction with the colonizing group up to the present (2). Of course this definition may be excessively broad to have import to Appalachia —after all the United States as a whole is classified as postcolonial by this definition. The authors continued, however, with a more nuanced definition that proves particularly useful to this analysis: "What each of these literatures has in common beyond their special and distinctive regional characteristics is that they emerged in their present form out of the experience of colonialization and asserted themselves by foregrounding the tension with the imperial power, and by emphasizing their differences from the assumptions of the imperial centre. It is this that makes them distinctly post-colonial" (2).

The textual resistance described here as a defining characteristic of a postcolonial literary work is palpable in the texts and literary characters of many Appalachian writers, who have resisted the flattening definition of Appalachians as hillbillies, nuancing and granting their voices a variety of valences. Indeed the assumptions of imperial centers are deeply rooted and deeply inhibiting; though Edward Said limited his discussion of Orientalism to the exploitative relationship between West and East, his concept of the imperial metropole defining the Other can likewise be observed in action between Appalachian and American culture. Said famously proposed that "because of Orientalism the Orient was not (and is not) a free subject of thought or action" (2). In this formulation one could insert Appalachia in lieu of Orient and be left with a legitimate construction, in which the cultural abstraction that is Appalachia is reduced to an unchanging entity based on notions of imperial cultural superiority. Rather than being a purely symbolic thought experiment, this exploitation of culture is not free of tangible effects, as it does not limit itself to defining what constitutes the culture in media, anthropological studies, and the popular imagination but also results in the economic abuse of the colonized region, which in Appalachia's case entails its exploitation for timber, coal, and tourism, among other industries that have been established in the area.

I am certainly not the first to draw connections between postcolonial theory and the structure of Appalachian culture. Though literary analysis of Appalachian writings from a postcolonial perspective has been relatively uncommon, historians and cultural critics have explored these frameworks for several decades. In 1978 Helen Lewis, Linda Johnson, and Don Askins published their revolutionary collection of essays *Colonialism in Modern America: The Appalachian Case,* which seeks to instantiate Appalachia among other regions exploited by corporate and industrial capitalism while simultaneously disentangling the region from the narratives of romantic primitivism and a culture of poverty that had long been used to explicate the area's qualities (1–5). Published in the same year, Henry Shapiro's *Appalachia on Our Mind* discusses the mountaineers, who are labeled as having a peculiar "otherness" as early as the 1870s, which he suggested challenged notions of a "unified," "homogenous" American culture (x). Populated by white Protestants who were descended primarily from Anglo-Saxons, Appalachia, Shapiro argued, suddenly in the late nineteenth century became a problem to be solved by integrating the mountaineers into the norms of an imagined, homogenous American life. At the same time Appalachia became a site for local-color writers, some of whom never visited the region, or if they did only for very brief periods, to inscribe and describe their understanding of the cultures and customs of the mountain people through magazine articles and novels (xiv). As in Said's conception of West-East relations, writers, in this case the local colorists, helped concretize the popular understanding of Appalachians as an Other that was "literally exotic" (4). Indeed the local colorists invented the hillbilly type, codifying a group of people as atemporal, a modern anachronism, existing not only in an isolated region but also, literally, of another time; in some local-color accounts, the trek into the Appalachians, as in the works of earlier writers like East India Company men traveling to Calcutta or James Cook in Tahiti, is presented as time travel (28). These early narratives created

Appalachians as a discursive entity for outside populations and posited them to embody unchanging, atemporal ideals, and, further, codified them in media for the consumption of the metropole.

There have been and still are hard-felt repercussions stemming from the codification of mountaineers as an atemporal or primitive entity. Rodger Cunningham posited an imbricated system beginning in the early twentieth century in which Appalachian backwardness and poverty were used as justification and pretext to colonize and educate mountaineers and solve the 'problem' of Appalachian culture (*Apples on the Flood* 102–3). The outcome, however, was an insertion of the mountaineer into industrialized modernity in which the economic exploitation of mountain subalterns in mines and timber camps became a desired part of the didactic enterprise.

At the same time, however, Appalachians had little voice of their own in this process of industrialization and modernization, as the concept of contemporary civilization in the late nineteenth and twentieth centuries was predicated dominantly on literacy (Cunningham, *Apples on the Flood* 104–5). In this framework mountaineers were defined as atemporal, unchanging, illiterate, and therefore infantile in both positive and negative lights. On the one hand, they were conceived as closer to nature, in an anachronistic, Arcadian space; on the other hand, they were held to be childlike, needing to be taught everything from basic hygiene to standard American English (116–20). Cunningham posited this as a double bind related to what he terms "double alterity"—that is, a double Othering from both southern sources, already the subject of Othering in mainstream American culture ("Writing on the Cusp" 41–53). This system creates a dual imperative for the mountaineer, the double bind. Thus there is the command to grow up and join modern society, while at the same time there exists a contradictory command to remain childlike in a romanticized past. Applying R. D. Laing's theory of inner-outer life, Cunningham further argued that the identity crafted by the dominant culture for Appalachians fails to map on to their own internal identity—a state of being Laing named "inauthentic existence" (qtd. in Cunningham, *Apples on the Flood* 117). This inauthentic existence, in turn, leads to the dominated person's perpetual feeling of lacking wholeness and impels him or her to seek validation in either conforming to the mandates of the dominant culture or in isolation from the hegemonic system; this insularity then feeds back into the dominant understanding of the mountaineer as backward and reclusive.

The stripping away of old identities and the inscription of new ones is what Cunningham via Laing referred to as a "disconfirmation of agency," a system in which the very ability of subaltern people, in this case Appalachians, to voice their mind or be cogent arbiters of their own world is denied on the basis of their cultural immaturity (Cunningham, *Apples on the Flood* 118). While this examination of Appalachian culture in a postcolonial mode has hereto remained within the bounds of historical and sociological critique, from the disconfirmation of agency Cunningham discussed we can begin to look at media and literary representations of the mountaineer, which have frequently infantilized Appalachians, objectifying them and flattening their existence to the monovalenced entity that is childlike and primitive. Accounts of Appalachian life from the perspective of authors and artists who are native to the mountains were sparse until the final three decades of the twentieth century; the growth of such native voices in literature, I would suggest, is concomitant with the growth of postcolonial resistance as voiced through scholars and authors like Said, Jacques Derrida, V. S. Naipaul, and others who were and are interested in recovering subaltern voices as literary agents against domination.[1] The persistent, infiltrative image of the mountaineer is perhaps best embodied in the long-running 1960s television show *The Beverly Hillbillies*.[2] Many of the show's plots center not around the active participation of the Clampetts in society, but rather on society impinging on them in business deals or culturally foreign activities, like dinner parties. The entertainment value—a reified commodity—of the Appalachian is then based in the passivity of their existence and their inability to account for and translate the modern world through cultural code switching.

As a remedy to the common characterization of Appalachians in the media, literary works can function as a discursive space to contest the reification and commodification of the subaltern body. In "Can the Subaltern Speak?" Gayatri Spivak posited that colonial control of the body exists at both a material and theoretical level. One can see this in the exploitation of Appalachian laborers as well as their commodified identity in television and other cultural goods. While Spivak cautioned against forcing meaning from the actions of textualized subalterns, she did, however, posit literary space as a locus for "interception" and "decipherment" of the complex agency speaking imparts in works (64). This search for textual voice so dear to postcolonial scholarship is not far removed from the injunctions of Appalachian studies scholars like Cunningham, who suggested that the "wholeness" of existence is polyphonic in that each person has his or her own existence and personal identity outside of the imperial identity inscribed by the Othering tendencies of the hegemonic power (*Apples on the Flood* 122, 132–56). There is currently a strong trend in scholarship looking to Appalachian voices in literature as resistant to the flattening of identity and to objectification and commodification. In 2012 the fall issue of the *Journal of Appalachian Studies* was devoted to questioning what it means to be Appalachian today. In a thought-provoking article in that same issue, Matthew Ferrence wrote about the search for subaltern voices in Appalachian texts, calling for readers to search for narratives that break the false notion that Appalachia speaks in "one voice" (129). With Spivak's caveat concerning the ventriloquism of subaltern peoples in mind, and with caution as to positioning an author as a speaker for objectified Appalachian peoples, it is from the angle of recovering agency and resistance to hegemonic, colonial culture that I suggest Ron Rash's *The World Made Straight* and *Serena* offer a polyphonic textual voice to Appalachians. The novels are connected by their localization in Appalachia, but also by a strong emphasis on language, silencing, heteroglossia, and objectification.

Ron Rash's The World Made Straight and Serena

In his books and short stories, Ron Rash has been committed to giving voice to the previously voiceless peoples of the Appalachian region. These voices do not speak with a unified diction or dialect, nor do they speak only of the folksy topics publications sometimes privilege.[3] Rash, like many other postcolonial writers, has offered his characters as individuals whose unifying quality is their shared involvement in the (post)colonial landscape of Appalachia. Likewise Rash has suggested in interviews that his view of regionalism and Appalachia's involvement on a global scale is transcendental and transregional; Appalachia, in this framework, is postcolonial in the way it has been bound to other exploited regions worldwide.[4] In particular Rash noted the influence that Irish writer Seamus Heaney, who is from one of England's first and most tumultuous colonies, has had on his own regional work. Rash has explained that one of his strongly held tenets is that his writing should always humanize the individuals in it and avoid stereotyping them, a testament to his desire to write Appalachians as polyphonic characters, rather than mountaineer caricatures.

The World Made Straight, in many ways, is a text resistant to the colonizing, monovalenced definitions of Appalachians that have permeated both media and previous literature discussed above. Throughout the work Rash sought to nuance the definition of contemporary Appalachians while simultaneously connecting and disconnecting them from the region's history vis-à-vis the modern implications of the Shelton Laurel Massacre in 1863. Furthermore the limits of the imperial archive as a means of describing the region are questioned continuously throughout the work. Travis, one of the novel's main characters, following a particularly trying conversation with Lori, his girlfriend, and Leonard, his mentor, states, "Words seemed to ruin everything"; he continues, quoting Nietzsche, whose words he had learned from Leonard, "*What can be spoken is already dead in the heart*" (143). These words suggest the dubious ability of text and even spoken words to accurately portray extant conditions, a concept explored repeatedly in the story. Related to this is a quote Leonard ruminates on while thinking of a particularly painful memory and which becomes a major theme of the novel as a whole: "*Landscape as destiny.* . . . He knew what it meant here, the sense of being closed in, of human limitation" (157). Two seemingly disparate forces, landscape and the power of words, conspire, in Leonard's and

Travis's understanding, to define or even ruin lives. As explored earlier Appalachia and the people living there have had codes written for them—ciphers through which they must live their lives. Appalachia, the landscape itself, has had a set of written codes—words—applied to it already, defining what the subaltern person can or cannot become. Throughout the novel Travis, though promising at school, seems unable to break away from the constraints poverty and familial problems have placed on his life, while Leonard, who was educated at the University of North Carolina, also ties his failure as a teacher to the codes of failure inscribed on the Appalachian landscape. Rash's project seems, in part, to consist of Travis's and Leonard's discursive attempts to resist and come to terms with the constraints of their mutual mountain home.

In their characterization Leonard and Travis, both Appalachian natives, subvert regional stereotypes: both are inquisitive and capable of learning, though their circumstances have led them to doubt their own intelligence and ability to succeed. Early in the novel, Leonard engages in conversation with Travis and accuses him of not knowing the definition of the word "empathy," to which Travis asserts that he, though a high-school dropout, is not ignorant and does know the meaning of words not commonly used in mountain dialect. Appalachians are represented throughout the novel as comprehending the Standard English of dominant American culture and turning preconceived notions of the region to their advantage through mimicry of the colonizer. Homi Bhabha offered a theoretical route to explore these acts of understanding, code switching, and mimicry; as he explained in *The Location of Culture,* mimicry is the action some subaltern peoples take in an attempt to become more like the dominant culture through a self-conscious appropriation of cultural characteristics. The image of the subaltern appropriating these characteristics is often disconcerting in some way for the colonizer, which Bhabha reads as a challenge to "narcissistic authority" (129). These acts of appropriation are attempts to secure for the colonized person part of the power associated with outward cultural signs like dress or speech. Bhabha refers to this phenomenon as "almost the same, but not quite"—the minor differences between a colonized and colonizing culture becomes a fetish for the colonizer, a place to assert the prestige of the colonizing culture lest the lines between outside and inside the colonized space become excessively blurred (122).

Notably Bhabhian mimicry is displayed by Carlton Toomey, an Appalachian drug dealer, who adjusts his grammar when speaking with different parties. With native Appalachians Toomey speaks a dialect of Appalachian English that would be impenetrable for many outsiders, yet he switches to Standard English grammar and syntax when he discusses Jimmy Carter's economic policy once alone with the university-educated Leonard (50). Toomey winks at Leonard "conspiratorially" in this scene—in the postcolonial understanding of this act, it is certainly a conspiracy. As Leonard approaches Toomey, who is reading a newspaper on his porch, the latter advises, "Don't tell nobody you caught me with a newspaper. . . . You get a fellow convinced he's smarter than you and he'll pretty much open up his bill-fold and give you whatever you ask for. Especially them from Charlotte or Atlanta" (195). The agency Toomey secures for himself is a reappropriation of the commodification of the Appalachian image, used to secure an economic advantage by inhabiting the stereotype that defines the region. Like Naipaul's mimic men, who are native Caribbeans that have embraced the culture of the colonizer for personal gain, Toomey secures his own success by using the appropriate codes. Ashcroft, Griffith, and Tiffin described the sort of mimicry set forward by Bhabha and exemplified in Toomey as extending from a hyperawareness of the objectified position and a desire to participate in the subjective, dominating position—hence the need to mimic the colonizing culture (4, 87).

Toomey's inhabitation of the hillbilly stereotype as a simultaneously resistant act and one designed for personal gain is connected to Leonard's idea of "landscape as destiny." Leonard wonders whether other mountain regions throughout the world—the transperiphery postcolonial world—"live in the passive voice" (157). The grammatical and ontological passivity Leonard describes impels passivity in Leonard's case and in Travis's case, but also a commandment, as in Toomey's case, "to be" or "to perform" a particular role. The historical implications of this passivity and objectification that the dominant culture inscribes on the region provides a narrative thread throughout the novel, especially in its focus on the Shelton Laurel Massacre of 1863. That the mountain regions of western North Carolina were passively thrust into the Civil War by outside forces is alluded to by Leonard early in the text (27). Rash suggested that Travis can transtemporally inhabit the mind of one of his young ancestors, albeit briefly, by imagining the scene of his execution by Confederate troops while wearing the young boy's wireframe glasses—an act that links the subaltern voice of past mountaineers to the present (87). The passivity on the part of the Appalachian victims of the massacre is reinforced through their being linguistically refashioned by outside forces, much like the hillbilly moniker reconfigures the identities of the novel's modern mountaineers. Citizens and soldiers were incorrectly labeled "bushwhackers," criminals, making their deaths more palatable to the executioners who were desperate to prevent any new Union gains in the mountains. Likewise the 1863 *New York Times* article detailing the massacre—a document Rash retrieved from the newspaper's archive—erroneously labels the massacre victims as Unionists and soldiers, rather than innocent, passive victims, some of whom were children (164). A theme that is explored frequently in Rash's works, the victims have their identities, hero or criminal, codified and inscribed by the northern and southern powers. Books, moreover, except for a few choice works of history, pass over the massacre. Travis had never heard the event discussed prior to meeting Leonard. Indeed even the doctor's notebook Leonard possesses from his ancestor present at Shelton Laurel left a blank page for the day of the massacre. One begins to see a pattern of the archive writing the identity of the mountain community and the people in it. Their identities become what history books and the outside world define them as, and multiple identities become a single identity as codes foreclose individuation.

Appalachians in *The World Made Straight* live life in the passive voice to such an extent that Leonard, while reading about the Civil War, feels a strong connection to a young soldier who, fearing death on the battlefield and the inability to write following the conflict, wrote "I was killed" in his diary (270). There is ambiguity in this act, as the man with whom Leonard empathizes is passive even in the grammatical construction of his death—he is killed rather than he dies. Yet archiving the death is in itself an act of subjectivity; for the soldier, announcing his own death becomes a resistant act of voicing that is preserved in the historical archive. Like the young soldier, Leonard's later inaction in the novel's climactic scenes following a car accident in the canyon that leads to his and Toomey's death but preserves Travis's life can be construed as action. Recursively the novel shows Leonard's passivity as productive in its ability to preserve life. Similarly Spivak famously questioned the ability of death to give voice to subalterns in her discussion of Bhubaneswari Bhaduri, whose suicide has been seen as both an act resistant to colonial-dominated power structures in South Asia and a meaningless act of abjection that was voiced by postcolonialists for their own ideological points. While I do not wish to make any claims as to Bhaduri's case, Rash explored the idea of subaltern voice by reminding the reader that passivity and even its ultimate end, death, is a means of communicating the experiences of those living within the precoded habitus of postcolonial societies like Appalachia.

While the characters of *The World Made Straight* inhabit a modern Appalachian community, *Serena* takes place in a semifictionalized version of 1930s western North Carolina in which prophetic visions like those of Galloway's mother coexist with the real history of the region's timber boom and the subsequent creation of the Great Smoky Mountains National Park. Reviews of the book have frequently noted that its Appalachian lumbermen form a "Greek chorus," commenting in an "awe-struck" way at the Pembertons' destruction of the land and Serena's menacing bearing.[5] I suggest, however, that Rash created this Appalachian chorus not as awe-struck witnesses but rather as active commentators who display the heteroglossia and polyphony of mountaineer feelings and responses, contravening the flattened, monovalenced stereotypes that have been used to define the region and its peoples in the past. Though a chorus in a traditional tragedy provides a unified voice of and for the community observing the dramatic action, Rash crafted a group that cannot be unified except in background in that its members come primarily from Appalachia, though their opinions and preferred topics of conversation prove to be the novel's primary discursive space owing to the chorus's range of understandings and experiences.

The chorus's carving out of discursive space is not, however, recognized by many of *Serena*'s outsider characters. Notably Serena and Buchanan, both outsiders, are interested not in the content of the lumbermen's speech but rather in its form—a fixation on the signifier rather than the signified. Buchanan even keeps a notebook of anachronistic speech patterns and words, like an anthropologist gathering data. These investigations aid in constructing the dominant conception of the mountaineers as anachronisms who are valued for their quaintness and physical ability to cut trees—one capable of being reified and sold in books, the other in lumberyards. Serena suggests an even stronger relationship between commodities like timber and books when she says of the conservationist Horace Kephart, "A librarian and an author . . . yet he'd stop us from harvesting the very thing books are made of" (35). Kephart, as a real author who published his ethnographic work *Our Southern Highlanders* in 1913 and then a second edition in 1922, reified and in many ways helped codify Appalachian culture in a print medium, much like Serena's project commodifies and eradicates the landscape that, as was suggested in *The World Made Straight,* formulates the destiny and culture of the mountaineers. A similar framework can be seen in the two novels, as Appalachians live in the passive voice; on the one hand, their speech patterns and culture are extracted, reified, and sold, while on the other they, commanded by the Pembertons, exploit and eradicate the very conditions that have gone to formulate their identity.

As I noted, the outsiders—including Kephart, who would have, in this semifictionalized universe, published both editions of *Our Southern Highlanders* by 1929—fixate on the forms of Appalachian speech. Yet upon closer inspection one finds a variety of contents and speech patterns at play beyond those the outsiders privilege. Snipes, one of the lumbermen, notes early in the book, "They's differences in every language in the world" (31). Snipes's dialectical conjugation of the verb "is" is demonstrative of the very principle the quote wishes to suggest. Moreover Snipes's utterance has implications beyond grammar as one can extrapolate that speech is varied not only all over the world but also in the lumber camp itself. Another lumberman, McIntyre, regularly speaks with references to biblical prophecy, as in a section where he suggests the Revelation of John has foretold the coming of one like Serena. McIntyre's viewpoints come into conflict with local folk knowledge that other members of the crew formulate, which interprets signs like wooly worms growing thicker coats and hornets building nests closer to the ground—a system McIntyre views as pagan in origin (62). Snipes, in the same discussion, speaks from a place of scientific and philosophical knowledge, using logic to parse out how the system of signs the folk culture posits are a valid system of belief and form a sort of natural language. However, one of the lumbermen, Stewart, must have the term "eminent domain" translated for him by another lumberman, as it comes from outside his normal sphere of knowledge; Ross, another lumberman, however, reduces its meaning from a legal term to an experiential one: "It means you're shit out of luck" (63). Outsider knowledge and terminology is assimilated into the conversation, forming a dialogic scene in which different forms interact and counteract one another, showing a range of mountain voices speaking in an Appalachian dialect but offering a variety of contents and carving out a discursive space.

These voices, however, are incapable of being heard by the outsiders. The language the Pembertons and other dominant outside forces speak is that of one interested in those products capable of being reified and removed. Sawyer, a crewman who dies in one of the camp's frequent accidents, is photographed lying in a wooden casket that he had cut that very morning (124). The image of the lumbermen's bodies placed inside the very product they have died to extract is more overtly presented later in the novel, suggesting the bodies of the men that are contained in a commodity are products themselves (246). The lumbermen are useful insofar as their bodies are useful to the Pembertons; their beliefs and voices remain uninvestigated, while their bodies and culture are extracted. The culture of the mountains, moreover, is disconcerting and frightening to Pemberton, who at one point states that the "*otherness*" of the mountains would always be "inexplicable" to him (118). Of course the otherness of which he speaks would be entirely explicable if any value were placed on the content of the lumbermen's speech rather than on their bodies and anachronistic grammar.

Near the end of novel, after the Pembertons have cleared nearly the entire mountain of its vegetation, the lumbermen contemplate their place in this newfound modernity. They ruminate on the role they have played in the destruction of their own homes. Rash presented a cycle gone awry: landscape is destiny as it formulates the culture of the subaltern Appalachians, and, as Snipes notes, there is a feeling: "Like there's been so much killed and destroyed it can't ever be alive again" (335). The heavy feeling hanging over the chorus's head is one of self-destruction. The Appalachian subalterns have played a part in annihilating the very thing that formulated their culture, which, as is shown in their conversation, is based firmly in a shared landscape. Whoever wins this battle, conservationist or timber company, there is no place left for these Appalachians in a modernizing world. Rash has given voice to the voiceless subalterns who were previously caught in the interstices of the triumphant rhetoric of the creation of the national park, but, like the young soldier in Leonard's book or Spivak's Bhaduri, the ultimate, passive utterance for subalterns is one that is ambiguous in its import: "we were killed."

Voicing the Hollers: What's at Stake?

Rash's treatment of Appalachia and its people frequently probes the impact of an exploitative and colonized past on its present culture and place in American and global society. Appalachia, as noted above, has been a region caught between opposing forces, a region not quite southern, nor entirely northern. A similar dichotomy is frequently at work in Rash's characters, who occupy both a geographical and cultural liminal space and who are caught between opposing forces that both threaten destruction. Postcolonial readings offer Appalachian characters as discursive entities, interacting with cultural codes and in some cases rejecting them, while in others succumbing to them. Likewise Rash has avoided the stereotypes that have been found in previous iterations of writing on Appalachia, replacing them with characters who struggle with the cultural codes thrust on them and exploitative systems that threaten both their corporeal and ontological existence. Moreover the characters in *Serena* and *The World Made Straight* function to deny ahistorical utopianism and singular cultural valences for Appalachians. Rash's Appalachians are, above all, humans. None are simple or subscribe to the dictates of the dominant portrayal of the "typical" Appalachian; rather they look, act, think, and have feelings in multitudinous configurations like any other group of people, though their experiences of exploitation and hardship have colored their past and present. While Lee Smith's "someplace else, a world away" reminds readers of both real and perceived variances between Appalachia and the South, the function of Rash's humanizing project that envisions Appalachia as part of a larger postcolonial world is to question how far away "someplace else" is when put into the context of a global human experience.

Notes

1. For a discussion of the rise of Appalachian voices in literature and media in the latter half of the twentieth century, see W. K. McNeil's introduction to *Appalachian Images in Folk and Popular Culture.*

2. *The Beverly Hillbillies* is, of course, only one example of culturally rampant images of the Appalachian as a simple and backward creature on the outskirts of mainstream society. Successful television shows like *Petticoat Junction, Hee-Haw, Green Acres,* and even minor characters like Cletus from *The Simpsons* show the stereotypical Appalachian as a reified commodity. Contemporary iterations of the hillbilly image in media, as in the ongoing *Hollywood Hillbillies* television series, admittedly allow Appalachian people to speak, but the situations the families are placed in are frequently designed for maximum comedy or discomfort.

3. The *Foxfire* series here comes to mind. The magazine, though written by and researched primarily by native Appalachians, carries with it an emphasis on folk activities that do not necessarily represent the realities of today's nor perhaps even yesterday's lived experience.

4. For this and the following discussion of Seamus Heaney's influence on Rash, see Lang, *Appalachia and Beyond,* 337–53.

5. As an example of description that became commonplace in reviews of the book, see Janet Maslin's "Couple Creates an Empire by Felling Trees and Anyone in Their Way."

Works Cited

Ashcroft, Bill, Gareth Griffith, and Helen Tiffin. *The Empire Writes Back: Theory and Practice in Post-colonial Literatures.* 2nd ed. New York: Routledge, 2002.

Bhabha, Homi K. *The Location of Culture.* London: Routledge, 1994.

Billings, Dwight B., Gurney Norman, and Katherine Ledford, eds. *Back Talk from Appalachia: Confronting Stereotypes.* Lexington: University Press of Kentucky, 1999.

Billings, Dwight B. "The Civil War Isn't Over." *Atlantic* (April 8, 2015). https://www.theatlantic.com/politics/archive/2015/04/the-civil-war-isnt-over/389847/. Accessed June 11, 2015.

Cunningham, Rodger. *Apples on the Flood: The Southern Mountain Experience.* Knoxville: University of Tennessee Press, 1987.

———. "Writings on the Cusp: Double Alterity and Minority Discourse in Appalachia." In *The Future of Southern Letters.* Ed. Jefferson Humphries and John Lowe. New York: Oxford University Press, 1996. 41–53.

Ferrence, Matthew. "You Are and You Ain't: Story and Literature as Redneck Resistance." *Journal of Appalachian Studies* 18.1/2 (2012): 113–30.

Hogan, Patrick Colm. *Empire and Poetic Voice.* Albany: State University of New York Press, 2004.

Kephart, Horace. *Our Southern Highlanders.* Knoxville: University of Tennessee Press, 1922.

Lang, John, ed. *Appalachia and Beyond.* Knoxville: University of Tennessee Press, 2006.

Lewis, Helen M., Linda Johnson, and Don Askins, eds. *Colonialism in Modern America: The Appalachian Case.* Boone: Appalachian Consortium Press, 1978.

Maslin, Janet. "Couple Creates an Empire by Felling Trees and Anyone in Their Way." *New York Times* October 5, 2008: C6.

McNeil, W. K., ed. *Appalachian Images in Folk and Popular Culture.* 2nd ed. Knoxville: University of Tennessee Press, 1995.

Naipaul, V. S. *The Mimic Men.* New York: Macmillan, 1967.

Newcomb, Horace. "Appalachia on Television: Region as a Symbol in American Popular Culture." *Appalachian Images in Folk and Popular Culture.* Ed. W. K. McNeil. Knoxville: University of Tennessee Press, 1995, 34–54.

Obermiller, Phillip J., and William W. Philliber. *Appalachia in an International Context: Cross-national Comparisons of Developing Regions.* Westport, Conn.: Praeger, 1994.

Rash, Ron. *Serena.* New York: HarperCollins, 2008.

———. *The World Made Straight.* New York: Henry Holt, 2006.

Said, Edward W. *Orientalism.* 2nd ed. New York: Vintage, 1994.

Shapiro, Henry D. *Appalachia on Our Mind.* Chapel Hill: University of North Carolina Press, 1978.

Sharp, Joanne P. *Geographies of Postcolonialism: Spaces of Power and Representation.* Los Angeles: Sage, 2009.

Smith, Lee. "White Columns and Marble Generals." *Lee Smith.* n.d. http://www.leesmith.com/works/columns.php. Accessed June 11, 2015.

Spivak, Gayatri Chaktravorty. "Can the Subaltern Speak?" *Can the Subaltern Speak? Reflections on the History of an Idea.* Ed. Rosalind C. Morris. New York: Columbia University Press, 2010. 34–54.

Stevenson, Sheryl. "Postcolonial Appalachia: Bhabha, Bakhtin, and Diane Gilliam Fisher's *Kettle Bottom.*" *CEA Forum* 35.1 (2006). http://www2.widener.edu/~cea/351stevenson.htm. Accessed June 11, 2015.

Whisnant, David E. *All That Is Fine and Native.* Chapel Hill: University of North Carolina Press, 1983.

CONTRIBUTORS

BARBARA BENNETT is an associate professor of English at North Carolina State University. Along with numerous articles on American literature and environmental studies, Bennett is the author of four books: *Scheherazade's Daughters* (2012), *Soul of a Lion* (2010), *Understanding Jill McCorkle* (2000), and *Comic Vision, Female Voices* (1998).

THOMAS ÆRVOLD BJERRE is an associate professor in American studies at the University of Southern Denmark. His research focuses on American popular culture with a particular interest in the American South, the western, and representations of 9/11 and the War on Terror. He coedited *The Scourges of the South: Essays on "The Sickly South" in History, Literature, and Popular Culture* (2014) and has published in various journals and contributed to *Still in Print: The Southern Novel Today* (2010), *Perspectives on Barry Hannah* (2010), *Larry Brown and the Blue Collar South* (2010) as well as *The Rough South: Artistic Representations* and *The South in Fiction and Film: Essays in Adaptation.*

MAE MILLER CLAXTON is an associate professor in the English Department at Western Carolina University. In 2012 she published *Conversations with Dorothy Allison,* a collection of interviews along with an introduction. She was a contributing editor to the *Heath Anthology of American Literature* (6th edition) and coeditor of the McMichael *Anthology of American Literature* (8th edition). Her most recent book is the coedited collection *Conversations with Ron Rash* (2016). Her scholarship focuses primarily on Eudora Welty, but she has recently expanded her interests to the Native South and Appalachian writer Horace Kephart. Her articles have appeared in *Mississippi Quarterly, South Atlantic Review,* and *Southern Quarterly,* among others.

MARTHA GREENE EADS is a professor in the Department of Language and Literature at Eastern Mennonite University. Her research and teaching interests include twentieth- and twenty-first-century drama, English modernism, and contemporary southern fiction, and her articles on those topics have appeared in the Carolina Quarterly, Christianity and Literature, the Cresset, Modern Drama, the Southern Quarterly, and Theology.

JAMES ERIC ENSLEY is a Ph.D. candidate in the Department of English at Yale University. He also holds a B.A. in English from Columbia University, an M.S. in library science from the University of North Carolina at Chapel Hill, and a M.A. in English from North Carolina State University. His research interests include Appalachian literature and culture as well as medieval studies and the history of the book.

JESSE GRAVES is an associate professor in the Department of Literature at East Tennessee State University. His poems and essays have appeared in *Prairie Schooner, Southern Quarterly, Connecticut Review,* and other journals, anthologies, and collections. His first book, *Tennessee Landscape with Blighted Pine,* was published by Texas Review Press in 2011 and won the Weatherford Award for Best Appalachian Book of Poetry. His second collection, *Basin Ghosts,* also published by Texas Review Press in 2014, won Graves a second Weatherford Award in March 2015. His most recent book is *Specter Mountain* (2018), cowritten with William Wright, from Mercer University Press.

JOHN LANG is professor emeritus of English at Emory and Henry College in Emory, Virginia, where he taught from 1983 to 2012. He is the author of *Understanding Fred Chappell* (2000) and *Six Poets from the Mountain South* (2010). He is also the editor of *Appalachia and Beyond: Conversations with Writers from the Mountain South* (2006), a collection of interviews from the *Iron Mountain Review,* which he edited for more than twenty years.

ERICA ABRAMS LOCKLEAR is an associate professor in the Department of Literature and Language at the University of North Carolina–Asheville. In addition to many articles and book chapters on southern and Appalachian literatures, she is the author of *Negotiating a Perilous Empowerment: Appalachian Women's Literacies* (2011).

TRIPTHI PILLAI is an assistant professor of English Renaissance literature at Coastal Carolina University. Her recent work focuses on theories of temporality and spatiality in the context of early modern drama. She is currently working on several critical and creative projects that also inform her teaching: a book-length study on Shakespeare and photographical logics; a critical-creative piece on cuteness and violence in Bollywood's "item" musicals and Christopher Marlowe's plays; and an essay on the onticology of shoes in *The Two Gentlemen of Verona.*

ADAM J. PRATT is an assistant professor of history at the University of Scranton. His research interests include Jacksonian America and the Civil War. Papers he has presented include "Georgia's Gubernatorial Election of 1831 and the Politics of Whiteness" and "'A curious compound of the hero and the dandy': George Armstrong Custer, the Cavalier Image, and Southern Masculinity in the Postwar South."

BRIAN RAILSBACK is the founding dean of the Honors College and professor of English at Western Carolina University. He is coeditor of two collections, including *The John Steinbeck Encyclopedia* (2006) and the author of numerous articles on John Steinbeck. Railsback's most recent novel is *A Going Concern* (2012).

JIMMY DEAN SMITH is a professor of English and chair of the Department of English and Communication at Union College. He has authored several articles and book chapters, most of which focus southern and Appalachian literatures. Smith was also selected as an NEH Summer Scholar by the National Endowment for the Humanities (2014) to participate in an initiative entitled "Reconsidering Flannery O'Connor."

FRÉDÉRIQUE SPILL is an associate professor of American literature; she teaches at the University of Picardy–Jules Verne in Amiens, France. She is the author of *L'Idiotie dansl'œuvre de William Faulkner* (2009). She recently contributed to *Critical Insights: The Sound and the Fury* (2014) and to *Faulkner at Fifty: Tutors and Tyros* (2014). She has also published articles in French and in English on Flannery O'Connor, Richard Ford, Cormac McCarthy, Robert Penn Warren, Jonathan Safran Foer, and Nicole Krauss.

DANIEL CROSS TURNER is an associate professor of English at Coastal Carolina University. He is the author of *Southern Crossings: Poetry, Memory, and the Transcultural South* (2012) and coeditor of *Undead Souths: The Gothic and Beyond* (2015) and of *Hard Lines: Rough South Poetry* (2016). Turner has also published numerous articles on contemporary writers and filmmakers, which have appeared in edited collections as well as journals, including *Mosaic, Genre, Southern Quarterly, Mississippi Quarterly,* and *Southern Literary Journal,* among other venues.

ZACKARY VERNON is an assistant professor of English at Appalachian State University in Boone, North Carolina. He has articles published or forthcoming in several journals and books, including *Studies in the Novel, Journal of Modern Literature, ISLE: Interdisciplinary Studies in Literature and Environment, Journal of American Studies, Mississippi Quarterly, Appalachian Journal, Fifty Years after Faulkner* (2015), and *The Bohemian South* (2016). He is also the editor of a forthcoming volume, *Ecocriticism and the Future of Southern Studies.*

EDWARD J. WHITELOCK is a professor of English and department head for Humanities and Programs in Fine and Performing Arts at Gordon State College. He is the author of many articles on American literature, culture, and music. Whitelock is also coauthor of *Apocalypse Jukebox: The End of the World in American Popular Music* (2009).

RANDALL WILHELM is an assistant professor of English at Anderson University. He is editor of *The Ron Rash Reader* (2014) and coeditor, with Jesse Graves, of the forthcoming *Conversations with Robert Morgan.* He holds degrees in both visual art and literature and has published articles on southern and Appalachian writers as well as interdisciplinary studies on the relationship between literature, music, and visual art. His work has appeared in *Mississippi Quarterly,* the *Faulkner Journal,* the *Southern Quarterly,* the *Hemingway Review,* and *Appalachian Journal,* among others, and he is a regular contributor to the *Casebook Series on Cormac McCarthy.*

INDEX

www.ingramcontent.com/pod-product-compliance
Lightning Source LLC
LaVergne TN
LVHW050150080826
844660LV00002B/155

* 9 7 8 1 6 1 1 1 7 8 3 8 8 *